the
trouble
with
billionaires

the trouble
with
billionaires

**How the Super-Rich
Hijacked the World
(and How We Can
Take it Back)**

LINDA MCQUAIG AND NEIL BROOKS

A Oneworld Book

First published in the United Kingdom and Commonwealth
by Oneworld Publications 2013

Copyright © Linda McQuaig and Neil Brooks 2013

Originally published in Canada by Viking Canada,
an imprint of Penguin Group (Canada)

The moral right of Linda McQuaig and Neil Brooks to be identified as
the Authors of this work has been asserted by them in accordance with
the Copyright, Designs and Patents Act 1988

ISBN 978-1-85168-994-1
Ebook ISBN 978-1-78074-220-5

Typeset by Tetragon, London
Printed and bound by CPI Group (UK) Ltd, Croydon, CR0 4YY

Oneworld Publications
10 Bloomsbury Street, London WC1B 3SR, England

For my precious Amy:
daughter, editor, best friend

—L. M.

To Marlane, with love

—N. B.

'Few tricks of the unsophisticated intellect are more curious than the naive psychology of the business man, who ascribes his achievements to his own unaided efforts, in bland unconsciousness of a social order without whose continuous support and vigilant protection he would be as a lamb bleating in the desert.'

R.H. TAWNEY

'The disposition to admire, and almost to worship, the rich and the powerful, and to despise, or, at least, to neglect persons of poor and mean condition...is...the great and most universal cause of the corruption of our moral sentiments.'

ADAM SMITH

contents

1
return of the
plutocrats

Imagine this: you are paid a pound every second.

After one minute, you would have £60. After one hour, you would have £3,600. If this spectacular rate of pay continued day and night, it would take twelve days for you to become a millionaire – something beyond most people's wildest dreams.

But how long would it take to become a billionaire?

Well, at that rate, it would take almost thirty-two years.

This little game helps illustrate that being a billionaire isn't just beyond most people's wildest dreams; it's likely beyond their comprehension. It also highlights how odd it is for society to regard the accumulation and retention of such vast material wealth by one individual as an appropriate aspiration.

Here's another thought experiment that illustrates how far beyond our regular comprehension the size of a billionaire's fortune is: imagine how long it would take Bill Gates, typically considered the world's richest man, to count his $53 billion. If he counted it at the rate of one dollar every second, and he counted non-stop day and night, he'd have it all tallied up in 1680 years. Still another way to look at it: if Bill Gates had started counting his fortune at that rate back in 330 CE – the year that the Roman emperor Constantine had his wife boiled alive and chose Byzantium as the empire's new capital – he'd just be finishing up now.

•   •   •

The fortunes of the wealthy, as revealed in the 2012 *Sunday Times* Rich List, are more opulent than ever before in history. Having recovered from the minor bruising they took in the 2008 financial collapse – which some in the City directly helped bring about – the rich now tower over the nation as financial behemoths. The combined wealth of the 1000 on the list totals £414 billion – an amount greater than a third of the UK gross domestic product (GDP), and higher even than their previous combined record of £412.8 billion, set just before the crash. Despite this cornucopia, Prime Minister David Cameron announced plans in early 2012 to send more their way by cutting the top marginal tax rate by 5 percentage points. This provided an average saving of £14,000 a week for some 40,000 UK millionaires[1] – an extra treat that was probably barely noticed by many in the far upper reaches of the 1 per cent.

Meanwhile, for the masses there would be no such mollycoddling, but rather a stiff dose of austerity, cutting deeply into health care services, education and welfare. With unemployment pushing three million, including one million young people, and incomes generally stagnant or falling, those in government were fierce in their resolve not to scrimp on austerity. So while the rich were indulged, despite their role in bringing about the financial collapse, the burden of dealing with the resulting recession and debt was shunted on to millions of ordinary Britons, who played no role whatsoever in bringing about the financial disaster. It's a replay of the brutal austerity medicine applied in Britain after the First World War – a disastrous era that bears striking similarities to today, and to which we'll return in Chapter Eight.

There's growing evidence that the current austerity, even apart from issues of fairness and justice, simply isn't working as an economic cure. Indeed, the IMF, an institution with a long record of imposing austerity on debtor nations seeking aid, forcefully condemned the austerity mania that has gripped Europe. In a lengthy report in October 2012, the IMF pointed out that austerity can be self-defeating, causing sharp contractions in an economy. It noted that Britain's austerity plans will likely suck £76 billion more out of the economy than expected by 2015, and move the UK from the camp of continental European countries, with their generous social welfare models, towards the stingy American model. Indeed, as the IMF data shows, the coalition government's austerity plans are projected to plunge Britain's government spending below miserly US levels by 2017.[2]

The ultra-wealthy in the UK are part of a new global super-elite that is capturing an unprecedented share of the world's resources. As a report by the charity Oxfam noted in January 2013, the 2012 income of the world's richest one hundred billionaires totalled £150 billion – enough to wipe out extreme global poverty four times over.[3] So excessive is the hoarding of resources in a small number of hands that it is hard not to gawk in disbelief. The *Onion* magazine astutely describes the gap between rich and poor as the 'Eighth Wonder of the World', and as 'a tremendous, millennia-old expanse that fills us with both wonder and humility…the most colossal and enduring of mankind's creations'.

The rich–poor gap is indeed a millennia-old project. But it's worth mentioning that there was once a blip. There was a brief period of about four decades when a small dent was made in the edifice of the rich–poor gap in the Western world – a small dent that made a significant difference to millions of people. What makes that brief interlude particularly significant is that it happened quite recently, from roughly 1940 to 1980, and that it coincided with an era of almost unprecedented prosperity and economic growth.

By any logic that brief interlude should have sparked serious inquiry into just how it happened. Instead, there's been an almost deliberate avoidance of the subject in official circles, an unwillingness to probe the cause of the dent in the rich–poor gap, how it coincided with such robust prosperity, and how we might emulate it today. Like the memorable scene from the movie *When Harry Met Sally*, in which Meg Ryan dramatically fakes an orgasm in a restaurant, surely the appropriate response is the one from the woman at a nearby table:'I'll have what she's having.' Instead, our ruling elites have tried to wipe out the notion that the widely shared prosperity of the postwar years is something we should aspire to create again, advising us to forget 'what she's having' and be content with the meagre bowl of gruel we're being served.

• • •

There might have been a time when it could honestly be said that we didn't know that the massive economic project – known as Thatcherism, Reaganism, modern conservatism or neoliberalism – was going to lead to a society dominated by billionaires.

Of course, many people always suspected that it would. After all, if you aggressively roll back state intervention aimed at protecting workers and at the same time dramatically reduce the taxes of the rich, it's reasonable to expect that you'll end up with a top-heavy society. On the other hand, there was always the possibility that things would turn out differently, that the trickle-down effect would, as promised, unleash a rising tide that would lift all boats.

But it's now a good thirty years since the neoliberal experiment was launched in the early 1980s. We've since seen that, while the tide did rise, it certainly didn't lift all boats. Vast numbers became submerged, sank, or ended up battered on the rocks, while a flotilla of diamond-studded yachts, appearing out of nowhere, sailed on by out to sea.

There can no longer be any confusion about the impact of the set of neoliberal economic policies that have been applied in the UK and the US over the past three decades. The results are unmistakable: these policies have led to a massive shift in income and wealth from the bulk of society to the already-privileged few.

Yet, strikingly, this dramatic rise in inequality – coming right after the most egalitarian era in modern Western history – has not led to an overthrow of the neoliberal agenda. There have been plenty of challenges to that agenda, plenty of brilliant critiques, but the agenda has not yet been rejected. The neoliberal economic orthodoxy of the last three decades continues to guide policy in the Anglo-American countries, perpetuating and aggravating levels of inequality that are already extreme by the standards of the developed world.

This book is about that dramatic increase in inequality – particularly the extraordinary concentration of wealth at the upper end. Although the glittering lives of billionaires may seem like a harmless source of entertainment, the extreme inequality that they represent amounts to a profound change in society with drastically damaging results. There is ample evidence that extreme inequality has negative consequences for the social well-being of a nation, as well as for its potential for economic growth. Notably, it has been well documented that an individual's prospects for upward social mobility – something that even conservatives consider essential – are greatly reduced in societies that are highly unequal. But, of all the destructive aspects of extreme inequality, probably the most serious is the impact it has on democracy itself.

Of course, the incompatibility of democracy and concentrations of great wealth has long been understood. As Aristotle noted in the fourth century BCE: 'Where the possession of political power is due to the possession of economic power or wealth…that is oligarchy, and when the unpropertied class has power, that is democracy.' In the early twentieth century, US Supreme Court Justice Louis

Brandeis put it succinctly: 'We can have democracy in this country or we can have great wealth concentrated in the hands of a few. We cannot have both.' Mark Hanna, a notorious Republican backroom operator of the late nineteenth century, made the same point more crudely: 'There are two things that are important in politics. The first is money, and I can't remember what the second is.'

What these diverse political thinkers are all pointing to is the fact that economic power inevitably translates into political power, and that enough economic power concentrated in a small number of hands can transform a theoretical democracy into what is, in reality, an oligarchy – that is, a nation ruled by the few. We think a more appropriate word to describe today's extreme inequality is plutocracy – that is, a nation effectively ruled by the wealthy few.

While an extremely wealthy elite has always posed a threat to democracy, the danger posed by such concentrated economic power is far greater today than ever before. That's because the human capacity for destruction has grown exponentially, as a result of industrial and technological advances. Whereas powerful kings and elites of earlier eras could wreak great havoc and suffering, today's corporate elite has a far greater capacity to imperil the public interest – by ruining the planet for human habitation through environmental destruction. For instance, the phenomenally wealthy set of interests comprising the fossil-fuel lobby is the driving force behind climate change, and is effectively blocking the world community from mounting a concerted global effort to tackle the potentially catastrophic problem. We will explore this connection between plutocracy and environmental destruction in more detail in Chapter Four.

The point to be emphasized here is that today's extreme inequality poses a fundamental threat to the world. Yet it is often treated as a mere peripheral issue. Indeed, while poverty is generally acknowledged as a significant problem, rising inequality is frequently dismissed as unimportant. Conservatives even celebrate inequality, saluting it as just desserts, and discounting complaints about it as mere sour grapes, the whining of the envious. Margaret Thatcher famously promoted inequality, proclaiming in her days as prime minister: 'It is our job to glory in inequality and see that talents and abilities are given vent and expression for the benefit of all.'

Even liberals and progressives sometimes turn a blind eye to extreme inequality, arguing that poverty matters, but the fortunes of the rich don't. Tony Blair's New Labour government, while declaring poverty reduction a central goal, showed an almost aggressive indifference to the galloping increase in inequality during his years in office. As Blair quipped: 'It's not a burning ambition of mine to make sure David Beckham earns less money.' Alistair Darling, as chancellor of the exchequer, similarly commented: 'I'm not offended if someone earns large sums of money. Is it fair or not? It's just a fact of life.'

We profoundly disagree. We don't think extreme inequality is fair, nor is it a fact of life. And, given what's ultimately at stake – nothing less than the future sustainability of the planet – raising objections to the transformation of our democracies into plutocracies is less a sign of envy and more one of sanity.

•   •   •

The good news is that the problem of extreme inequality is solvable: through the tax system.

In saying this, we are not minimizing the political difficulty of bringing about changes to the tax system, particularly of bringing about a return to more progressive taxation. We are simply noting that these difficulties are exclusively political – and not economic. Nor are we ignoring the many other social reforms that could – and should – be implemented in order to increase equality and social inclusiveness, including improvements to education, health care, child care, housing and social welfare systems. In addition, stronger minimum wage laws and labour laws protecting unionization rights are reforms that would significantly help reduce inequality.

Many progressives who are concerned about inequality argue that these reforms – not the tax system – should be the central focus of the campaign for greater equality. But while we wholeheartedly agree with all these reforms, we note that they involve fighting many battles on many fronts. This means that progress is likely to be difficult and slow, with reductions in inequality at best piecemeal and only realized in the long term. The goal of reducing inequality can be achieved more quickly, efficiently and comprehensively through changes in the tax system. With its sweeping reach over all citizens, the tax system is quite simply the most powerful tool for achieving greater equality. This is, of course, why modern conservatives have been so determined to render it off-limits, to turn 'tax' into a dirty word that even progressives fear to be associated with.

We must restore the notion that the tax system has a central, honourable role to play in a democracy. It is, in fact, one of the most basic tools of democracy. It allows us to make decisions collectively about what kind of society we want, and to finance the programmes and services necessary to create that society. In addition to the essential revenue-raising function, the tax system allows us to tackle directly extreme inequality. Through progressive taxation – in which a heavier burden is placed on those with larger incomes – it is possible to reduce the damage of extreme inequality and the risk of plutocracy. A progressive tax system can ensure that more of society's resources end up in the hands of ordinary citizens, who have a legitimate claim to a larger share than they currently receive (as we will argue in the next chapter), and ensure that the wealthy are prevented from capturing such an enormous portion that their economic power allows them to ride roughshod over our democracies.

Over the past three decades, conservative ideologues in Anglo-American countries have made an extensive list of arguments that boil down to 'governments bad, markets good', with the resulting conclusion that taxes should be reduced. The two assertions they have made most incessantly are that government programmes financed with taxes are generally ineffective in achieving their social objectives, and that increased taxes have huge economic costs. Therefore, they hope to convince us that we would all be better off if taxes were reduced.

If these assertions were true, one would expect countries with high taxes to be no better off in terms of social outcomes than countries with low taxes, and also to be economic basket cases. But the evidence suggests the opposite. In fact, countries with high taxes tend to have significantly better social outcomes than those with low taxes, and their economies appear to be unaffected or even improved by the higher taxes required. We review this evidence in Chapter Three, with a series of graphs.

Our graphs provide evidence, across a broad range of countries, to support the case for higher taxes – and not just on the rich. The graphs show that, throughout the developed world, there is a clear correlation between high total tax levels and better outcomes in social well-being, as well as a correlation between high total tax levels and as good or better economic outcomes. In other words, if we look at real-world results – not economic theories – we find powerful evidence that high tax levels are overall beneficial to society.

This clearly flies in the face of the anti-tax arguments we've heard in recent decades. Conservatives always present taxes in isolation, restricting the focus exclusively to the impact of taking money away from taxpayers, thereby reducing their disposable income. With this limited focus, it is hard to see much benefit in taxation. But this ignores what happens to the money that is taken away. Governments don't just dump it down a deep hole; they spend it.

Conservatives deal with this reality by restricting the focus to wasteful government spending. Needless to say, there is wasteful government spending and bureaucratic inefficiency. But, overall, governments spend on programmes and services that are enormously beneficial to the public. Taxes have brought us high quality schools that remain our democratic treasure, low tuition fees at world-class universities, excellent medical services, public parks, libraries, safe streets, liveable cities and freedom from fear of crippling health bills. None of these things come cheaply.

Taxes also assist us in spreading our incomes over our lifetimes to maximize our well-being by, for example, transferring income from our high-income years to our retirement years, from times in our lives when we don't have dependents to support to times when we do, and from periods when we are well and able to take care of our own needs to periods when we are ill or suffering from a disability.

Just as importantly, the public goods and services that we pay for with taxes leave working people healthier, better educated and more economically secure, and therefore less vulnerable in the face of lay-offs and plant closures. With this greater security, working people are more able to demand and win their fair share of the national income that we all collectively produce.

Ultimately, what is at stake with taxes is the question of who will exercise power in society. In low-tax countries, a small class of wealthy people tend to exercise power through their dominance over private markets; in high-tax countries, a majority of citizens tend to exercise it through democratically elected governments.

Despite all the right-wing jaw-boning to the contrary, the almost universally condemned notion of higher taxes turns out to be a very sensible approach.

●　　●　　●

Of course, many people will strongly object to the suggestion of higher taxes. In the course of this book, we will deal with the main objections. Right now, however, we want to highlight one objection that many people seem to find particularly compelling – the fear that higher taxes will prompt capital flight and the departure of the best and the brightest. We want to deal with this objection up front, not just because it seems to capture the attention of many people, but also because it is, quite simply, highly overrated as a concern.

Certainly, the mention of higher taxes quickly provokes speculation about the departure of the well-heeled. In June 2012, David Cameron seemed almost gleeful at the prospect of luring France's wealthy elite to Britain when the newly elected French government moved to raise taxes on the rich. 'If the French go ahead with a 75 per cent top rate of tax, we will roll out the red carpet and welcome more French businesses to Britain and they will pay taxes in Britain and that will pay for our health service, and our schools and everything else.'

First, it's worth noting the malice Cameron is directing towards the people of a neighbouring country, which is also a valued trading partner and ally. The French people had just elected François Hollande, who had run on a platform of higher taxes on the rich. And yet Cameron is urging the French elite to punish their fellow citizens – depriving them of revenue for French health care and education – for exercising their democratic rights. As Richard Murphy pointedly noted in the *Guardian*, Cameron was seeking 'to undermine a decision that the people of France have democratically chosen. That's what tax havens do – they hold democracy in contempt.'[4]

The threat of exodus has always been a powerful trump card in the pockets of the wealthy. And they haven't hesitated to make use of it by threatening – often through spokespeople such as tax lawyers and business associations – to use it. The extent to which they actually move to another country to avoid high taxes is less clear. Some evidence suggests that, except for a small number of high-profile, loudly proclaimed cases, few rich people leave their native lands primarily as a result of taxes. But, whether or not they actually do leave, the threat of their departure – made by them or by their proxies, or simply invoked by politicians explaining the need to cater to the demands of the wealthy – has undoubtedly served as a mighty weapon in warding off high taxes on the rich.

What is rarely mentioned is that, even when the rich actually do carry out their threats and depart, the negative impact on society is small or non-existent. In other words, while the wealthy have managed to induce fear in the public and to keep politicians in line with threats of their departure, there is little or no evidence that their exodus actually hurts us.

In the mid-1970s, there were frequent claims in the British press that many senior managers were considering moving abroad due to raised tax levels. But a survey of corporate executives conducted by the Institute for Fiscal Studies concluded that 'the changes in the income and tax levels of senior staff in the United Kingdom during the 1970s had very little impact on their ability to retain, recruit, or transfer the managers required to fill senior positions'.[5] More recently, a 2011 report from the High Pay Commission found that global mobility among the elite is more limited than is widely believed. The independent commission, sponsored by the Joseph Rowntree Charitable Foundation, found 'only one successful FTSE 100 chief executive officer poached in five years – and even this person was poached by a British company'.[6] Contrary to the hype about the perils of a brain drain, departing professionals and business executives are not common, nor would they be difficult to replace with equally talented individuals, including people who never had the advantages of nepotism that likely greased the careers of many of those they'd be replacing.

Nor is there evidence that we would suffer from wealthy individuals leaving and taking their capital with them. It might be different if we lived in a world where citizens were prevented from investing beyond their borders, or were required to invest their savings in enterprises within their country. But this is not even remotely the case in modern Western nations. Keeping the wealthy in their native lands thus has little influence over where they invest their fortunes, given the rules of the global economy. The financial industry – backed up by mainstream economic thinking – is deeply committed to the notion that the rich should ignore the concept of citizenship when they invest. Indeed, one of the central tenets of 'globalization' is that citizenship is no longer relevant to those who control pools of capital. Why, then, the big fuss about where billionaires call home?

It may seem that the very wealthy, even if they aren't obliged to invest where they live, are at least obliged to pay taxes where they live. But there isn't even much truth in this, given that so much of the wealth of the mega-rich is stashed in offshore tax havens, beyond the reach of national tax authorities. According to compilations by the Tax Justice Network, the global rich have hidden some £13 trillion in tax havens – as much as the combined GDPs of the US and Japan.[7] This raises the question of whether Britain's extensive effort to woo the rich to British soil even makes sense economically. Britain actually acts as a tax haven for rich foreigners, offering them significant tax advantages as 'non-domiciled' residents. So David Cameron's keenness to lure the French elite to Britain isn't just an insult to French sovereignty; it is also pointless if the goal is more revenue for British health services and schools. Rich French exiles living in the UK would qualify as 'non-doms' and therefore pay shockingly low rates of tax (more on this later).

Of course, the presence of a wealthy elite in our midst means lots of work for butlers, chauffeurs, tax professionals, cosmetic surgeons, gardeners and all those whose work relies on catering heavily to the rich. Another likely outcome is higher real estate prices, as the rich invest in local luxury properties. This is a mixed blessing; it benefits other property owners, but also pushes home ownership beyond the reach of most citizens. In any event, higher real estate values and an economy dependent on servicing the rich are probably the only two certain consequences of living in a country with a lot of wealthy people. These benefits, themselves dubious, should be weighed against the well-documented negatives. In their highly acclaimed book *The Spirit Level: Why More Equal Societies Almost Always Do Better*, Richard Wilkinson and Kate Pickett draw on a vast body of social science evidence, as well as their own research, in revealing the long list of problems that large income inequalities exacerbate, including poor physical health, mental illness, drug use, violence, obesity, shorter life spans, diminished social relations and reduced prospects for upward social mobility.

Accordingly, an appropriate response to threats of departure from the rich might be: have a safe trip.

One might also point out the sheer selfishness involved in their decision to depart, considering all the privileges they have enjoyed and the huge extent to which society has helped them get to where they are. As the Paris newspaper *Libération* declared in a front-page headline after ultra-wealthy French fashion tycoon Bernard Arnault applied for Belgian nationality, apparently to avoid higher taxes: 'Get lost, you rich bastard!'

Back in the 1890s, William Jennings Bryan, the firebrand American populist leader, made the case more eloquently in an address to the US Congress, after 400 top business leaders threatened to leave the country if income tax became law. Bryan memorably shrugged off fears of dire consequences caused by their departure, noting: 'we can better afford to lose them and their fortunes than risk the contaminating influence of their presence...Let them depart, and as they leave without regret the land of their birth, let them go with the poet's curse ringing in their ears!'

•   •   •

After years of basking in the glow of a flattering limelight, by the autumn of 2010 the very rich were experiencing something new and altogether jarring: the glare of a harsh spotlight trained menacingly on them. Those operating the spotlight were swarming through dozens of cities and towns across the UK, behaving like the sort of unruly mob one finds in faraway places where the ways of the free world are not sufficiently appreciated. In London, just before Christmas, on one of the busiest shopping days of the year, the swarmers, furious at reports of massive tax avoidance by the rich, were staging protests in some of the leading fashion stores on Oxford Street. They honed in on those owned by multi-billionaire retail magnate Sir Philip Green, a keen supporter of the austerity agenda, and his wife Tina, whose distaste for personal austerity is reflected in her decision to reside in the tax haven of Monaco.

Unrest even erupted in the US the following year. All of a sudden, in September 2011, being wondrously, fulsomely, voluptuously rich was no longer a badge of honour, something to be announced gleefully to the world by squealing the tyres of one's Lamborghini at pedestrians who were in the way. Wall Street – the nexus of ambition, greed, glamour, the very g-spot of the American Dream – was no longer something to be glorified, but rather to be occupied.

Being the target of all these protests was no doubt baffling to members of the financial elite, who still had trouble grasping the notion that they were supposed to feel culpable for the 2008 financial crash.

That bewilderment had been evident in January 2009, only months after the crash, at the elite get-together held every year in the Swiss town of Davos, where bankers, business leaders, political shakers and other big thinkers gather to celebrate the globalized world of liberated financial markets, shrunken government and reinvigorated capitalism. The headline on a dispatch that appeared on the website *Slate* captured the mood: 'Davos Man, Confused.' Journalist Daniel Gross explained in the piece that there was a broad consensus at Davos that '[s]uccess is the work of Great Men and Women, while failure can be pinned on the system.' Or as Julian Glover noted in the *Guardian*: 'The shock is real, the grief has hardly begun, but no one in Davos seems to think [this] means they should be less important or less rich.'

That would involve a change of mindset, which was not what this group seemed inclined toward. After all, a key concept behind the economic order of the past few decades has been the central importance of individual talent – and the need to bestow upon 'talented individuals' abundant rewards in order to lure them to the all-important jobs on Wall Street and in the City. The fact that these same individuals were, in part, behind the disastrous global economic meltdown didn't seem to make a dent in the sky-high-pay mentality.

And so the Royal Bank of Scotland, on government life support in the wake of the financial crash, still paid out £340 million in cash bonuses in February 2009. In Manhattan, then-CEO of Merrill Lynch John Thain explained that he was paying $4 billion in executive bonuses in order to keep the 'best' people – right after those same overachievers had steered the company to a staggering net loss of $27 billion. The decision by the Wall Street crowd to pay themselves collectively a record $140 billion in 2009 – outstripping even their 2007 record – may have seemed odd under the circumstances, but then no one ever accused Wall Street bankers of being modest or prone to self-doubt.

Away from the rarified air of Davos, Edinburgh, London and New York, doubts were beginning to appear. Some 'less-gifted' types were now clamouring for reform, even suggesting that cutting executive pay might induce the hyper-talented to seek more socially useful employment in areas such as teaching or health care. But a letter to *The New York Times* drew attention to the danger of this approach, making a compelling case for maintaining extravagant pay, even huge executive bonuses: 'Without them, Wall Streeters will all look for other jobs. Do we really want these greedy, incompetent clowns building our houses, teaching our children or driving our cabs?'

•   •   •

Before going any further, we should point out that we are not against all rich people. Our criticism is directed at those who have supported the aggressive drive in recent years to redirect society's rewards towards themselves at the top, particularly those who use the threat of their departure to intimidate governments into keeping their taxes low. Furthermore, we note that among the critics of this aggressive advocacy for the wealthy are some wealthy individuals themselves. Eduard de Rothschild, of the famous banking dynasty and a major shareholder in *Libération*, backed the newspaper's attack on Bernard Arnault for threatening to give up his French citizenship after France raised its top tax rate. Rothschild noted that he himself would pay the new taxes 'wholeheartedly'. Similarly, multi-billionaire investor Warren E. Buffett has been a key backer of Barack Obama's attempt to raise taxes on high-income Americans, endorsing Obama's 'Buffett rule' to ensure that the rich face tax rates at least as high as Buffett's secretary.

We should also point out that we are not against all inequality. On the contrary, some reasonable degree of inequality is not only acceptable and inevitable but also desirable, because it allows for different rewards for different levels of individual effort, contribution and risk-taking. But what exists today in the UK is a level of inequality that is extreme compared to most of the nations in the advanced, industrialized world.

It's also extreme by the recent historical experience of Britain itself. England has, of course, a long history as a plutocracy, in which a small propertied elite has enjoyed a virtual monopoly on wealth and power. But there was remarkable progress towards reducing income inequality in Britain, starting in the 1940s. The notion that 'the rich always get richer' was shown to be quite untrue in the decades that followed the crash of 1929 and the Depression of the 1930s. The great banking barons who had ruled the City in the 1920s found their wings clipped in the new era of financial regulation and progressive taxation. While there were more than a thousand millionaires in Britain in 1939, there were only 36 by 1953.[8]

The declining ranks of millionaires coincided with the rising fortunes of the rest of the population. From 1940 to 1980, national income kept growing, but it was much more widely shared. While the affluent crowd comprising the UK's top-earning 1 per cent captured fully 16.9 per cent of national income in 1937, that share declined significantly in the early decades after the Second World War. By 1955, the top 1 per cent captured just 9.3 per cent, and by 1978, the top 1 per cent's share of national income had declined to an all-time low of merely 5.7 per cent. Not surprisingly, this early postwar period has been dubbed the 'Golden Age of Capitalism' because it was an era in which capitalism delivered the benefits of economic growth not just to those at the top but broadly across the social spectrum.

At the time, this rising level of equality was typically viewed as simply part of the march of progress, part of the evolution towards a more advanced, modern way of life. A similar historical progression towards greater equality can be seen in other areas – in the evolution of legal and political rights. This general advance towards greater equality and social inclusiveness has continued, as legal and political rights have kept on evolving. In recent decades, there have been significant breakthroughs, for instance, in the recognition of rights for disadvantaged groups – racial minorities, women, gays, lesbians, the transgendered and the disabled.

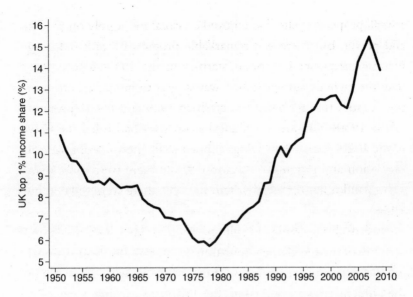

Fig. 1 The rise of the super-rich in the UK[10]

But while the *general* march towards greater equality has continued and advanced considerably in recent decades, the march towards greater *income* equality has been firmly halted, and turned sharply around.

In the past three decades, real incomes (with inflation factored out) have stagnated for most Britons. Virtually all the income growth has gone to the top 10 per cent, with particularly large gains going to the top 1 per cent, and spectacularly large gains going to the top .01 per cent. As a report by the Resolution Foundation noted in 2011, the bottom half of workers in the UK have seen their share of the national income fall by a quarter over the past thirty years. At the same time, the share going to the top 1 per cent has increased by half.[9] Figure 1 illustrates this dramatic surge in the share of national income going to the top in recent decades.

Of course, the rise of the super-rich has been even more pronounced in the United States. Between 1980 and 2008, the incomes of the bottom 90 per cent of Americans grew by a meagre 1 per cent (or an average of $303). Over those same years, the incomes of the top .01 per cent of Americans grew by 403 per cent (or an average of $21.9 million). The top 300,000 Americans now enjoy almost as much income as the bottom 150 million.[11]

To put this in perspective (as much as it's possible to put something like this in perspective), let's stack up today's top US incomes against the income of John D. Rockefeller, who in his day and for many decades afterward served as the legendary Richest Man Imaginable. In 1894, at the height of the Gilded Age when grand mansions lined Fifth Avenue, Rockefeller had a staggeringly large income of $1.25 million ($30 million in today's dollars). This was 7000 times the average US income at the time. But in 2007, hedge fund manager John Paulson had an income of $3.7 billion – more than 80,000 times the average US income.

Another way to look at it is this: Paulson, whose actions betting against the sub-prime mortgage market helped trigger the 2008 financial collapse and global economic meltdown, received as much income as did 80,000 nurses, who provided essential health care for more than six million Americans.

Fortunately, we have the teachings of modern economics to help us make sense of such a gap. Otherwise, we might be left struggling to understand by what logic Paulson could possibly be worth as much as 80,000 nurses – or, for that matter, as much as a single nurse.

•   •   •

The financial figures become numbing after a while. To get a clearer sense of how very rich the top income earners have become – and how dramatically they've pulled ahead of the population at large – it's helpful to create a visual image. To do so, we've borrowed a concept created by Dutch statistician Jan Pen. Pen's idea was to present the distribution of income as a national parade in which everyone in the country marches. The height of the marchers is determined by their incomes. The entire parade takes one hour, during which time the entire nation marches by very quickly, in order of height, starting with the shortest marchers (the lowest income earners) and ending with the tallest ones (the highest income earners).

The parade illustrates inequality, and it can be adapted to show the level of inequality in any country at any time. So, before we take a look at the British national income parade today, let's put things in a really broad context by looking at what a national income parade would have looked like in pre-industrial Britain.

There's a tendency to think of extreme inequality as a relic of a less advanced age. But while kings and nobles of pre-industrial times enjoyed a standard of living that was wildly lavish compared to the poor of their day, that gap was actually considerably smaller than that which exists today between billionaires and the homeless living on the streets of major UK cities. The lives of the destitute probably haven't changed that much over time, but the rich have become vastly richer than their pre-industrial counterparts. Here, then, is what the national income parade would look like for England and Wales in the late seventeenth century (1688, to be exact).[12]

At the outset, we'd see some very tiny characters – vagrants, gypsies, rogues, vagabonds – who manage to collect about £2 a year by begging or performing magic tricks at village gatherings. These extremely small people are followed by a large number of paupers and cottagers, who are still very low to the ground. Following close behind, about fifteen minutes into the parade, are household servants and common labourers, with incomes of about £15 a year, measuring about sixty centimetres tall.[13] Eventually, we start to see the 'middle class' – blacksmiths, silversmiths, masons, tinkers, tailors, weavers, cobblers, cordwainers (leather workers) – all earning about £38 to £40 a year and standing about average height. Just slightly taller are prosperous shopkeepers, ale-sellers and innkeepers. Next, there are naval officers, about three metres tall. Only in the last few minutes do we start to see some giants – successful merchants and sea traders, measuring about fifteen metres. Then in the last second, a cavalry of heavily armed knights appear, thirty-three metres tall (standing on the ground). Behind them, in weighty church garb, are pious-looking bishops and archbishops, earning £1300 a year and soaring up to fifty-three metres, even as they proclaim that the poor will inherit the Earth. Finally, a couple of dozen magnificently attired dukes and earls, with incomes above £6000, stretch a lofty 248 metres into the air.

Now let's see what a national income parade would look like in Britain today. What is striking is the much greater height discrepancies in today's parade, reflecting the fact that income inequality is now considerably more extreme than it was some three hundred years ago.

For the first six minutes of today's parade we see nothing but very tiny people – less than thirty centimetres tall. This low-income crowd, all earning less than £4500 a year, includes people on government assistance, part-time workers and senior citizens on fixed incomes. The height of the marchers rises ever so gradually. After about fifteen minutes, there are fast-food workers, retail shop workers and parking attendants, all less than ninety centimetres tall Eventually, slightly taller receptionists, factory workers and lorry drivers appear, but they're still awfully short, generally measuring less than 130 centimetres high. Their ranks seem never-ending.

The parade goes on for almost forty minutes before we start to see people of normal height, reflecting average income levels of around £25,000.[14] It is only in the last ten minutes that tall people start to appear. These are typically high-income professionals – lawyers, doctors, accountants, architects, engineers – and they stand well above the crowd, 3 to 3.5 metres in height. In the last minute, the marchers are much taller still – surgeons, corporate lawyers, advertising executives – standing over 4.5 metres tall.

Just before we come to the very end of the parade, let's recall that we're measuring inequality of income. If we were measuring inequality of wealth – that is, net worth – the size differences would be even more dramatic. In that parade, a good portion of the marchers would actually be underground, reflecting the fact that their debts are larger than the value of their assets.

But in this parade we're measuring income inequality, so the height differences reflect the differences in what individual Britons earn in a year as they go about working and contributing to the overall economy. For the most part, everybody works and contributes in some way. The varying height levels reflect the fact that some individuals earn more because they work harder, are smarter, more talented, better educated or just ended up in better jobs than others. But, towards the end, the marchers soar to such great heights that it's hard to account for the vast discrepancy between them and the others in the parade.

With a few seconds to go, we begin to spot some famous faces in the crowd. There's supermodel Kate Moss, with an annual income of £5.74 million, stretching half a kilometre into the air. Less stunning but taller, measuring 1.5 kilometres, is Rupert Murdoch, who collected £18.7 million from his News Corporation, even in the wake of the company's phone-hacking scandal. Also recognizable among this group of giants is former Barclays chief executive Bob Diamond, measuring 1.9 kilometres high, who collected £23 million in share options (which he surrendered under public pressure over his disgraced role in the LIBOR scandal, leaving him with total compensation of £100 million since 2006).[15] David Beckham, with an income of £28.7 million (including endorsements), jogs by at a height of 2.3 kilometres. Then there's media mega-star Simon Cowell, standing 4.6 kilometres tall, with an income of £57 million.

Now, with less than a second to go, we get a glimpse of some of the hedge fund crowd – or at least of their lower legs. Their bodies stretch so far above us, we can't see their faces. Chris Rokos, co-founder of Brevan Howard Asset Management, with a take-home income of £100 million, stands a gigantic 8.1 kilometres tall. David Harding of Winton Capital Management, with an income of £390 million, shoots up to a towering 31.6 kilometres.

Then finally, there he is – the very tallest person in the parade, Alan Howard, the key fund manager and co-founder of Brevan Howard. The recipient of the nation's largest income, Howard relocated to Geneva in June 2010. His firm said the move was for lifestyle reasons, but there was widespread speculation he was trying to avoid the 10 percentage point increase in the top British tax rate. His firm also caught some attention last year with accusations from a fired RBS trader that Brevan Howard had requested the bank make changes in the LIBOR rate.[16] Nonetheless, Howard, with an income of £400 million, stands a phenomenal 32.4 kilometres tall. A high-cruising airplane would fly past him at thigh-level. His head juts into the stratosphere, well beyond view of the millions of Britons still mired in recession and austerity down below.

●　　●　　●

As we've noted, there is strong evidence that a more equal distribution of resources would provide significant social and economic benefits. But the case for a more equal society also rests on compelling moral grounds.

It is our contention that the concentration of resources in the hands of a small elite amounts to a profound moral wrong that cries out for correction. The distribution of economic resources in a society is one of its most influential social structures. In a market economy, to have money is to have freedom. Income and wealth confer extraordinary freedom and advantages. Conversely, inadequate income and wealth give rise to exceptional disadvantages and the denial of freedoms. Indeed, the concentration of income and wealth, and in particular the wide gap between rich and poor, shapes every aspect of society. Vast numbers of citizens are effectively denied entry to the main activities of our society because they lack money, the basic ticket of admission.

Furthermore, it is our contention that there is no moral legitimacy to the claim of the rich to such a large share of the nation's resources. Perhaps stung by charges of moral illegitimacy coming from protest groups including UK Uncut, the mega-rich have strained to come up with fresh justifications for their oversized portion. One line of argument that has gained currency, at least among the rich, is the notion that today's vast fortunes were earned in a 'meritocracy'. The argument emphasizes the notion that inherited wealth plays a smaller role today than in the past. In particular, the rise of 'self-made' billionaires and the emergence of a wealthy class of corporate and financial professionals has led some observers to conclude that today's rich are deserving of their huge rewards, that income is now meted out in a ruthlessly competitive global economy where the best and the brightest rise to the top because of their own worth and contribution.

Not surprisingly, the meritocracy concept has become a staple in the literature on which members of the new elite rely. In a special report in January 2011 – shortly after the launch of UK Uncut – *The Economist* heralded the rise of what it described as 'the few': 'Societies have always had elites...The big change over the past century is that elites are increasingly meritocratic and global. The richest people in advanced countries are not aristocrats but entrepreneurs such as Bill Gates.' The magazine went on to celebrate today's super-rich, arguing that 'to become rich in the first place, they typically have to do something extraordinary. Some inherit money, of course, but most build a better mousetrap, finance someone else's good idea or at least run a chain of hairdressers in a way that keeps customers coming back. And because they are mostly self-made, today's rich are restless and dynamic.'

In fact, entrepreneurs make up a very small portion of today's top earners, estimated at less than 4 per cent.[17] Today's super-rich elite is composed mostly of corporate and financial professionals, who account for some 60 per cent of those in the top-earning 0.1 per cent (with lawyers and real estate developers accounting for another 10 per cent). In the past, corporate and financial professionals were regarded as agents who managed the enterprises of the owning class. In recent decades, however, these management professionals have moved centre-stage, grabbing more power for themselves – and a much larger share of the financial rewards.

The result, according to John C. Bogle, founder and former chairman of US-based Vanguard Group mutual fund organization, has been 'grotesquely excessive compensation paid to executive chiefs' – compensation that is 'unjustified by any remotely comparable business achievement'.[18] Bogle argues that the corporate world is now riddled with conflicts of interest, leaving little check on the cosy relations between CEOs and corporate directors, compensation committees and auditors. Similarly, in the UK, the High Pay Commission concluded that 'pay at the top has spiralled alarmingly to stratospheric levels in some of our biggest companies'. It also found that corporations were attempting to '"camouflage" executive pay' and hide 'ever more complicated pay arrangements... within reams of remuneration reports'.[19]

Nowhere has the money grab by the professional class been more evident than in the financial world, whose top players are members of an elite group that financial historian Charles Geisst has called 'the highest earners of all time'.[20] Among the top-earning 0.1 per cent of Britons, fully 30 per cent now work in finance.[21] This not only reflects how big the rewards have become at the top in the financial world, but also the changing nature of finance and its role in the economy. Traditionally, the role of finance was to raise capital for business ventures, to 'finance someone else's good idea' – as *The Economist* put it. But today's financial barons mostly avoid the slower, riskier rewards to be won in financing good ideas. Instead, they concentrate on financial speculation (also known as gambling) where the rewards can be much quicker and truly stupendous, and where there is often little at risk, since governments end up bailing out massive losses. Hedge fund managers have used financial speculation to catapult themselves into a stratosphere of income compensation that is in a league all of its own, vastly higher than even the wildly extravagant CEO pay levels at leading corporations. In 2009, the top twenty-five hedge fund managers in the world made a total of $25.3 billion – averaging a little more than $1 billion *each*.

Images of the super-rich financing good ideas or building better mousetraps or hairdressing salons cast these characters in an attractive light. But, outside the pages of *The Economist*, members of the new global elite aren't actually doing much of this. Nor are they especially talented or indispensable – or even particularly beneficial to society. More often, they are receiving gigantic rewards because of brute luck, ruthlessness, speculation, cheating, or simply because they were well positioned to direct income towards themselves or to capitalize on socially created opportunities that could have (and would have) been taken by others in their absence. Certainly there is no evidence that members of today's elite are any smarter, more talented or harder working than were the elite of a generation ago, who received a fraction of the pay for doing work that was at least as good and as valuable to society.

In fact, the sums of money earned by the rich – and everyone else for that matter – are hugely influenced by the particular laws and institutions that govern a society and that have been put in place by those with the power to make the rules (a subject we'll return to in the next chapter). It is often argued that today's big incomes are the result of 'globalization'. In fact, what is referred to as 'globalization' is simply the particular set of laws that govern the global economy, codified in trade deals and enforced by bodies such as the World Trade Organization. And these laws, conceived and put in place by the elite, have tended to favour the elite. Furthermore, while globalization has been experienced by all advanced nations, it is really only in the Anglo-American countries that the rewards at the top have grown so spectacularly. Continental European nations, and in particular the Nordic countries, remain more equal societies – because they have continued to redistribute incomes more equitably, as a result of the laws that make up their tax-and-transfer systems.

As we will argue in this book, the biggest factor in explaining today's colossal pay at the top isn't better performance or the effects of globalization. Rather, it's that our highest earners have managed to shape the agenda in the past thirty years, using their influence to put in place laws – domestically and internationally – that favour their own interests. Rather than wealth creation, their main achievement has been ensuring the diversion to themselves of an enormous share of the wealth created, what is known in economics as 'rent-seeking'.

The growing concentration of income and wealth at the top is thus largely the product of deliberate policy changes affecting the corporate and financial world, as well as the gutting of labour laws and social programmes that protected those lower down the income ladder. The rise of a hugely rewarded class of financial professionals has been greatly facilitated, for instance, by the dismantling of financial regulations that were wisely put in place in the 1930s, following the 1929 crash. And no discussion of how the rich manage to rig the rules in their favour would be complete without highlighting their role in convincing governments to reduce their tax burden.

Most crucially, the elite has managed, through a pervasive propaganda campaign, to convince much of the public that the huge redirection of rewards to the top is simply not an issue. This campaign – reflected in the media and in public discourse – has effectively changed social norms and expectations, putting forward a new social creed that celebrates greed and personal acquisitiveness (particularly in those at the top). With business-funded think-tanks churning out pseudo-theories about how enriching the rich benefits us all, rapacious behaviour on the part of the elite has come to be regarded as natural and healthy, even something to be admired and rewarded.

This is a sharp departure from the more egalitarian values of the postwar era, when such gluttonous conduct would have been frowned upon. Back then, there was a largely unspoken agreement in society as to the acceptable levels of remuneration for jobs at all levels, including at the top. Thus, business executives and the corporate boards overseeing them had a sense of the boundaries. They didn't reward themselves with princely compensation, because such behaviour would have been regarded by the public as inappropriate and improper, even vulgar. This social disapproval was reflected in the very high top marginal tax rates that prevailed in the postwar era, defining the limits of what was considered reasonable pay for even those performing the top jobs. Anything beyond that was seen as excessive, and society weighed in by taxing it almost all away.

In recent decades, those social constraints have been all but wiped away, silencing the popular outrage that would surely have otherwise accompanied such a massive heist of national income by the richest members of society. The propaganda campaign selling the virtues of unbridled acquisitiveness seems to have convinced large segments of the public that mind-boggling greed is acceptable or at least 'a fact of life', an inevitable, pointless-to-resist aspect of the postmodern age. With public outrage largely muted or deflected onto gazing breathlessly at the lifestyles of billionaires, there has been little to deter those at the top of the corporate and financial world from dipping ever deeper into the till.

The implications of all this – for social equity and harmony, for the well-being of individual citizens, for British democracy and for the very survival of the Earth's ecosystem – are clearly mammoth, and are the subject of this book. But let's start with some clarity about what's taken place and not be sidetracked by misconstruing as a 'meritocracy' a system that is delivering the largest rewards in history to a group whose main distinguishing characteristic is an unusually fierce determination for self-enrichment.

2
why pornography is the only true free market

In December 2009, the Labour government slapped a one-time 50 per cent tax on bankers' bonuses, prompting howls of protest from the banking elite, including foreign banks operating in the UK.

As the furore grew, the legendary Wall Street firm Goldman Sachs quietly informed a key British media outlet that it was considering relocating its massive London operation to Geneva, signalling that its top officials had no intention of submitting to the 'super-tax'. Goldman CEO Lloyd Blankfein, who received $73 million in compensation in 2007 and had amassed some $500 million in Goldman stock, had previously revealed how little the crash of 2008 had diminished bankers' perception of themselves and their place in society. In an interview with the *Sunday Times* in November 2009, Blankfein steadfastly defended his company and himself, explaining that he was just a banker 'doing God's work'.[1]

The tax hike that raised the top income tax rate to 50 per cent earlier that year had led to similar threats of departure from members of the UK elite. Theatre impresario Sir Andrew Lloyd Webber had appealed to the public to reject what he characterized as a tax increase on those who create wealth: 'The last thing we need is a Somali pirate-style raid on the few wealth creators who still dare to navigate Britain's gale-force waters.' Film star Sir Michael Caine echoed the outrage, threatening to leave Britain if taxes at the upper end went even 1 percentage point higher.[2] In a sympathetic *Telegraph* article about Michael Caine's tax complaints, journalist Iain Martin noted that Micahel Caine, the son of a charlady and a Billingsgate fish market porter, personified the rags-to-riches success that the government should be trying to encourage. What we need is not higher taxes, Martin asserted, but to clear 'the rubble of the interfering state out of the way'.[3]

In fact, Martin – and just about every other critic of high taxes on the rich – conveniently overlooks one key fact: without 'the rubble of the interfering state,' the rich would have nothing.

It's a simple and unassailable point, but it's almost always ignored: it is only possible for anyone to own anything – money, land, jewellery, yachts – if there is a state to create laws and enforce those laws. This is the logical starting point for any serious discussion about income and wealth and who is entitled to what.

Without government, there would be chaos and anarchy, or what seventeenth-century English philosopher Thomas Hobbes called 'a war of all against all'. Not only would life under such circumstances be rough and disorderly – or, in Hobbes's words, 'nasty, brutish, and short' – but there would be no reliable way to enforce ownership. As another English philosopher Jeremy Bentham succinctly put it: 'Take away the laws, all property ceases.' Under such conditions, everyone's welfare would be fairly minimal – and roughly equal. Accordingly, philosophers Liam Murphy and Thomas Nagel argue that it is wrong to 'pretend that the differences in ability, personality and inherited wealth that lead to great inequalities of welfare in an orderly market economy would have the same effect if there were no government to create and protect legal property rights'.[4]

By imagining the complete removal of government, we can quickly dispose of the notion that the 'interfering state' has been hard on the rich. On the contrary, that interfering state has been their best friend. Without it, they'd be scrounging around in the bush with the rest of us, worried about when the next marauding gang was going to pounce on the buffalo they had just speared in an attempt to feed their children. Only with the complex set of laws governing property, inheritance, contracts, banking, stock exchanges, and other commercial relations – not to mention criminal prosecution of those trying to seize their buffalo – can the rich be secure in holding their possessions and enjoy the comfortable lives that come with those possessions.

Indeed, a government-enforced system of property rights, while theoretically benefiting all, provides far greater benefits to the rich than to the rest of us. As American legal scholar Robert Hale put it: 'One owner, as the result of the entire network of restrictions inherent in property rights, gets the benefit of finding that liberty to use a particular ragged suit of clothes will not be interfered with by the acts of non-owners. Another owner gets the liberty of wandering over a large estate and using a large number of automobiles without interference from others...The benefits conferred by these rights are not equal in any important sense.'[5] It could be added that the police would likely respond somewhat differently to a call from the homeless man saying that someone was making off with his ragged suit than they would to a call from the estate owner reporting that his mansion was being robbed. While the state theoretically serves us all, it serves some more readily and fully than others.

In fact, those who lack resources will quickly find the state and all its resources lined up against them. Hale notes that while no law forbids a man to eat food, 'there is a law which forbids him to eat any of the food which actually exists in the community – and that is the law of property.' Unless the individual has the money to afford the food available, he will have to go without. Similarly, he can't take possession of the delightful swing set in someone's garden and then tell the police that he was simply exercising his right to acquire private property. Private property is a special privilege, backed up by state power, and conferred exclusively on those who have control over sufficient resources.

Of course, the rich have no quarrel with government interference when it comes to enforcing property rights. They are only irked when the government interferes by imposing taxes on their incomes, particularly when those taxes are progressive, that is, impose a higher marginal rate on higher levels of income. But in protesting this taxation as unjust – in suggesting that it amounts to a 'Somali pirate-style raid' – the rich are implying that the income they received before tax was somehow just. There they were, minding their own business, receiving their just compensation due to their talent and effort, and then along came the tax system and disturbed this otherwise intrinsically fair distribution. The assumption is that the way the 'market' distributes income is fair.

This assumption is based on the notion that the market operates according to basic, natural principles – such as the laws of gravity – that are not subject to the sort of human pressure and political manipulation that presumably shape the tax system. In other words, the market is what would just happen if the interfering hand of government were removed, if things were simply allowed to happen, based on the laws of nature. Hence, the term *laissez-faire* ('let act' or 'leave alone'). In fact, this is a bit of fiction. The 'market' is a creation of the state every bit as much as the tax system is. Both are based on an elaborate series of laws devised and put in place by humans. Accordingly, those with the power to make the laws are able to mould them to their own benefit.

The profit level of a company, for instance, is determined by a whole range of laws covering property and contractual rights – copyright laws that prevent competitors from copying an innovation; environmental laws that determine how much a company may pollute or what fines it will face if it exceeds those levels; labour laws that determine whether its employees are allowed to form a union and whether they are permitted to withdraw their services; contract laws that determine what it can collect from a client who fails to live up to the terms of an agreement or what it must pay a landlord if it wants to break the lease held on its factory. After these (and many other) laws determine the company's profit level, there is a whole different set of laws governing how owners of the company will transfer those profits to themselves – what rights shareholders have in determining how the profits will be divided, who will get paid and who won't in the case of the corporation's bankruptcy, and so on. (The very existence of the company, for that matter, is made possible by laws that allow for incorporation, thereby limiting the personal financial vulnerability of the company's officers and owners in the event of a lawsuit.)

Once a shareholder is allotted her share of the company's profits, she may perhaps invest some of this money in bonds. Once again, the hand of government will be involved in determining how much she will profit from her investment, since the return she receives on her bonds will be determined by interest rates, which are determined by the actions of government-appointed central bankers. Their decisions affecting interest rates will hinge on whether they (and, ultimately, the government that appointed them) give priority to controlling inflation (as wealth-holders tend to want) or to encouraging employment (as those without wealth tend to want).

For that matter, lawyers, doctors, accountants, engineers, architects and other professionals enjoy elevated incomes because of laws that give these groups monopoly power over their occupations. By giving them the legal power to license those practising in their fields, governments enable these professionals to restrict the number of participants, thereby ensuring high demand and high prices for their services. While such laws may be necessary to protect the public from quacks and charlatans, they also clearly bolster the incomes of a small group of professionals. Certainly, these professionals are operating in tightly controlled situations governed by a set of laws – far from what is conjured up by the expression 'free market'.

The same is true in the international sphere. An international set of laws governs the world economy, shaping outcomes and determining winners and losers. Those with the power to make the laws are able to shape them to their own advantage. Thus, in recent decades, increasingly powerful corporate interests have revamped international trade laws and put in place 'free trade' treaties that eliminate or reduce national tariffs and establish a set of investor rights facilitating capital flows and limiting government interventions. It is these legal changes that have enhanced capital mobility, with negative consequences for labour. Of course, we're told capital is mobile today because of 'globalization'. In fact, capital could have been highly mobile in the postwar world as well, but international trade laws placed more restrictions on capital mobility back then. It is today's international laws – not the nebulous forces of 'globalization' – that have loosened the restraints on capital, thereby reducing the bargaining power of labour.

The point is that there's no simple, natural thing called 'the market'. The market is the result of the complex set of national and international laws that regulate commerce and financial exchange. It can take any number of forms, depending on decisions made by government officials and parliamentarians who design, approve and implement those laws. If the government tilts toward the interests of business owners, it may ensure strong property rights by, for instance, enacting laws that make it very difficult for workers to unionize or that make work stoppages or strikes illegal. In doing so, the government is not simply letting nature take its course, as implied by the phrase laissez-faire; rather, it is actively intervening in a way that restricts the rights of workers, preventing them from combining with other workers or from withdrawing their labour in order to maximize their bargaining power.

If a new government takes over and tilts more toward workers' interests, it might revise those laws to ensure the right to unionize, thereby strengthening the bargaining power of labour in its struggle with business owners. There is a wide range of legal possibilities just on issues dealing with unionization – and unionization represents just one area of the vast array of laws that determine how any particular 'market' will operate. All these variations represent ways that the goalposts can be moved around and each variation will produce a different result, with different winners and losers.

So, for instance, the stagnation in workers' wages in recent decades is largely a result of the enactment of conservative policies that have tilted the playing field against labour, by weakening laws protecting workers' incomes and their right to unionize and strike, and by strengthening laws protecting corporate rights. At the same time, changes in other laws – particularly ones governing financial regulations and taxation – have made it possible for those at the top to earn vastly more than it was possible for their counterparts to earn a few decades ago.

How much less, for instance, would Goldman Sachs CEO Lloyd Blankfein have earned in 2007 had there been a different set of laws governing financial markets?

To answer this question, it's useful to briefly review some recent history. Only a few decades ago, financial markets were much more carefully regulated. It was because of changes in the rules governing the financial marketplace that firms in the City and on Wall Street grew to become so colossal and wildly profitable.

In the early postwar period, the major investment houses in both the UK and the US were considerably smaller, operating as private partnerships. This meant that a firm was owned by its senior partners, who shared the profits but who also were jointly responsible for all the firm's debts and liabilities. As a result, the partners were careful in their investing practices, knowing that they would personally be on the hook in the event of big losses.

They also held each other in check, since the reckless behaviour of one individual could lead to losses that affected all partners in the firm.

But things changed in the 1970s and '80s – because the rules governing the marketplace changed. In 1970, the New York Stock Exchange lifted its ban on investment banks becoming public corporations with listings on the stock exchange. As a result, the major US investment banks gradually switched over to the public model. In Britain, with the sudden financial deregulation of the Big Bang in 1986, small partnerships were also replaced by large investment houses.

In both countries, investment banks, no longer constricted by the responsibilities inherent in partnerships, were able to raise huge amounts of cash and grow much larger in size. 'The Big Bang generation became millionaires at the same time as they were freed from the responsibility of looking after the partnerships,' notes former British investment banker Philip Augar in *The Death of Gentlemanly Capitalism*.[6] Senior bank executives were no longer personally liable for their firms' debts. So when individuals within a firm – or whole trading divisions – indulged in rogue behaviour in pursuit of ever-bigger profits, there was none of the vigilance that had existed in the days when the finances of all the firm's partners had been at stake. Now bankers could use other people's money, gamble recklessly, and siphon massive pay packages for themselves out of the profits, with little on the line.

Indeed, as a result of the bigger size of the banks and the fact that they were raising money from the public, government now regarded the banks as 'too big to fail'. If their irresponsible behaviour risked undermining the stability of the entire financial system, government would have to step in and bail them out. For bankers, it was a dream world: they could take enormous risks, knowing that whatever gains they made would be theirs alone, while losses would be covered by the taxpayers.

All this of course suggests that the more stringent laws that governed financial markets in the early postwar period had been eminently sensible, and their removal greatly contributed to the 2008 financial crash. The point here, however, is that today's plutocracy earns much of its income in ways that would not have been possible under the particular set of market rules that existed only a few decades ago. Without a whole new set of man-made laws governing the financial marketplace, Blankfein would undoubtedly have earned considerably less than £45 million in 2007, and his Goldman Sachs stock would be worth a lot less than £300 million today – probably hundreds of millions less.

Under the laws of the early postwar era, doing 'God's work' would have been a lot less profitable.

● ● ●

We may never know how well Michael Caine would have fared had he become a porn star, but his income would have certainly been smaller.

This is relevant because it helps unpack the mythology that allows Michael Caine, Andrew Lloyd Webber and other big earners in the entertainment world to believe that their large incomes are simply the result of the exercise of their talents in the free market. Make no mistake about it: their good fortune has come about because of government intervention in the marketplace. And no, we are not talking about government subsidies for the arts but rather something much more basic and enriching – the elaborate set of copyright laws that allow artists and performers to receive royalties for their creative efforts. Without these laws, the movies in which Michael Caine appears could be copied and sold to people all over the world, without Michael Caine receiving a penny. Under such a wide-open system, no film production company would be willing to pay him a substantial fee for his performance, or much of a fee at all.

This indeed is the fate of porn stars. No matter how great their talent, porn stars earn far less than stars in the regular movie business. That's because the porn business, with its dubious legal status, hasn't been able to take advantage of the huge protection the state offers 'legitimate' filmmakers and other creative artists in the form of copyright laws. Given the social disapproval of pornography, porn producers have assumed they would have little success in the courts, and have therefore been reluctant to bring legal action against those who reproduce their videos without permission (although some recent court challenges indicate this may be changing). As a result, porn videos are constantly ripped off: the Internet abounds in freely available pornography. This unregulated system is closer to what an actual 'free market' in the film industry would be like.[7]

But it's not a market that allows performers to get rich, as American economist Dean Baker has noted. The huge incomes enjoyed by stars such as Michael Caine and Andrew Lloyd Webber would be impossible without an elaborate set of government laws that provide them with property rights over their own artistic works – rights that are enforced by police and the courts. Baker notes that copyrights and patents are really government-granted monopolies, and that they have their origins in the feudal system of guilds.

It's straying a bit from our point, but it's worth briefly noting that it would be possible to do without copyright and patent laws, which form a large part of our legal system. The justification for these laws is that, without them, there would be little investment of time and money in creating new works of music, film or writing – or, for that matter, developing new pharmaceutical drugs. But, as Baker argues, there are other forms of government intervention that could ensure adequate investment in these areas, while creating fewer negative consequences due to the monopoly power of copyrights and patents. For instance, laws permitting generic equivalents of brand-name drugs can help restrain brand-name manufacturers from using their monopoly power to extract astronomical profits, with increased government funding covering research costs into drugs badly needed by the public. The consequences of monopoly power are less serious in the field of the creative arts, but Baker argues that the monopolies created by copyright laws are enormously costly to enforce, and becoming more so as the technology for video and music reproduction becomes ever easier. He proposes instead a system of individual vouchers, under which each taxpayer would be given a fixed sum that he or she would pass on to individual artists each year through the tax system. That may sound like it would involve a great deal of government intervention, but then so does the system of copyright and patent laws.

The point here is that government intervention in the form of copyright laws benefits stars such as Michael Caine and Andrew Lloyd Webber. They have become rich, not by exercising their talents in some mythical 'free market' but by exercising those talents within a tightly regulated, government-enforced monopoly, heavily enforced at great cost by police and the courts. Without the interfering rubble of this aspect of the modern state, Michael Caine and Andrew Lloyd Webber would be no richer or more famous than the giants of the porn world, no matter how much natural talent they were endowed with.

So it is bizarre to isolate the possible tax increases faced by Lloyd Blankfein, Michael Caine or Andrew Lloyd Webber and condemn them as the actions of an interfering government. The market is nothing but a complex web of government interventions. The income-tax hike stands out in these people's minds only because it's an intervention that goes against their interests, whereas so many of the other laws and government policies favour them. As Murphy and Nagel wryly put it: 'people care more about what unjustly harms them than about what unjustly benefits them'.[8] The favourable interventions tend to become invisible to their beneficiaries, as if they were just part of the natural order of things.

•   •   •

The notion that it should be possible to become a billionaire is rooted in the idea that there are some uniquely talented people whose contribution is so great that they deserve to be hugely, fabulously rewarded. Some fabulously wealthy individuals, such as American businessman Leo J. Hindery Jr, have articulated this point themselves. Hindery, whose contribution was to found a cable television sports network (a clear example of a government-granted monopoly, by the way), put it like this: 'I think there are people, including myself at certain times in my career, who because of their uniqueness warrant whatever the market will bear.'[9] Similarly, Lew Frankfort, chairman and chief executive of the high-end handbag company Coach, argues that today's extraordinary pay packages can be justified because of the extraordinary skills required by the individuals running corporations in the 'technological age'. As he told *The New York Times* in 2007, 'To be successful, you now needed vision, lateral thinking, courage, and an ability to see things, not the way they were but how they might be.' Sanford I. Weill, long a towering figure on Wall Street, is also impressed with the contributions of billionaires like himself: 'People can look at the last twenty-five years and say that this is an incredibly unique period of time. We didn't rely on somebody else to build what we built.'

What is so striking about such statements, beside the absence of modesty, is the lack of acknowledgment of the role society plays in the accumulation of any great fortune. These men apparently fail to see society's role in constructing a market that favours their interests. More broadly, they seem unaware of the pervasive role played by society in general (as well as by specific other people) in every aspect of their lives – in nurturing them, shaping them and teaching them what they know, performing innumerable functions that contribute to the operation of their businesses and every other aspect of the market and indeed every part of life around them.

Those justifying large fortunes tend to see the individual in splendid isolation, achieving great feats on his or her own. In fact, no such reality exists. There is no such thing as the 'self-made man'. Humans are, above all, social beings who make their way in the world with the assistance and involvement of countless others who play roles of varying importance. This point is so obvious that it seems ridiculous, even trite, to mention it. Yet it is typically left out of the formulations of those invoking the inherent right of individuals to accumulate large fortunes.

Philosophers have conjured up the notion of the individual, alone in a state of nature, choosing to enter into a contract with society. But this is clearly a metaphor with no basis in reality. No individual ever existed first in a state of nature and then decided to join society. Her involvement with society came first and, except in the most unusual circumstances, continued throughout her life. The primacy and ubiquity of society – so casually erased by billionaires and others justifying their fortunes – must be restored if we are to have any meaningful discussion of income and wealth, and where an individual's claim ends and society's begins. The restoration of society into the equation allows us to meaningfully explore the question of the proper relationship between the individual and the community – and who owes what to whom.

One of the crucial ways that society assists individuals in their ability to generate wealth lies in the inheritance from previous generations. This inheritance from the past is so vast it is almost beyond calculation. It encompasses every aspect of what we know as a civilization and every bit of scientific and technological knowledge we make use of today, going all the way back to the beginning of human language and the invention of the wheel. Measured against this immense human cultural and technological inheritance, any additional marginal advance in today's world – even the creation of a cable television sports network – inevitably pales in significance.

The question then becomes this: who is the proper beneficiary of the wealth generated by innovations based on the massive inheritance from the past – the individual innovator who adapts some tiny aspect of this past inheritance to create a slightly new product, or society as a whole (that is, all of us)?

Under our current system, the innovator captures an enormously large share of the benefits. Clearly, the innovator should be compensated for his contribution. But should he also be compensated for the contributions made by all the other innovators who, over the centuries, have built up a body of knowledge that made his marginal advance possible today?

It is our position that society – and, by extension, all of us – should be entitled to a much larger share of the benefits. This could be accomplished through a decision to raise taxes at the upper end, thereby adjusting the economic goalposts – a decision no more arbitrary than the decisions that determined the current location of the goalposts.

The sums involved are potentially colossal. Virtually all the economic gains of the past few decades have gone to the top; that's where the money is. Furthermore, the goal is not just to find a new revenue source. The goal is more basic: to determine a morally valid basis for the distribution of income, rather than accepting on faith the moral validity of the way income is distributed by the set of man-made laws that make up the current version of the 'market'.

●   ●   ●

We maintain that billionaires do not deserve their massive fortunes, that members of the ultra-wealthy elite are not morally entitled to keep the large share of their gains permissible under today's tax laws. In taking this position, we are not denying the enormous contribution made by some of the mega-rich, including innovators such as Bill Gates and Mark Zuckerberg. These men have truly changed the way people live today – a fact that perhaps puts them in a category quite different to, say, the stars of the handbag industry or the world of cable TV sports.

Bill Gates may be the hardest case to contest, given that he is credited with nothing less than making the computer revolution accessible to hundreds of millions of people and donating billions of dollars to worthwhile causes. We will look at his case in more detail later. For now, though, let's take a quick look at Mark Zuckerberg, who became a multi-billionaire in his twenties by inventing the social media network Facebook, which has an estimated five hundred million users worldwide.

In questioning the moral legitimacy of Zuckerberg's fortune, our point is simply to note that he has received a staggering fortune – estimated today at about $12 billion – for producing a product in which his role was, by any reasonable measure, fairly marginal. Certainly, Zuckerberg couldn't have made that $12 billion all on his own, or even remotely on his own. He made it, as a mere university student, by taking advantage of the technological inheritance provided by all those who had developed the Internet and, before that, the personal computer and, before that, the mainframe computer and, before that, the punched-card tabulating machine and, before that…all the way back to the invention of the wheel.

It is estimated that about 90 per cent of any wealth generated today is due to this 'knowledge inheritance' of the past. If this sounds unlikely, imagine whether Zuckerberg could have created the Facebook empire if he had, say, been a student thirty years ago in the pre-Internet age, if he hadn't attended college in the early 2000s, when computer advances had reached a certain stage of sophistication. Given these advances, he and a number of other bright students spotted the opportunity to develop a social networking program. If Zuckerberg hadn't got Facebook off the ground in early 2004, any of his competitors would have soon got theirs off the ground and probably gone on to dominate the field.

So, to whom does the massive knowledge inheritance that made Facebook possible logically belong? Does it all belong to Zuckerberg? We argue that a very significant portion of it belongs to society, and that society should capture its rightful share through a more progressive tax system.

It could be added that a more progressive tax system would have done little to discourage Zuckerberg's enterprise. While he was scrambling to develop Facebook, it's unlikely that he was devoting much time to worrying about what taxes he might eventually pay if he were to become phenomenally, incomprehensibly rich. It's certainly hard to imagine him simply abandoning his quest, had he thought that success might leave him with an after-tax fortune of only, say, $5 billion – or, for that matter, $500 million or even just $5 million. And if he had abandoned the quest, it's clear that his competitors, hot on the same entrepreneurial trail, would have simply finished the job.

With or without Zuckerberg, we would all today be experiencing the benefits of social networking.

●　　　●　　　●

So higher taxes on the rich are certainly in order. And the case for such an adjustment of the economic goalposts is particularly compelling today, since a huge proportion of the wealth currently being generated stems directly from the many computer-related technological breakthroughs of the past half century. Individual entrepreneurs, including Gates and Zuckerberg, have been able to utilize these technological advances to develop the wide array of information-age and Internet-related products that flood our markets, enabling them to become wildly rich.

In the early decades of the 1900s, there was also an impressive set of technological breakthroughs related to the development of the internal combustion engine. This led to mass consumer markets for cars and airplane travel following the Second World War, creating vast new wealth and many private fortunes. However, there was an important difference. Back in that early postwar period, the enormous economic gains were more widely shared, as a result of the more egalitarian ethos that produced more powerful unions, more progressive taxation and more generous social programmes. Today, the stupendous economic gains made possible by the technological advances of the computer age have been almost entirely captured and retained by a tiny elite, with little of the wealth flowing back to society through the tax system.

This seems grossly unfair. It also appears to have led some of the lucky few to develop a false sense of their own contribution. We take issue, for instance, with Lew Frankfort, the CEO of Coach, who argued that today's billionaires deserve their fortune because they had the 'vision, lateral thinking, courage and an ability to see things' that was necessary to succeed in the 'technological age'. We think he's got things backwards. The enormous rewards at the top haven't come about because today's elite has been particularly far-sighted, visionary or courageous in the technological age. Rather, the technological age has produced spectacular breakthroughs, and the elite has been adroit at seizing a particularly large portion of the resulting economic gains for itself, and lobbying to ensure that the tax system retrieves little back for society.

Today's gigantic fortunes seem to be less a reflection of the innovative genius of current billionaires, and more a reflection of how exceptionally adept they've been at elbowing their way to the front of the trough.

3
paying for a
civilized society

The most reliable applause line for politicians in recent decades has been calling for lower taxes. Since anti-tax sabre-rattling became all the rage with Margaret Thatcher and Ronald Reagan, the Anglo-American countries have slashed their taxes deeply. Meanwhile, another group of developed economies, led by the Nordic countries, has maintained high tax levels. So we have two groups of developed countries with very different approaches, creating what could be considered almost a laboratory for testing the impact of high and low tax levels.

The results of this thirty-year experiment amount to a staggering repudiation of the anti-tax arguments that have dominated public discourse in the Anglo-American countries. The Nordic countries have pulled dramatically ahead in achieving greater social well-being and equality, better health and stronger economic security for their citizens. Tax-cutting advocates tend to deny or ignore these achievements – or, when they do acknowledge them, insist that they have come at a great economic cost. This is simply not true. High-tax countries have enjoyed just as good or better economic results and material prosperity as low-tax countries.

We hear exactly the opposite, of course. The dreadful financial crises in Greece, Spain, Portugal, Ireland and Italy are routinely cited as proof that high-tax, high-spending countries end up in some Faustian hell of their own making. All the more reason to stay the Anglo-American low-tax course, we're told.

What is rarely acknowledged is that these basket-case countries (with the exception of Italy) are not high-tax, high-spending countries at all. On the contrary, they belong in the low-tax category, alongside the Anglo-American countries. Furthermore, as Nobel-winning economist Paul Krugman has pointed out, the financial problems of Greece, Spain and the other nations in southern Europe are not related to their tax levels but rather to their membership of the EU single currency system, which severely limits their ability to adjust their exchange rates downward to restore their international competitiveness.[1]

The financial crisis in countries in southern Europe tells us nothing about the impact of high tax levels. Rather, these cases are being cited deceptively in an attempt to perpetuate myths about the menace of taxation.

• • •

A broad consensus emerged during the 1950s and '60s about the role of government and the goals of public policy, including taxation. Based on the experience of citizens during the Great Depression and the Second World War, it was widely accepted that governments should correct the pervasive failures of the market, stabilize the economy, ensure rising living standards, guarantee workers a degree of economic security, provide access to health and education services, and promote social equality. While the precise nature of what was often called the 'social contract' varied from country to country, citizens in most Western industrialized nations opted to rely upon the economic decisions of democratically elected governments rather than purely on the market. In order to empower governments to carry out their vital tasks, taxes were increased substantially. In the UK, total tax levels as a percentage of GDP increased from 30.4 per cent in 1965 to 34.9 per cent in 1975 and then to 37 per cent in 1985. This was broadly in line with increased total tax levels in the average Western European country at the time.

In the mid-1970s, the rich became increasingly concerned about the threat that a strong, active state posed to their power and privileges, and sought to rewrite the terms of the social contract. The basic thrust of their agenda has been to marginalize the democratic political system and to concentrate power in the private sector, where they can operate free from serious constraint. To achieve this end, they have denigrated and cut back every democratic policy instrument that citizens use to achieve their collective goals: state enterprises have been privatized; industrial and financial sectors have been deregulated; environmental and consumer regulations have been abandoned; social security programmes have been reduced; union power has been curbed; and public institutions such as universities and health facilities have been partially privatized.

The main focus of their attack, however, has been on the tax system. They have campaigned to disable the tax system as a vehicle for redistributing income and wealth, and furthermore, have attacked the very idea of taxes. Demonizing taxes has become red-meat standard fare for conservative politicians in Anglo-American countries since Thatcher's election in 1979 and Reagan's in 1980, with liberal and progressive politicians continually conceding ground to the tax-cutters. The assault on taxes has been supported and co-ordinated by business-financed think thanks, and justified by right-leaning economists.

● ● ●

In this chapter, we try to rehabilitate the idea of taxes by showing that the 99 per cent have derived significant benefits through more generous social programmes and more developed democratic institutions financed by taxes, and that higher taxes have not harmed the economy. We show that countries with higher taxes tend to have significantly better social outcomes and that their economies have been unaffected, and indeed arguably have benefited, from the increased government spending that higher taxes have financed.

Some readers will note that our findings are similar to those of Richard Wilkinson and Kate Pickett in their 2009 book, *The Spirit Level*. Wilkinson and Pickett revealed that more equal countries tend to have better social outcomes. We measure tax levels (instead of equality) and find that there is also a strong correlation between high tax levels and better social outcomes. The overlap is perhaps not surprising since countries with higher tax levels tend to have greater equality. Arguably, in the Western high-income countries we examine, the chain of cause-and-effect runs like this: higher tax levels (and the increased income transfers and government services that taxes finance) lead to better social outcomes, including greater equality.

Before we go any further, we feel it is important to point out that, based on our findings, the UK's current austerity programme and commitment to low taxes are propelling Britain like a high-speed train in the wrong direction. The international evidence suggests that reducing government expenditures will greatly diminish the quality of life of ordinary Britons, and that lower taxes will do nothing to bring them greater material prosperity.

Until fairly recently, the UK has been roughly in the middle of the pack of industrialized countries when it comes to levels of taxation and government spending. However, the coalition government's austerity programme is changing that profoundly, leaving Britons increasingly reliant upon markets, family and charity for goods and services that were previously provided by government. The UK is moving towards the notoriously inadequate social contract that has long prevailed in the United States, one of the lowest-taxed countries in the OECD, the international economic organization comprised of thirty-four of the world's largest market economies. What will be the implications of this dramatic rewriting of the UK social contract? If the American model is to be the future, a straightforward way of predicting the consequences for the UK is to examine the quality of life for the 99 per cent in the United States today.

As we will show in this chapter, on almost every social indicator, the US is at or near the bottom of the major OECD nations.

- Poverty is widespread, afflicting about 17 per cent of all Americans, and about 22 per cent of children.[2] A greater percentage of citizens, by a substantial margin, live in poverty in the US than in any other industrialized country in the world.
- The gap between the income of vulnerable citizens, such as the elderly and those with disabilities, and the income of other citizens in the US is greater than in almost all other industrialized countries.
- When it comes to infant mortality, the US lags behind forty countries, according to the World Health Organization. Newborn children in the US die at roughly the same rate as newborns in Qatar, Croatia and the United Arab Emirates.
- Ordinary workers in the US have less personal economic security than workers in any other industrialized country.
- As an indication of gender inequality, women in the US still hold a relatively small percentage of positions in the professions, legislative bodies and senior civil service, and otherwise lag behind men in many respects.
- As a proportion of GDP, the US spends more than twice as much on health care than many European countries and yet US health care outcomes remain far worse. For example, the percentage of children who die at birth in the US is the highest among industrialized countries.

- Although the US spends a greater percentage of its GDP on education than most other countries, American fifteen-year-olds rank near the bottom of OECD countries when it comes to science and maths skills, and rank relatively low on reading skills, too.
- On a comprehensive index of the degree of social justice, which measures the extent of equal opportunity for citizens, the US scored twenty-seventh out of thirty-one countries.
- On almost every index of environmental sustainability, the US ranks about the lowest of the Western industrialized countries.
- Living conditions in the US are shockingly unequal. By any measure, income is distributed more unequally in the United States than in all other industrialized countries. The richest 1 per cent of Americans capture over 17 per cent of national income – more than twice the percentage of national income captured by the top 1 per cent in many European countries.

In contrast to the United States, the social outcomes in high-tax countries, such as the Nordic countries, rank near the top of the industrialized world. Denmark, for instance, does well on almost every social indicator.

- Only 6 per cent of the general population and less than 4 per cent of children live below the poverty line.
- The elderly and those with disabilities have incomes that are close to those of the rest of the population.
- Women hold about 50 per cent of the positions in legislative bodies and in the senior ranks of the civil service.
- Workers in Denmark enjoy one of the highest levels of economic security among workers in the industrialized world.
- Income is distributed relatively equally, with the top 1 per cent capturing only 4 per cent of national income.

To provide a more systematic review, we compare low- and high-tax countries along a number of dimensions generally regarded as important to a high quality of life. For the purposes of this comparison, we have chosen twenty of the highest-income countries of the OECD. Since 1965, the United States has been a very low-tax country, while the Nordic countries have been very high-tax countries. In 2009, the total tax level in the US was 24.1 per cent of GDP. That same year, the total tax level in Denmark was almost twice as high: 48.1 per cent of GDP. The UK's total tax level was 34.3 per cent of GDP, putting it roughly in the middle.[3]

Among the twenty countries, the median total tax level over 2006 to 2010 was 36 per cent. As shown in Figure 2, the countries below the median were categorized as low-tax, and those above the median as high-tax.[4]

High-tax Countries		Low-tax Countries	
Denmark	48.6	United Kingdom	35.5
Sweden	46.9	Spain	33.9
Belgium	43.8	New Zealand	33.5
France	43.4	Canada	32.3
Norway	43.2	Portugal	31.8
Italy	43.1	Greece	31.1
Finland	42.9	Ireland	29.5
Austria	42.1	Switzerland	29.3
Netherlands	38.8	Australia	27.9
Germany	36.3	United States	26.2

Fig. 2 Average annual tax revenue as percentage of GDP in selected high-income OECD countries, 2006–10

As the table shows, Anglo-American countries – the UK, New Zealand, Canada, Ireland, Australia and the US – all fall under the low-tax country category, with an average tax level of 31 per cent of GDP. The Nordic countries – Denmark, Sweden, Norway and Finland – are all in the high-tax country category, with an average tax level of 43 per cent.[5]

TAXES AND SOCIAL OUTCOMES

Overall, our findings show that high-tax countries perform significantly better than low-tax countries on a wide range of social indicators. The UK, which is just below the average in terms of tax levels, scores about average on a number of these measures. It is striking to note that the lowest-tax country, the United States, is at the bottom or near the bottom in every social measure. This would appear to be the UK's future once the austerity programme is fully implemented. Perhaps the coalition government officials are assuming that Britain can make severe cuts in social spending while avoiding the poor social outcomes of the US. They may believe so, but there is no evidence from cross-national studies to support this hope.

Poverty

The causes of poverty are undoubtedly complex. But high-tax countries, through their far more extensive social security systems (paid for by taxes), have much better records in reducing poverty than low-tax countries. This is especially true in the case of child poverty.

The United States has the highest overall poverty rate in the Western industrialized world, with 17.3 per cent of its citizens living in poverty (that is, living on incomes that amount to less than 50 per cent of the country's median income). On average, in low-tax Anglo-American countries, the poverty rate is 12.5 per cent (11 per cent in the UK). By contrast, in high-tax Denmark,

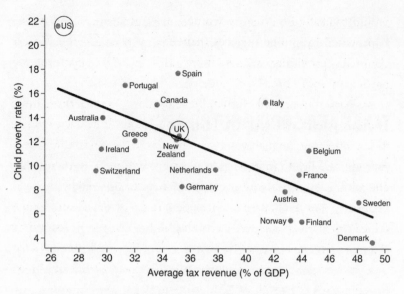

Fig. 3 The higher the tax level, the lower the rate of child poverty[7]

the poverty rate is only 6.1 per cent, and the average poverty rate for the Nordic countries is just 7.6 per cent.[6]

Over one-fifth of American children – 21.6 per cent – live in poverty. In Anglo-American countries, the average child poverty rate is 14.5 per cent (12.5 per cent in the UK). By contrast, in the Nordic countries, the percentage of children living in poverty is 5.4 per cent – about one-third of the Anglo-American average.

Figure 3 reveals how closely rates of child poverty are related to tax levels. For almost all countries, the higher the tax level, the lower the rate of child poverty.

Gender equality

Every country in our sample is officially committed to equality for women. Although progress has generally been slow, countries with higher taxes have had much greater success in nearing this goal. For example, a considerable amount of the care-giving work that would typically be done by women in Anglo-American families is provided by public services (paid for by taxes) in the Nordic countries, providing women there with greater opportunity to participate more broadly in society.

As part of its annual Human Development Report, the United Nations publishes a Gender Inequality Index. It is a composite index reflecting inequality between men and women in three areas: reproductive health (measured by a nation's maternal mortality ratio and adolescent fertility rate), empowerment (measured by the proportion of women in parliament, and by their secondary and higher education attainment levels), and the labour market (measured by women's participation in the workforce). The index measures the percentage loss in national achievement in these aspects of human development as a result of gender inequalities.

The Gender Inequality Index indicates that the potential human development loss as a result of gender inequality is only 5 per cent in high-tax Sweden. By contrast, it is almost 30 per cent in the

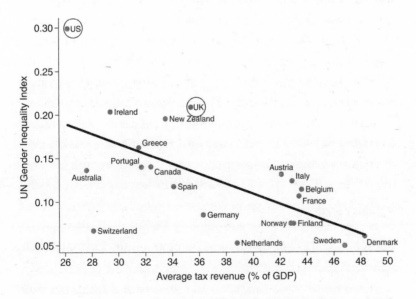

Fig. 4 The higher the tax level, the greater the degree of gender equality[8]

low-tax US. Indeed, the US has by far the most extreme gender inequality of the countries surveyed; it is well outside the pack. The UK is the next worst, with a 21 per cent human development loss as a result of gender inequality. The average among Anglo-American countries is 20 per cent. By contrast, the average for Nordic countries is just 7 per cent.

Economic security

Personal economic security is a key factor in determining the ability of individuals to develop to their full potential. It enables them to plan for the future, protect themselves and their families against hardship, and allows them to maintain a sense of self-worth and well-being. It also puts them in a stronger position to press for a larger share of the national income that all members of society collectively produce. A lack of economic security leads to stress, low self-esteem and difficulty in maintaining personal relationships. It also often results in poor planning choices, as people accept low-paying employment rather than risk spending time searching for a better job or retraining. Enhancing economic security has been a central focus of social movements over the years.

Not surprisingly, high-tax countries have a much stronger record in providing the government services, programmes and supports that contribute to economic security for their citizens. The International Labour Office (ILO) published a major report in 2005 on economic security as part of its programme *Economic Security for a Better World*. The ILO identified a number of forms of work-related security, including employment opportunities, protection against arbitrary dismissal, protection against accidents and illness and protection against income loss. It developed these into a single index, the Economic Security Index.

According to the index, the Anglo-American countries provide far less economic security than the Nordic countries. The US ties

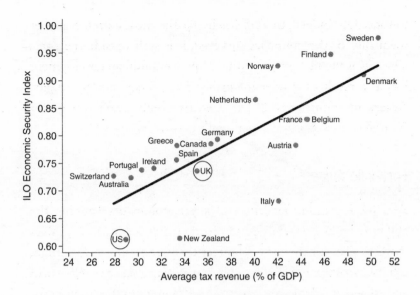

Fig. 5 The higher the tax level, the greater the degree of the economic security of workers[9]

with New Zealand in providing workers with the lowest level of economic security among industrialized countries, or 0.61 on the index. The average score for Anglo-American countries is 0.70. The UK scores slightly above the Anglo-American average at 0.74. The average score for Nordic countries is 0.94, with Sweden providing the highest degree of economic security at 0.98.

A recently published study reveals an even stronger relationship between tax levels and economic security more broadly defined across the industrialized countries. The Centre for the Study of Living Standards (CSLS), a Canadian-based research organization, has since 1998 produced a sophisticated composite index of economic well-being that measures per capita consumption, per capita wealth, economic equality and economic security.[10] Of the fourteen major OECD countries measured by the CSLS index in 2009, the US ranks near the bottom, with an overall score of 0.482, just slightly better than Spain with 0.451. The Anglo-American countries are all near the bottom of the scale, with the United

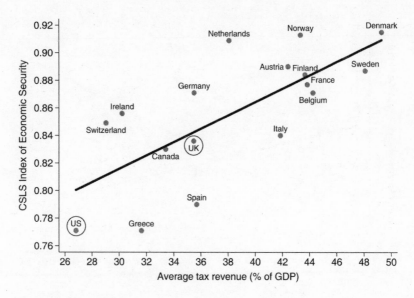

Fig. 6 The higher the tax level, the greater the degree of economic security[11]

Kingdom at 0.562. By contrast, the Nordic countries all have scores indicating a high degree of overall economic well-being: Finland (0.626), Sweden (0.637), Denmark (0.684) and Norway (0.799). On the specific measure of economic equality alone, the US has a number so low that it is almost off the scale (at 0.123).

In a 2012 working paper, the CSLS specifically measured economic security in seventy countries, focusing on economic risks associated with unemployment, sickness, widowhood and old age. Figure 6 shows the results for major OECD countries.

Even among this much larger sample, which included less developed nations, the US ranks among the lowest, sandwiched between Egypt, and Trinidad and Tobago. The UK also ranks on the lower end of the industrialized countries, although considerably higher than the US. The relatively higher-tax countries, such as Germany and France, rank much higher and, once again, Nordic countries all rank near the top.

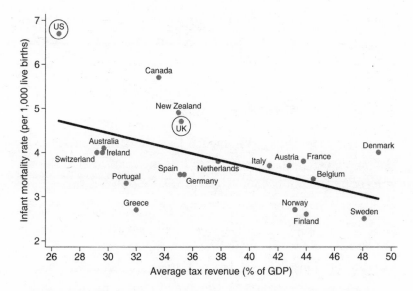

Fig. 7 The higher the tax level, the lower the rate of infant mortality[12]

Health

A key measure of a nation's health is infant mortality, that is, the death rate of children under the age of one. As Figure 7 shows, infant mortality is higher in low-tax Anglo-American countries than in high-tax Nordic countries.

Social well-being

German think-tank the Bertelsmann Foundation has compiled one of the most comprehensive and sophisticated indexes of a country's social well-being. It measured the degree of what it calls 'social justice' in thirty-one OECD countries by looking at six key factors: poverty prevention; access to education; labour market inclusion; social cohesion and non-discrimination; health; and intergenerational justice. In many ways, the index is an indication of how well the 99 per cent are faring. The low-tax US is a dismal twenty-seventh in the rankings (near countries such as Turkey and Slovakia), while the high-tax Nordic countries are bunched together at the top.

Environmental sustainability

The Yale Center for Environmental Law and Policy publishes an Environmental Performance Index that measures how a country is meeting pollution control and natural resource management challenges. The twenty-two performance indicators cover a broad range, measuring effects on human health, impact on ecosystems, preservation of habitat and biodiversity, and efforts to combat climate change. Once again, as Figure 9 shows, the US ranks very low for an industrialized country – forty-ninth out of the 132 nations, with a score of 57 out of 100. The Nordic countries do better, with Norway scoring 70. Switzerland is somewhat of an outlier. Even though it is a low-tax country, it scores an impressive 77 on the environmental sustainability scale.

Another highly regarded index of environmental performance, prepared for the David Suzuki Foundation, finds an even stronger relationship between a country's environmental performance and its tax level.[15] Out of the twenty-five countries measured, the three top spots are filled by Nordic countries, with the UK ranking ninth. Once again, the US was ranked last, with Canada and Australia close to the bottom.

Income equality

Finally, there is a strong association between tax levels and income equality. Interestingly, there is even a strong relationship between tax levels and the share of market income (that is, pre-tax income) going to the top 1 per cent. In other words, taxes appear to play a role in reducing the concentration of market income at the top

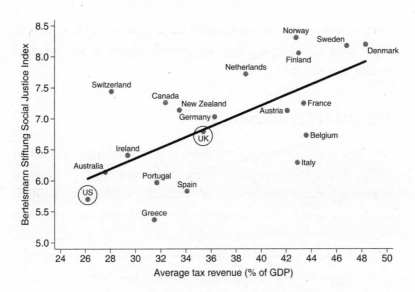

Fig. 8 The higher the tax level, the greater
the degree of social well-being in a society[13]

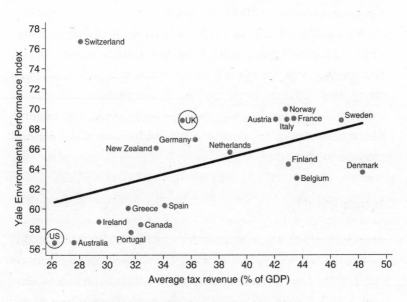

Fig. 9 The higher the tax level, the greater
the degree of environmental sustainability[14]

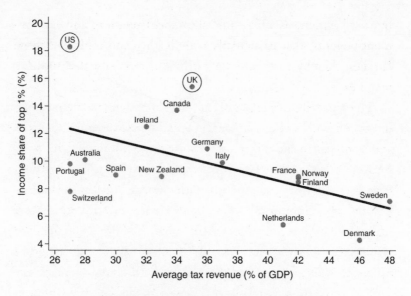

Fig. 10 The higher the tax level, the lower
the share of income going to the top 1 per cent[16]

(even before taxes are applied to this income). This might be because in high-tax countries, the 99 per cent have more control over the democratic process. This makes it more likely that laws favouring working people – such as minimum wage laws or stronger union protections – will be enacted, allowing workers to win a larger share of market income.

This relationship between pre-tax income and tax levels is illustrated in Figure 10. In the mid-2000s, the top 1 per cent of Americans captured more than 18 per cent of national income (not including capital gains); in the UK, the top 1 per cent captured 15 per cent. By contrast, in Denmark, the top 1 per cent captured only about 4 per cent of national income. On average in the Nordic countries, only about 7 per cent of national income went to the top 1 per cent, compared to an average of about 13 per cent in the Anglo-American countries.

In addition to making market incomes more equal, countries with high tax levels are able to provide more extensive government transfer payments (such as child allowances, pensions and employ-ment benefits) that particularly benefit low- and middle-income families, thereby further reducing inequality in final, disposable incomes.

The redistributive effect of the 'tax-and-transfer' system can be illustrated with a chart showing inequality, before and after taxes and transfers. To show this, we have used the Gini coefficient as a measure of inequality. The Gini coefficient is a number between 0 and 1, where 0 corresponds with perfect equality (everyone has the same amount of income) and 1 corresponds with perfect inequality (where one person has all the income). Hence, the higher the number (the closer to 1), the greater the degree of inequality. Before taxes, Italy has the greatest degree of inequality, with a Gini of 0.47. It is followed closely by the United Kingdom (with a Gini of 0.46) and the United States (with a Gini of 0.45). Sweden and Denmark have the most equal distribution of market income (with a Gini of about 0.37), followed by Norway (with a Gini of 0.38).

However, after taxes and transfers, low-tax countries still have a very high degree of inequality. So, for instance, after its minimal taxes and transfers, the US still has a very high Gini of 0.37, leav-ing Americans with the most unequal distribution of disposable income. The UK's tax-and-transfer system does somewhat more redistribution, but not much, leaving Britain with one of the most unequal distributions of disposable income.

The Nordic countries – who would have guessed? – distinguish themselves once again with impressive tax-and-transfer systems that substantially reduce inequality. For instance, in Denmark, the tax-and-transfer system reduces the Gini coefficient by more than one-third from 0.37 to only 0.24, leaving Denmark with the most equal distribution of disposable income.

Figure 11 ranks countries according to the inequality in the distribution of disposable income, but it also shows the important

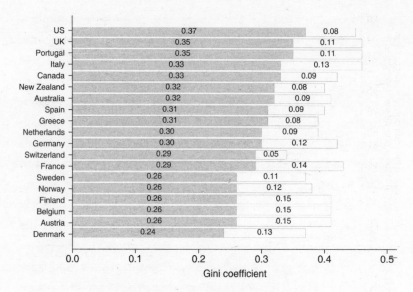

Fig. 11 The tax-and-transfer system plays an important role in reducing income inequality[17]

role of the tax-and-transfer system in achieving the final result of a more equal society. The grey bars represent a country's Gini after taxes and transfers, with the white bars representing the reduction of inequality in a country's Gini before taxes and transfers.

Figure 12 shows how much more significantly inequality is reduced by the tax-and-transfer system in high-tax countries than in low-tax countries.

TAXES AND ECONOMIC GROWTH

Even if high-tax countries are able to achieve greater social equity and quality of life, conservatives typically argue that these countries pay for their better social outcomes by sacrificing economic benefits. High taxes, they argue, diminish the incentive to work, save and invest, thereby reducing economic growth and ultimately shrinking

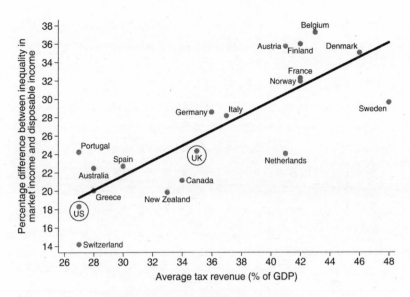

Fig. 12 The higher the tax level, the more redistribution is done by government[18]

the material well-being of the population. There is only one thing wrong with this argument – there are no facts to support it. The evidence suggests that there is no trade-off between the pursuit of social benefits and material prosperity. Indeed, when it comes to economic and material outcomes, high-tax countries do as well or better than low-tax countries.

Taxes and GDP per capita

The most common way of measuring the economic performance of a country and the material well-being of its citizens is simply to divide the country's GDP by its population.[19]

By this measure, Luxembourg is the richest country in the world, by far, with an astonishing GDP per capita of $89,164 in 2011. We can't resist noting that the richest country in the world has a tax level of about 37 per cent of GDP, higher than the OECD average.

The next richest is another high-tax country, Norway, with a GDP per capita of $61,870. Third is low-tax United States with a GDP per capita of $48,043. The UK is in the middle of the OECD pack with a per capita GDP of $35,642.

Furthermore, on average, the GDP per capita of the Nordic countries, $45,477, is much higher than the GDP per capita of the Anglo-American countries, $39,566.[20]

Figure 13 compares the average tax levels in twenty of the most prosperous Western democracies over the 1975–2008 period with their GDP per capita in 2011. The line trends gently upward, suggesting that, if anything, higher taxes correlate with better material living standards. However, the relationship is not statistically significant (which is why we mark it with a broken line). At the very least, as the graph shows, there is no evidence that higher taxes lead to reduced material well-being.

Although GDP per capita is the most frequently used measure of national material well-being, it is a flawed measure in many ways.

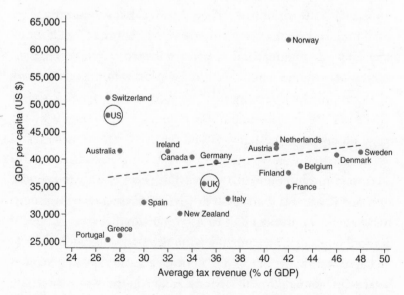

Fig. 13 Lower tax levels do not increase the material well-being of citizens[21]

Correcting for these flaws would further reduce the apparent material well-being of citizens in low-tax countries such as the United States.

First, GDP measures the market values of activities carried on in a country without considering whether these activities contribute to material well-being. In the US, for instance, the extra costs associated with the country's exceptionally high rates of incarceration, of police and private security guards, and of inefficiently delivered health care services, add considerably to the national GDP, without in any way adding to the material well-being of Americans.

Second, a country's GDP is a function not only of the productivity of its workers, but also of how many hours they work. Workers in Nordic countries have been able to produce goods and services per capita that exceed the value of the goods and services per capita produced by workers in Anglo-American countries – while working on average 144 hours less a year! Indeed, workers in the United States typically work an extra five weeks a year more than workers in Nordic countries. While this drives up US GDP per capita, it doesn't make Americans better off (indeed, by any reasonable measure, it makes them considerably worse off).

Third, and most importantly, the simple measure of GDP per capita reveals nothing about how income in the country is distributed, and therefore who is benefiting from the wealth produced in the economy. GDP per capita is a figure that is arrived at simply by taking the total income of the country and dividing it by the total population. The figure would remain the same whether all of the income went to one person or was distributed equally to everyone in the country. In fact, GDP per capita is high in the US largely because there are some extraordinarily rich Americans whose enormous incomes bring up the national average. Surely, a more important measure of a country's economic success is the material well-being of the typical or median family (a real family, exactly in the middle of the income ladder), not the average family (a statistical construct).

It is revealing, for instance, to compare income growth in the United States and France in recent decades. Between 1975 and 2006, growth in per capita GDP was stronger in the US (32.3 per cent) than in France (27.1 per cent). However, if we remove the richest 1 per cent of citizens in both countries from the calculations, the growth of typical incomes is only 17.9 per cent in the US compared to 26.4 per cent in France. In other words, although the US had higher growth in its GDP per capita, the bottom 99 per cent in France experienced much better growth in their material well-being than did the bottom 99 per cent in the US.[22]

Similarly, in Britain, the real incomes of the top 1 per cent increased on average by 168 per cent from 1960 to 2010, while the real incomes of the bottom 90 per cent increased by only 37 per cent. On the other hand, in Sweden, real incomes for the top 1 per cent grew by 144 per cent, while real incomes for the bottom 90 per cent actually grew more – by 149 per cent. As these examples show, measuring growth in GDP per capita tells us very little about the material well-being of most citizens.[23]

A more meaningful measure of material well-being can perhaps be found in the Legatum Prosperity Index, published each year by the UK-based Legatum Institute. Surveying 142 countries, the index factors in traditional indicators such as material wealth, but also indicators such as entrepreneurship and opportunity, social capital, personal freedom, quality of education and health care. In its 2012 index, high-tax Norway was in first place (for the fifth year in a row), followed by Denmark and Sweden. The US, for the first time, dropped out of the top ten, coming in at twelfth place, followed by the UK in thirteenth place.

Taxes and rate of economic growth

Countries sometimes experience unusually fast periods of economic growth. If they happen to be low-tax countries, conservatives are quick to attribute the growth spurt to low taxes. Such was the case with Ireland. From 1990 to 2004, the Irish economy grew at an astonishing rate of about 6.6 per cent a year on a per capita basis. Even including the recent downturn, it grew at a rate of almost 4.7 per cent a year on a per capita basis between 1990 and 2010.[24]

Ireland has always been a relatively low-tax country, but after 1995 its tax level fell even further, to below 30 per cent. This, along with its low corporate tax rate of 12.5 per cent, led tax-cut supporters in Anglo-American countries to urge their governments to follow the Irish model.

However, the Irish 'economic miracle' was due to a number of factors. Tax cuts undoubtedly played some role in attracting foreign investment. But Ireland also reaped the advantages of huge European Union subsidies in the 1970s, '80s and '90s, and invested those subsidies wisely in infrastructure, including in free higher education. It had an English-speaking, well-educated, under-utilized labour force, and aggressively courted foreign investment through industrial development agencies.

In any event, the Irish miracle appears to have been built on an unsustainable foundation. Ireland's annual real growth rate declined by almost 5 percentage points in 2007–8 and by almost 8 percentage points in 2008–9, and it remains deeply mired in recession.

The Irish example is a reminder that economic growth tends to be highly cyclical, making it necessary to consider growth rates over a long period of time. From 1970 to 2010, annual GDP per capita growth in both the low-tax Anglo-American countries and the high-tax Nordic countries averaged slightly over 2 per cent. As Figure 14 illustrates, there appears to be no relationship between tax levels and rates of economic growth over time.

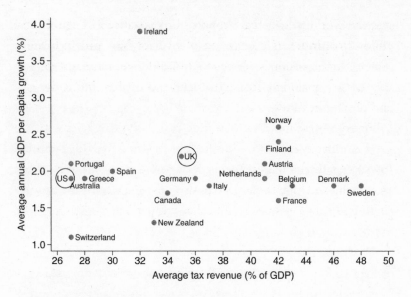

Fig. 14 Lower taxes do not lead to higher rates of economic growth[25]

Taxes and innovation

There is wide agreement that innovation is a main driving force behind long-term prosperity. A country's capacity for innovation depends upon a broad range of factors, including having a strong education system, high quality researchers and creative thinkers, government funding for basic research, political stability, and a social safety net that encourages risk-taking. It turns out that high-tax countries do as well as low-tax countries in sowing the seeds for innovation.

The European Business School, in collaboration with the World Bank, has produced an elaborate Innovation Capacity Index that is made up of sixty-one variables.[26] According to this index, three of the top six most innovative countries are Nordic: Sweden ranks first, Finland fourth and Denmark sixth. The other countries in the top six are Switzerland, Singapore and the US.

Perhaps the most comprehensive index of innovation is prepared annually by INSEAD, a European-based business graduate school, and the World Intellectual Property Organization.[27] Their Global Innovation Index is comprised of over eighty-four indicators. Three Nordic countries (Sweden, Finland and Denmark) rank in the top seven, along with Switzerland (no. 1), Singapore, the UK and the Netherlands.

As both these innovation indexes reveal, the countries with the greatest capacity for innovation are found among both high-tax and low-tax countries. Figure 15 shows that the relationship between innovation and high tax levels is positive, as indicated by the upward sloping line, but it is not statistically significant.

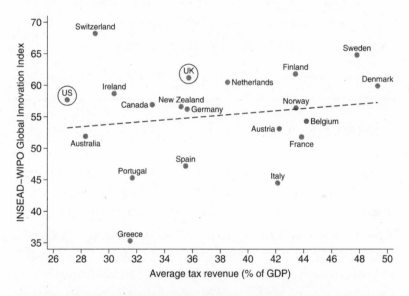

Fig. 15 Lower taxes do not lead to greater innovation[28]

Taxes and international competitiveness

While it is frequently alleged in the business press that high taxes destroy a country's competitiveness, the Nordic countries prove otherwise. The World Economic Forum, a business-financed, Geneva-based organization, releases an annual Global Competitiveness Index that measures countries according to a wide range of indicators, including economic institutions, infrastructure, education, training, labour market efficiency, and innovation, as well as financial market and business sophistication. On average, the high-tax Nordic countries invariably rank as more competitive than the low-tax Anglo-American countries. In 2012–13, for instance, the Nordics had an average score of 5.4 versus 5.2 for the Anglo-American countries. Both Finland (no. 3) and Sweden (no. 4) were ranked as more competitive than the US (no. 7) and the UK (no. 8).

Figure 16 suggests that there is a positive, but statistically insignificant, relationship between tax levels and global competitiveness among the high-income 20 OECD countries.

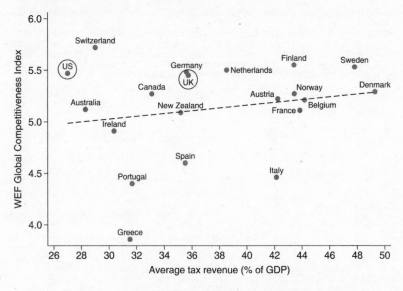

Fig. 16 Lower taxes do not lead to more global competitiveness[29]

TOP TAX RATES AND ECONOMIC GROWTH

In light of the compelling evidence that high tax levels do not stunt economic growth, conservatives sometimes argue that it is not overall tax levels that matter, but rather marginal tax rates. In particular, they argue that high marginal tax rates on high-income earners impede economic growth.

One obvious difficulty with this argument, as noted earlier, is that the top marginal rates in all Anglo-American countries were extremely high – often exceeding 80 per cent – throughout the postwar period, and yet the economic growth rates of these countries during this period were also very high.

Conservatives insist that the world has changed, that globalization and increased capital mobility now make it necessary to keep the top marginal tax rate low. But, once again, the evidence does not support this claim.[30] Since the mid-1970s, top marginal tax rates, particularly in the Anglo-American countries, have declined dramatically. While this has prompted other countries to cut their marginal rates as well, the cuts haven't been as deep elsewhere. Yet, as Figure 17 shows, there is no relationship between cuts in the top tax rate and per capita GDP growth.

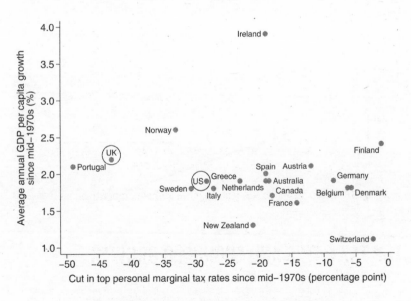

Fig. 17 Cuts in top personal marginal tax rates do not lead to increased rates of economic growth[31]

However, while there is no relationship between lower marginal tax rates on the rich and rates of economic growth, there is a strong and statistical significant relationship between lower taxes on the rich and the share of national income that the rich are able to capture.

As Figure 18 reveals, countries that cut tax rates on the rich the most, such as the UK and the US, experienced the greatest increase in income concentration at the top. For example, since the mid-1970s, the top marginal tax rate in the UK was slashed by more than 40 percentage points, while the top US rate was cut by almost 30 percentage points. The share of income captured by the top 1 per cent in these countries increased dramatically. In Germany and France, however, where the top rate was reduced by fewer than 10 percentage points, the increased share captured by the top 1 per cent rose very little.

The findings reflected in the previous two graphs undermine the case that lowering taxes on high-income earners increases

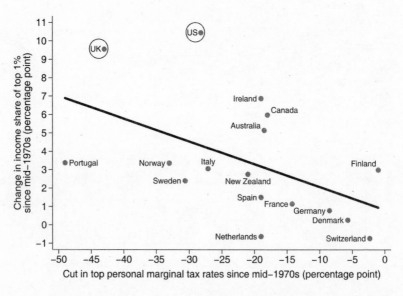

Fig. 18 Cuts in top personal marginal tax rates do make the rich richer[32]

economic growth (by motivating them to work harder). Rather, the findings suggest that lower taxes on the rich do nothing for economic growth; they simply make the rich richer.

Surprise, surprise.

While taxes have been vilified throughout the Anglo-American world in recent decades, the evidence suggests that the case against them has been fabricated. The public goods and services that citizens purchase with their taxes – in the areas of health, education, and insurance against job loss and disability – leave them healthier, better educated and more economically secure. As we've seen, countries with strong tax-and-transfer systems have better overall social well-being, and at least as strong economic growth. As Britain's austerity programme weakens its tax-and-transfer system, it risks ending up with the sort of dismal social results that afflict America.

4
plutocracy, climate change and the fate of the world

The approaching climate change disaster is, appropriately, the focus of intense concern. Yet, despite all this attention, the issue of climate change has been largely absent in the discussion of the negative consequences of inequality and concentrated economic power. While the discussion of rising inequality has included concerns about the negative impact on democracy, these concerns have largely been confined to the economic sphere, examining how the ultra-rich exert undue influence over areas such as tax policy or financial regulations. By contrast, there's been little focus on the impact of concentrated economic power on the environment – a sphere ultimately even more important than the economy. Indeed, there's been disturbingly little attention devoted to how the increasing concentration of economic power has created an elite so dominant and unrelenting that the public may be losing its capacity to ensure its own survival on Earth.

The failure to tackle the climate change crisis is the most potent illustration of how the rise of a global plutocracy in the last few decades has profoundly changed the global power dynamic, undermining democracy to the point that the world community appears to be losing its ability to protect itself. An exceptionally powerful elite is now able to act in ways that potentially threaten human survival. We can see this deeply disturbing development if we compare today's inaction over climate change with the success of the world community in dealing with the global environmental crisis of the 1970s – ozone layer depletion.

There is a surprising degree of similarity between the ozone layer crisis of the 1970s and the current climate change crisis. In both cases, there was a sudden awareness of an emerging problem with extremely serious global consequences. Also in both cases, the problems were solvable, but the solutions required significant changes that threatened to diminish the profits of some of the world's most powerful corporations. Furthermore, in both cases, there was consensus within the scientific community about the action needed and considerable mobilization by the public, but severe pushback from the corporate interests.

In the ozone case, however, the public effectively triumphed. Within about a dozen years of the onset of public awareness about the crisis, a global treaty was put in place that has been hailed by former UN Secretary-General Kofi Annan as 'perhaps the most successful international environmental agreement'. Yet, in the case of climate change, a quarter century after the world became aware of the crisis, there is still no meaningful treaty in place and the chances of achieving one seem to slip further from reach with each passing year.

Before addressing the question of why the outcomes have diverged so sharply, let's consider how, in the early stages at least, both cases were handled in ways that provide positive examples of how well-functioning democracies work.

In the case of the ozone layer, chemists Mario Molina and F. Sherwood Rowland published a ground-breaking article in *Nature* magazine in 1974 sounding the alarm about the dangers of chlorofluorocarbons (CFCs). The article showed that these chemical compounds, widely used in aerosol sprays and as solvents and refrigerants, had the capacity to break down the ozone layer, the crucial atmospheric shield that protects us from the harmful ultraviolet rays of the sun. Environmental groups, led by the Washington-based Natural Resources Defense Council, quickly got the issue national media coverage and launched an effective public campaign for a CFC ban.

The work of Molina and Rowland also sparked considerable scientific interest and further research into the problem. Particularly important was the role played by Robert Watson, a British scientist with a Ph.D. in atmospheric chemistry, who grasped something crucial early on: the real obstacles to a solution lay outside the realm of science. Powerful industrial interests stood to lose financially from the changes that would be required, and counteracting their influence would be the central problem. What was needed, then, was a highly credible process for assessing the scientific data so that it couldn't be easily dismissed by the companies. Working with the United Nations Environment Programme (UNEP), the US space agency NASA and the British Meteorological Office, Watson launched a massive international process that consulted with scientists from all over the world who specialized in the field of atmospheric chemistry. Hundreds of scientists were asked to critically review the data, and to do so quickly and comprehensively. The process resulted in a stunning degree of co-operation and consensus about the seriousness of the problem and the nature of the solution.

As Watson had predicted, there was a strong industry counter-attack, led by DuPont, one of the world's largest chemical manufacturers and producer of about half of global CFCs. Along with Dow Chemical, General Electric, General Motors and others, DuPont launched an intense lobbying and advertising blitz attacking the credibility of the case against CFCs, and even found a few scientists willing to lend their names to the industry campaign. The companies also argued that restricting the use of CFCs would have a devastating effect on the $8 billion industry, leading to serious job losses. DuPont lambasted CFC opponents for their 'ban-now-find-out-later' approach, insisting that the impacts on the ozone layer were simply projections and that proof in the form of a thinning ozone layer wouldn't be evident for decades. 'Businesses can be destroyed before scientific facts are assembled and evaluated,' cautioned DuPont chairman Irving Shapiro.

However, the well-funded corporate campaign was soon overwhelmed by the strength of the scientific consensus and pressure from environmental and consumer groups. By 1978, non-essential aerosol sprays were banned in the United States, with similar action following in Canada, Sweden and Denmark (although Britain and France, major CFC producers, were initially unwilling to implement restrictions). However, CFCs were still widely used in refrigerators and air conditioners. So the debate raged on, both in the media and behind the scenes at the UN. A turning point came in 1985, when scientists with the British Antarctic Survey discovered a 'hole' in the ozone layer near the South Pole – proof that the ozone layer was indeed thinning as predicted. With this discovery, new levels of media and public scrutiny were focused on estimates that, without serious and immediate government action, there would be tens of millions of additional skin cancer cases within a few decades.

In the face of mounting public concern, particularly in the US, Washington felt obliged to act. The Reagan administration, despite its well-known hostility towards environmental regulation, publicly endorsed plans to develop international regulations limiting the production of CFCs. With this crucial backing from Washington, twenty-four nations came together at a UN-sponsored conference in Montreal in September 1987 to sign the Montreal Protocol, a far-reaching agreement to phase out industrial compounds that threaten the ozone layer. Under the protocol, the main burden is borne by the industrialized countries, with a ten-year grace period for developing nations and a fund to help them adapt to the changes. (Today, almost two hundred nations have ratified the protocol.)

With the international community moving decisively to tackle the ozone depletion problem, industry shifted its stance, its fierce resistance giving way to compliance. Although companies had insisted there were no alternatives to CFCs, there were in fact alternatives but they were costly to develop. Once the Montreal Protocol removed CFCs as an option, and incentives were provided to develop alternatives, the industry adapted, and even actively co-operated. As a result, the ozone layer is recovering. Refrigerators and air conditioners still operate today, but without ozone-depleting CFCs. (The CFCs have been replaced by hydrofluorocarbons or HFCs, which are harmless to the ozone layer. However, it turns out that HFCs are powerful greenhouse gases. There is now growing pressure to replace HFCs with environmentally safer alternatives.)[1]

Still, the story of how some of the world's foremost democracies came together to tackle a complex problem requiring global co-operation is impressive. The first truly global attempt to stop damage to the Earth's ecosystem had been a significant success.

•   •   •

In its early stages, the response to the climate change crisis also looked promising. Scientific understanding of the global warming phenomenon actually began to take shape as far back as the 1820s. But it wasn't really until the mid-1980s – about a decade after the ozone depletion issue surfaced – that the scientific community became aware of the scope of the problem, and how it was being driven by the excessive consumption of fossil fuels by the industrialized nations. This new awareness led to the organization of an international scientific conference on global warming in Toronto in June 1988, with Canadian Prime Minister Brian Mulroney underlining the importance of the event by giving the opening address. At the end of the conference, the scientists attending released a consensus statement declaring that 'humanity is conducting an unintended, uncontrolled, globally pervasive experiment whose ultimate consequences are second only to global nuclear war'.

The Toronto conference helped sound a worldwide alarm. And, coming less than a year after the signing of the Montreal Protocol, there was reason to believe that the world would proceed to address this newly discovered problem. With evidence suggesting that global warming was already under way – melting icebergs, rising sea levels, unexplained weather extremes – the United Nations and the World Meteorological Organization moved quickly, setting up an independent body called the Intergovernmental Panel on Climate Change (IPCC) to review the scientific understanding of the problem. Robert Watson, fresh from his effective handling of the ozone scientific review process and now a senior scientist at NASA, was enlisted as a key figure in the IPCC, eventually becoming its chairman.

From his experience with the ozone process, Watson understood that the key resistance to tackling global warming would come from industry, and would be fierce – even fiercer this time around, given the greater clout of the fossil fuel industry interests. Tackling global warming would involve taking on the most profitable and powerful set of business interests on Earth.

Watson's response was to be even more thorough and comprehensive in establishing the scientific review process. He put in place a relentlessly rigorous system for the preparation and peer review of scientific reports. Reports were drawn up after extensive research, which included consultation with industry. A draft was first sent to a few experts and then redrafted and sent to every relevant scientist in the world – about two and a half thousand. After feedback from these experts, it was redrafted and sent back to them for another look. 'Without any question it's the most intense peer review system ever,' Watson said in an interview.[2]

The IPCC's first assessment report, released in 1990, was a powerful statement of the problem, effectively a scientific throwing down of the gauntlet to the world. It laid out clearly that the 'greenhouse effect' was real, and that, after ten thousand years without a significant change in temperature, the Earth's surface had been getting detectably warmer since the beginning of the Industrial Revolution. At a 1992 UN-organized conference in Rio de Janeiro, which became known as the Earth Summit, the leaders of 154 countries responded by signing a legally binding convention committing themselves to address global warming.

Sadly, despite this impressive start, more than twenty years later, progress towards a solution seems to be largely stymied. Why was the world able to tackle ozone depletion but not climate change?

•　　•　　•

In a thoughtful analysis comparing the two environmental crises in the journal *Solutions*, science writer Matthew Cimitile argues that the efforts to tackle ozone depletion were successful because they managed to link the issue to human health concerns, notably the possibility of millions of skin cancers. 'It seems that the major difference between a successful ozone treaty and an out-of-reach climate agreement is the weak connection made between climate change and human health,' Cimitile concludes. Yet opponents of global warming have always highlighted its impact on human health – through severe weather, which can bring drought, famine and freezing conditions, as well as rising sea levels, which threaten to flood low-lying, densely populated regions. A 2012 report, commissioned by twenty governments and prepared by the humanitarian organization DARA, concluded that more than 100 million people will die by 2030 if the world fails to tackle climate change.[3]

Hard to imagine a much bigger impact on human health than 100 million deaths.

Cimitile also points to the impact of the discovery of the 'hole' in the ozone layer as a pivotal factor leading to the signing of the Montreal Protocol. No doubt this was true, but similarly dramatic discoveries have become almost common on the global warming front, from the ever-accelerating melting of the polar ice cap to the many extreme weather events. As James Hansen, director of the NASA Goddard Institute for Space Studies, noted in August 2012: 'our analysis shows that, for the extreme hot weather of the recent past, there is virtually no explanation other than climate change. The deadly European heat wave of 2003, the fiery Russian heat wave of 2010 and catastrophic droughts in Texas and Oklahoma last year can each be attributed to climate change.'[4]

Richard Elliot Benedick, chief US negotiator to the Montreal Protocol, suggests that the ultimate factor determining the successful completion of the ozone treaty was leadership. 'Individuals can make a surprisingly significant difference in the course of long and difficult negotiations,' he wrote in an analysis of the ozone case. 'From the overall leadership on ozone provided by UNEP's Mostafa Tolba to the roles of individual scientists, negotiators, environmentalists, and industrialists, it was personal ideas, decisions, and actions at a given critical moment that determined the successful outcome.'[5]

Again, this is undoubtedly true. And yet this doesn't really account for the abject failure of the climate change process. There seems to have been no shortage of talented, passionate and influential individuals who have devoted themselves to the cause.

Clearly, there are many things that help explain the difference between the world's response to ozone depletion and to climate change, but perhaps the most important factor is the one that is the central concern of this book: the rise of a globally dominant plutocracy.

Certainly, the role of a powerful and resistant industry lobby is central in both of these environmental crises. To some extent, the corporate world's success in blocking action on climate change simply reflects the fact that a more powerful set of corporate players has been involved in climate change than in ozone depletion. While DuPont and some of the other major chemical producers are huge, powerful companies, they aren't in the same league as the oil lobby. Topping the list of oil mega-giants is Exxon Mobil, which ranked no. 1 on the Fortune 500 corporate chart for 2012, with a reported profit of $41.6 billion – an amount that is bigger than the GDP of many nations.

Furthermore, while eliminating CFCs threatened to destroy one stream of profits for the chemical giants, CFCs weren't central to their business operations. Curbing fossil fuel emissions, on the other hand, would cut right to the heart of the business interests of Exxon, BP, Chevron, ConocoPhillips and Royal Dutch Shell, whose central function is producing and selling oil. In a major investigative report in *Rolling Stone*, environmental activist Bill McKibben cited figures showing that fossil fuel companies currently have proven reserves of oil, gas and coal worth $27 trillion.[6] If the world were to reduce carbon emissions enough to keep the temperature increase below 2 degrees Celsius (which the international community has agreed is the critical threshold), 80 per cent of those reserves would have to stay in the ground! McKibben notes that this means the fossil fuel industry would 'be writing off $20 trillion in assets' – not something corporate moguls are wont to do, especially when it involves their core business. As author Naomi Klein puts it, 'with the fossil-fuel industry, wrecking the planet is their business model. It's what they do.'

Given the stakes, it was almost inevitable that the opposition to climate change mounted by the fossil fuel lobby would be a campaign staggering in its size, scope and sophistication.

At the same time, the campaign to tackle climate change was also considerably more sophisticated than the campaign to save the ozone layer, and was backed up by a more rigorous scientific process and a more engaged global public, including tens of millions of people who came to appreciate the enormity of the stakes for humanity. Exxon and its oil allies, even with (almost) all the money in the world, had a fight on their hands.

But, crucially, there has been a profound change in the zeitgeist between the era of the ozone battle and the current era in which the climate change battle has been raging. Although the time periods involved are very close together, practically overlapping, they represent two eras with very different political cultures. The ozone crisis (1974–87) includes the last few years of the egalitarian postwar era and the early days of the current neoliberal era, before the rising corporate elite had moved fully into its ascendancy. The climate change crisis (from 1988 on) has been played out when corporate power has been at its zenith and has gained a virtual stranglehold over important public policy decisions. The difference in the political cultures, even over this short time span, is enormous.

It would be misleading to overemphasize the egalitarian nature of the postwar era. Corporations were always immensely powerful, given their centrality to the economy. But, as we explain in greater detail in Chapter Nine, the period roughly spanning 1940 to 1980 did involve a far more equal distribution of national income in the Anglo-American countries than has been the case in recent decades. Beginning in the early 1980s, the share of national income going to the top 1 per cent, and particularly the top 0.1 and 0.01 per cent, has grown significantly, as has the share going to corporate profits rather than wages.

At the most basic level, this has put considerably more money into the hands of the richest individuals and into the coffers of the corporations they own, giving them more resources to champion their own self-interests in the political realm – something they've done with vigour. At the same time, rising inequality has diminished the resources available to ordinary citizens. Thus, while the stakes for both sides are higher in the climate change contest than in the ozone depletion battle, the corporate side has seen its resources soar in recent decades, while ordinary citizens and the groups and institutions that represent their interests have seen their resources decline relatively.

More importantly, along with this changing distribution of resources has come a change in the public mindset and culture. The rising wealth and power of the corporate elite has allowed it to reshape public discourse, and to influence popular attitudes about the economy and government. Through its well-funded think-tanks and media empires as well as its increasing influence within universities, the elite has managed to establish the ideology of neoliberalism as the dominant paradigm. This has led to the celebration of the rich as 'wealth creators' whose goodwill must be constantly cultivated, lest they be discouraged from investing. The central theme of this ideology has been the need to free up (so-called) market forces from the controlling hand of government. This has boiled down to a simple notion – government bad, private sector good – that has become the mantra of our times, and the guiding force in reshaping public policy.

This new ideology has had an enormous impact on the political battle over climate change. Nowhere is this more evident than in the domain of the United Nations, where much of the climate change battle has taken place. With the rise of the new anti-government, pro-market paradigm, the UN underwent a transformation from being a body tasked with regulating corporate behaviour to one that 'partners' with the corporate sector. In an insightful report entitled *Corporations, Climate and the United Nations*, Sabrina Fernandes and Richard Girard observe: 'During the 1970s and into the early '80s the UN was actually mandated to regulate and monitor the activities of multinational corporations who were perceived to be unduly pressuring states in the Global South and in turn responsible for certain aspects of underdevelopment.'[7] This began to change in the 1980s, they note, as illustrated by the replacement of the UN's regulatory body, the UN Centre on Transnational Corporations, with a new body whose goal was to encourage foreign investment in the developing world, the UN Conference on Trade and Development.

This significant transformation at the UN took place just as the global warming problem was coming to world attention in the late 1980s. By 1992, global warming had moved to the forefront as one of the most pressing global issues, prompting world leaders to come together for the Earth Summit in Rio. After the 1995 release of an even stronger second report from the IPCC, pointing to the human 'fingerprint' in climate change, world leaders reconvened in Kyoto, Japan, in 1997. Following marathon negotiating sessions in Kyoto, an international treaty was reached to reduce greenhouse gas emissions, with US Vice President Al Gore playing an important mediating role.

Surprised by the tenacity of the international commitment to action, some key industry players – including BP, Royal Dutch Shell and General Motors – announced they were withdrawing from the anti-Kyoto coalition, leaving Exxon virtually alone in carrying on the struggle. While this seemed to be the beginning of the end, in fact, it was the beginning of an even greater level of engagement and resistance by the oil lobby. The lobby now shifted gear, relying less on increasingly difficult efforts to discredit the scientific evidence and more on taking advantage of the fiercely pro-corporate political culture fostered by the rise of plutocracy.

Inside the UN, which faced serious financial shortfalls by the late 1990s, there was an increasing openness to the idea of partnering with the corporate world rather than attempting to regulate it. An important step in this direction happened in 1998, with the establishment of the Global Compact, a UN–industry partnership programme that asked multinationals to promise to act responsibly, without requiring them to make any binding commitments.

Similarly, a major initiative known as Caring for Climate (C4C) was established specifically to promote UN–industry partnership on climate change, again without imposing any binding targets on corporations participating. Significantly, the C4C also invited corporations right into the UN policy-making process, providing tools, according to one UN document, for 'the business community to contribute inputs and perspectives to key governmental deliberations'.[8] As Fernandes and Girard note: 'The C4C is a prime example of the United Nations helping corporations greenwash socially and environmentally damaging practices while at the same time providing the private sector with greater access to policy makers.' Indeed, it's hard to imagine a henhouse providing the fox with a more wide-open invitation.

The fossil fuel lobby fully took advantage of this opening, becoming deeply embedded in the climate change negotiation process known as the UN Framework Convention on Climate Change (UNFCCC). Corporate involvement in this process is pervasive, ubiquitous and takes many forms. Corporations are welcomed to participate in the process as non-governmental organizations (NGOs). While the public tends to think of NGOs as non-profit, low-budget organizations dedicated to defending the public good, industry lobby groups have been allowed to take on the guise of NGOs at the UN. Designated as 'Business and Industry Non-Governmental Organizations' (BINGOs), industry associations qualify for privileges and tools for participating in UN climate change meetings and deliberations. 'By attaining consultative status, business-driven NGOs are provided with a direct line to influence policy at the UN thereby hiding or replacing the voices of smaller, grass-roots not-for-profit organizations,'[9] insist Fernandes and Girard. They note that BINGOs constitute one of the biggest of nine NGO categories admitted into the UNFCCC, with some four thousand two hundred individual BINGO lobbyists having participated in UNFCCC international meetings since 1995.

Of course, there is nothing wrong with the UN encouraging corporations to adopt socially responsible policies, and even to 'partner' with them to achieve results. What does seem misguided, however, is to assume that co-operation and partnership are adequate substitutes for regulation. Corporations are created to generate profits for their owners. If good stewardship of the environment helps them sell products to consumers, presumably they will be willing to be good environmental stewards (or at least *appear* to be – another problem). But if corporate executives see a conflict between their ability to generate profits and protecting the environment, they will consider their prime responsibility to be ensuring corporate profitability. To expect them to behave differently is naive. And to leave the public interest dangling, dependent on the decisions of business executives devoted to ensuring corporate profits, is highly irresponsible.

In addition to involvement in UN negotiations, the fossil fuel lobby has been intensely active in influencing governments directly, particularly in the Anglo-American countries. Its success on this front can be seen in the disengagement of governments in these countries from global efforts to tackle climate change. It is striking that in the early years of the climate crisis, even conservative governments – led by George H. W. Bush, John Major and Brian Mulroney – responded to pressure from their electorates and participated in the 1992 Earth Summit. Since then, however, the political dynamic has changed significantly, with the corporate world increasingly dominant and aggressive in pushing its pro-market dogma. This has allowed right-leaning governments to ignore urgent calls for action from the scientific community, environmental groups and the broader public to tackle climate change.

So, for instance, George W. Bush announced the US withdrawal from the Kyoto process just two months after he took office in 2001. His administration, notoriously close to the oil lobby, remained resistant to efforts to tackle climate change, even in the face of a hair-raising secret report to the Pentagon predicting that climate change would have deadly consequences for US security. The 2003 report was commissioned by influential Pentagon advisor Andrew Marshall and co-written by Peter Schwartz, a CIA consultant and former head of planning at Royal Dutch Shell. It warned that European cities would be sunk beneath rising seas, Britain plunged into a Siberian climate, and North America subjected to brutal storms and prolonged droughts, while other parts of the world would suffer from typhoons, mega-droughts and famine, leading to widespread human strife. According to the report, which was leaked to the *Observer:* 'Humanity would revert to its norm of constant battles for diminishing resources...Once again, warfare would define human life.'[10]

In the recent years of corporate dominance, Canada has also departed sharply from its earlier environmental activism on climate change under Conservative Prime Minister Mulroney to a role of actively obstructing progress in the crisis under Stephen Harper, another Conservative prime minister. Championing unlimited development of Alberta's high-polluting oil sands, Harper has gutted national environmental regulations and been accused of deliberately undermining international negotiations on climate change, withdrawing Canada from the Kyoto Protocol in 2011. Meanwhile in Britain, David Cameron, after promising to lead the 'greenest government ever', has mostly been silent on the issue since taking office, allowing Chancellor of the Exchequer George Osborne to brand green campaigners as 'the environmental Taliban' and to hint at a watering-down of the UK's commitment to cutting carbon dioxide emissions.

As the political landscape has changed profoundly over the past twenty years, efforts to tackle climate change have gone from initially promising to hopelessly stalled, even as time is running out for any hope of heading off potential catastrophe. 'The lasting symbol of this failure is the Kyoto Protocol, passed with much hope in 1997 and then rendered ineffective by 2007 and virtually dead four years later,' conclude Fernandes and Girard. 'In many ways the trajectory of the Kyoto Protocol has been dictated by multi-national corporations through their direct influence on individual country delegations and incessant lobbying during UNFCCC meetings.' The rise of plutocracy, with its sweeping changes to the political culture and the global policy agenda, has allowed a tiny but immensely powerful corporate elite to derail a well-organized global campaign aimed at saving the planet – a campaign that should have been unstoppable.

•   •   •

Plutocracy has led to the derailment of Kyoto not just because the corporate elite has grown more powerful, but also because the rest of the population has lost power. In other words, the threat that extreme inequality poses to democracy – and to democracy's ability to deal with global threats – lies not just in the over-empowerment of the elite, but in the disempowerment of ordinary citizens.

The stagnant or declining incomes of much of the population in Anglo-American countries in recent decades have left citizens scared and less in control of their own lives. With fewer resources, reduced labour protections and diminished government social support, tens of millions of workers have been left less confident that government will help them and potentially more susceptible to corporate arguments that tough environmental regulations will hurt the economy and destroy jobs. Their sense of economic insecurity also undoubtedly leaves them feeling overall less self-assured and, therefore, less willing or able to mount a political challenge to the agenda of an extremely powerful corporate elite.

Political scientist Frederick Solt has studied the impact of economic inequality on political engagement and concluded that high levels of inequality lead ordinary citizens to disengage from the political process. Using data from more than a dozen national surveys of the world's rich democracies, Solt found that 'economic inequality powerfully depresses political interest, discussion of politics, and participation in elections among all but the most affluent and that this negative effect increases with declining relative income'.[11] Solt's work suggests that the predominance of a wealthy elite leaves the rest of the population feeling uninterested and disinclined to participate in politics, sensing it is hopeless to try to affect the outcome. 'Greater economic inequality increasingly stacks the deck of democracy in favor of the richest citizens,' he notes, 'and as a result, most everyone else is more likely to conclude that politics is simply not a game worth playing.'

Ordinary citizens appear to be correct in their assessment that their wishes are ignored by policy makers. Certainly, in the United States, there is growing evidence that elected officials are unresponsive to the policy preferences of the broad public. Martin Gilens, a politics professor at Princeton University, reviewed almost two thousand survey questions put to the public in the last three decades, correlating them against what policy changes were actually made. Gilens found that the chances of a policy change being enacted depended on the income level of those supporting it, and that 'influence over actual policy outcomes appears to be reserved almost exclusively for those at the top of the income distribution'.[12]

Conversely, when income is distributed more equally in society, there is broader participation in the political process and, it seems, greater responsiveness on the part of politicians. This is reflected in the greater responsiveness of politicians – even conservative ones – to public concerns over ozone depletion than to those over climate change.

As noted, the ozone case, played out between 1974 and 1987, took place largely before the dramatic rise in income inequality and the emergence of an overwhelmingly rich and dominant corporate elite. Back then, ordinary citizens in the developed economies had just come through the postwar economic boom, in which average incomes had grown at rapid rates. The role of government had expanded dramatically, enlarging the sphere for collective action and enhancing the notion that political institutions reflected the popular will and should serve the public good. Although the transformation to plutocracy was already under way by the 1980s, there was still a strong overhang of postwar attitudes; the public had not yet been worn down into a state of submission and disempowerment by years of corporate triumphalism.

We can see the impact of the rise of plutocracy on the two environmental crises particularly clearly in the US, which went from playing a leading role in bringing about the Montreal Protocol to being a major opponent of global efforts to stop climate change. When the ozone issue surfaced, the American public reacted with alarm and engagement. Millions of Americans boycotted aerosol sprays, reducing the market by two-thirds by 1977. Despite opposition from industry, the US Congress moved quickly to show its responsiveness to public concern by including in the 1977 Clean Air Act an authorization for the US Environmental Protection Agency to regulate any substance that 'may reasonably be anticipated to affect the stratosphere, especially ozone in the stratosphere'. It empowered the government to regulate CFCs even without conclusive proof that they were harmful. The government needed only to have a reasonable expectation that they were harmful.[13] This was bold action, aimed at satisfying an aroused public.

This stands in marked contrast to the Congressional response to the even more troubling issue of global warming in the 1990s. It's not that the public didn't care about climate change as much as it had cared about ozone depletion; public opinion polls have consistently shown that a large majority of Americans are aware of the danger posed by climate change and want government action to deal with it. But, as corporate domination became deeply entrenched in the 1990s and the business community became more assertive in insisting on its agenda, citizens became largely passive, resigned to accepting the outcomes demanded by the corporate world, whose vision was reinforced by the media. Indeed, the business agenda became pretty much the political mainstream, with dissenters increasingly pushed to the margins.

Certainly, the business agenda was the gospel of the Republican Party, which won control of Congress in the 1994 mid-term elections. As a result, the fossil fuel lobby found a warm reception on Capitol Hill. Congressional hearings held in 1995 became a veritable showcase for global warming deniers and a dragon's den for serious scientists trying to lay out the scope of the problem the world faced. Arch-conservative congressmen vilified the IPCC process as a UN attempt to impose world government on the United States. By May 1996, members of the House of Representatives Science Committee, insisting that they had heard enough whining about global warming, voted to cut funding to the government's climate research programmes, eliminating some programmes completely. Congressman Dana Rohrabacher, whose subcommittee had set up the hearings, explained: 'I think that money that goes into this global warming research is really money right down a rat hole.'[14]

•   •   •

Over two millennia ago, Aristotle had already figured out an important truth about politics: 'When the possession of political power is due to the possession of economic power or wealth... that is oligarchy, and when the unpropertied class has power, that is democracy.' Aristotle probably wouldn't have been surprised by the concentration of wealth and power in today's leading Western nations, although he might have found it curious that we call these nations 'democracies'.

What surely would have surprised Aristotle, however, is the way in which the modern industrialized world has brought itself to the brink of destroying the Earth's ecosystem, and therefore our ability to survive and flourish on this planet. That we seem powerless to stop ourselves from doing so – despite our awareness of what we're doing and the consequences of it for human life – reveals the extent to which democracy has been compromised in our times.

As we prepare to amble off the cliff together, it's time we at least acknowledge the role played by oil billionaires, quietly, invisibly marshalling us into line.

5

why bill gates doesn't deserve his fortune

Bill Gates's fortune is worth well over $50 billion.

One of the key arguments of this book is that Gates, like other billionaires, only 'deserves' a fraction of his fortune. Of course, even if his fortune were much smaller – say, just a couple of billion – Gates would still be a fabulously wealthy man, and his other billions could be spent in ways that would dramatically improve the lives of millions of others.

Let's start by noting that there's a difference between the concept of what one deserves and the concept of what one is legally entitled to. Presumably, Gates has good tax lawyers, so he probably hasn't broken any tax laws. And if he were to run afoul of any tax or other laws affecting property, the matter would be sorted out through proper legal channels. Therefore, we can assume that his billions are legitimately his, under the law. So he is entitled to them. But the question remains: does he deserve them? The question is essentially a moral one, a question about what society considers fair.

Gates is, in many ways, a good test case for the question of whether billionaires deserve their fortunes because he sets the bar high. As billionaires go, he seems like a rather deserving one. He didn't just inherit a fortune; he went out and made one on his own in the marketplace. He not only has great natural talents, but, by all accounts, worked extremely hard to get where he is, making full use of his abilities and every opportunity he encountered. Furthermore, his accomplishment is nothing less than coming up with the operating system for the personal computer – the most widely used innovation of the past century and one that few of us would want to do without. So Gates has made a substantial contribution to society. And, to top it off, he's become one of the world's foremost philanthropists, donating $28 billion to the Bill and Melinda Gates Foundation, which has directed huge sums of money to help truly needy people, such as African victims of AIDS and other diseases. He's become almost a mythical character. It wasn't surprising then that *Time* magazine elevated him to one of the one hundred most influential people of the twentieth century, and, in 2005, chose him (along with wife Melinda, and rock star Bono) as Person of the Year. If there's anyone who seems to deserve his fortune, it's Bill Gates. He's kind of a poster boy for billionaires.

Like most legends, of course, there's more to the story. Certainly the point has been made, including by Malcolm Gladwell in his bestselling book *Outliers*, that Gates's success was dependent on luck, which immediately makes him seem less heroic. Indeed, Gates had the great luck of being born into a well-to-do family, opening up possibilities that would almost certainly not have been available to a child of low-income parents. His father was a successful Seattle lawyer, and his maternal grandfather a rich banker. As a result, he was sent to a private school, Lakeside, which happened to have a computer club – something unusual in the late 1960s. A fundraising drive by the savvy mothers of Lakeside students didn't just raise small change for hockey sweaters or school outings. Rather, drawing on the school's wealthy clientele, they raised enough money – and were sufficiently forward-looking – to buy a $3,000 computer terminal for the school. This made Lakeside one of the few high schools in the country, and probably the world, with a computer terminal in the 1960s. And it was a particularly good one. Gates, who hadn't been very interested in schoolwork, took readily and enthusiastically to the technology and was soon spending all of his time in the school basement playing with the exciting new machine.

As it turned out, his timing was perfect. Society was on the cusp of a revolution that would shortly bring computers into the lives of millions of people. Decades of technological advances had led to the development of giant IBM mainframe computers, which had spectacular powers but were enormously costly and big enough to fill a room. By the late 1960s, the technology was evolving rapidly. In particular, a project that had been undertaken for the US Air Force in the early 1960s, called 'Augmenting Human Intelligence', made possible the development of miniature computers that could be programmed to process data in response to commands. This created the possibility that, in addition to giant machines used by government and the military, computers could be personal devices used by individuals in their own lives. The prospects were breathtaking. Gates, at just thirteen years old, was getting ample access to rare and expensive computer time, enabling him to experiment for hours on end with a technology that was about to change the world.

Over the next few years, Gates had a number of important lucky breaks that greatly helped him to get a grounding in the emerging technology. The mother of one of the Lakeside boys happened to be involved in computer programming at the University of Washington. She and some colleagues had set up a small business developing software for sale to companies wanting to lease time on the university computer. They decided to let the students in the Lakeside computer club come down to their office and test out the company's software programs after school and on weekends.

That meant more access to free computer time, and Gates and the others grabbed the opportunity. Soon they had an even better deal with another Seattle company, Information Services Incorporated (ISI), which had its own mainframe and was willing to give them free time in exchange for testing out software it was developing for processing company payrolls. In addition, the Lakeside gang discovered that they could get free time on the computer at the University of Washington in the middle of the night. Again, they jumped at the chance, becoming regular nocturnal visitors.

The ISI connection proved crucial. When Gates was in his final year of high school, a company looking for programmers to help it develop a computer system for a state power station approached ISI. The assignment required experience with a particular type of software – software now very familiar to Gates after hours of work on the ISI computer. He managed to convince the teachers at Lakeside to let him move to the southern part of the state to work on the power project as an independent study programme. The following year, Gates went off to Harvard, where computers remained his obsessive focus. After a couple of years there, he dropped out and, in 1975, set up Microsoft with former Lakeside computer pal Paul Allen.

For the first few years, Microsoft was a relatively small, aggressive technology company with several dozen employees – one of a number of such companies working in the emerging field of desktop computers. At this point, these were fairly primitive machines and hard to operate, and the market for them, while growing, was still limited. Gates was successful in the field, but not a leading figure. He was certainly far behind Gary Kildall, a brilliant computer innovator thirteen years his senior who had already developed an operating system, known as Control Program for Microcomputers or CP/M, which was the most widely used operating system for desktops at the time. Kildall's company, Digital Research, had sold hundreds of thousands of copies of CP/M, and was pulling in revenue of more than $100,000 a month. Microsoft's main business was selling computer-programming language that ran on Kildall's CP/M.

But Microsoft caught a huge break in 1980 that was to launch it into the stratosphere of corporate success as the dominant force in the computer industry. That year, IBM had set up a secret internal task force, code-named Project Chess, to consider developing a desktop computer for the mass market. Crucially, the company would need an operating system for its new minicomputer. By any logic, the task force should have turned to Kildall, who was the acknowledged leader in the field. As writer Harold Evans puts it: 'Everybody in the computer field knew that Kildall had created CP/M – everybody, it seems, except the biggest beast in the mainframe jungle, in which personal computers had hitherto been invisible.' Instead, oddly, the IBM task force headed to Seattle to see a secondary player, Bill Gates.[1]

Gates received members of the IBM team enthusiastically, but when they tried to buy the licence for CP/M from him, he told them that it wasn't actually his. He referred them to Kildall, whom he knew personally; he'd been to dinner with Kildall and his wife at their home in Monterey, California. The IBM project team flew down to see Kildall the next day to negotiate a licensing deal. There's some dispute over exactly what happened when they showed up at Kildall's office. Kildall later claimed that there'd been an agreement in principle that day, confirmed by a handshake. However, there were no follow-up negotiations. Instead, the IBM team was soon headed back to Seattle, where Gates now assured them that Microsoft would be able to come up with an operating system to meet their requirements. He then quickly bought the rights to another operating system – an adaptation of Kildall's CP/M developed by Tim Paterson and produced by a Seattle company.

Gates flew down to IBM's southern headquarters in Boca Raton, Florida, to meet with the IBM project team for lunch. The meeting went well. Project leader Don Estridge told Gates that the new IBM chief executive, John Opel, was delighted to hear that the company might be doing a deal with Gates, whose mother he knew personally. (Opel sat on the board of the United Way NGO with Mary Gates.) Bill and his mother certainly fitted much more comfortably into the upscale corporate culture of IBM than the hippie-like and free-spirited Gary Kildall.

In the end, IBM did a deal with Gates – even though Kildall's system was clearly superior. Indeed, Kildall, who was years ahead of everyone else in the field, had already developed the capacity for multitasking – a function that it would take another decade for IBM and Microsoft to come out with. According to Evans, Kildall was 'the true founder of the personal computer revolution and the father of PC software'.[2] But, of course, it was Gates who was to get the credit, and in the process become one of the world's most famous and celebrated men – and the richest person on the planet.

•   •   •

But does he deserve that fortune?

Although Gates was a go-getter who maximized every opportunity that came his way, he wasn't the actual inventor of the operating system of the personal computer, as he's often celebrated for being. If anyone deserves that title, it's Gary Kildall. Of course, this is by no means the first time an actual inventor has been nudged aside by a rival who was simply more adept at manoeuvring himself to the front of the line. The history of inventions is full of such stories. But the point isn't that Kildall should have ended up with $50 billion (in fact, Kildall, although not in the same league as Gates, did do very well financially). Rather, the point is to question whether anyone should end up with such a vast fortune as a reward for inventing a system that was actually developed through the collective contributions of many, many people.

Our culture inculcates us with the notion that important advances are the product of individual genius. We tend to see the development of human civilization over the centuries as the history of spectacular achievements by individuals, virtually eliminating the role that society plays. This notion gives credibility and legitimacy to the accumulation of immense wealth. If Gates – or for that matter, Kildall – was responsible all by himself for an invention that changed the world, then our winner-take-all system of rewards might make sense. But the personal computer didn't just spring whole from either of their brains. On the contrary, it was the product of a long series of technological developments going back decades (or even centuries), each one making possible the advance of science to the point that the next breakthrough became possible, indeed almost inevitable.

In many ways, the story of the personal computer begins in France in the early 1800s with the invention of a superior loom for weaving silk. The intricately brocaded fabrics that were fashionable at the time could be produced by an instrument known as a drawloom, but only with extremely difficult and complex hand-weaving. Joseph Marie Jacquard, the fifth of nine children of a master weaver from Lyon, devised a loom that allowed the weaving function to be done without manual effort. The key to his invention was a series of punched cards. These were inserted into the loom, where metal rods attached to individual threads would hit against them. If a rod encountered a hole in a card, it would activate a thread; if it encountered solid card, it would do nothing. So the actions of the loom were determined by the placement of a series of holes in the punched cards. With the insertion of the cards, the loom could effectively be programmed to carry out the complex weaving tasks on its own. The Jacquard loom, notes technology historian James Essinger, 'was a machine of a caliber and sophistication that had never been seen before. In fact, when it was patented in 1804, it was unquestionably the most complex mechanism in the world'.[3] Its punched-card technology was the germ of the idea for the computer. (Indeed, the first computers Gates worked on as a student still used punched cards.)

Jacquard's loom was the inspiration for an ambitious calculating machine that is now considered to be a Victorian-age 'computer'. Developed by British scientist and mathematician Charles Babbage, the machine was an attempt to adapt the punched-card technology of Jacquard's loom for the tedious task of mathematical calculation.

At the time, for instance, tables used to calculate the move-ment of stars and planets were prepared slowly and painstakingly by clerks who were known, interestingly enough, as 'computers'. Babbage wanted to create a machine that would avoid this time-consuming manual process, and also produce more reliable results. In the same way that Jacquard had used punched cards to control the metal rods on his loom, Babbage's machine used punched cards to control metal rods that in turn activated cogwheels carrying out calculating functions. His 'Analytical Engine' even had a memory, which he called 'the store', and a processor, which he called the 'mill'. Babbage openly acknowledged that his idea was derived from Jacquard, even displaying a magnificent portrait of the French weaver in his home, made of silk using the Jacquard loom. While Babbage developed highly sophisticated portions of his machine, as well as detailed plans and drawings for its completion, he failed to make it actually operational. More than a century and a half later, in 2004, scientists built a full model of his extraordinary appa-ratus – with eight thousand parts and weighing five tons – based faithfully on his drawings. Babbage is now considered the father of the modern computer.

The next key step was taken by Herman Hollerith, an American engineer who used the punched-card technology of Jacquard's loom to create a machine that was actually able to process information. Hollerith originally developed his machine, known as the 'tabula-tor', to simplify the massive task of processing data gathered by the

US census. Hollerith had some success adapting his machine for commercial purposes, and his company later merged with three others and surfaced under a new name in 1911: International Business Machines, or IBM. It was under IBM, and specifically its high-powered, sales-oriented president, Thomas John Watson, that Hollerith's punched-card tabulating machine became a widely used business tool. By the 1930s, IBM had developed an advanced automatic tabulation machine and was manufacturing some fifteen hundred of them a year. The Depression hurt sales, but the introduction of the Social Security Act in 1935 as part of the New Deal created a bonanza for IBM. Suddenly, the US government needed to automate the employment records of the entire nation, and it soon ordered five hundred machines from IBM.

IBM got even more help from the government during the Second World War, when the US Army funded it to carry out special projects. In January 1943, IBM produced its first real computer – the first automatic digital calculating device – for use by the US Navy. The device consisted of a massive steel frame fifty-one feet long and eight feet high containing five hundred miles of wire and three million wire connections, but it was still based on the central punched-card technology.

Meanwhile, two engineers from the University of Pennsylvania, J. Presper Eckert and John Mauchly, again with funding from the US government, succeeded by the late 1940s in developing an all-electronic computer. It could carry out five thousand operations per second – compared to just three thousand for IBM's wartime computer. The development of transistors in the late 1940s allowed computers to get more powerful still, and they could soon perform up to one hundred thousand tasks per second. At the same time, the devices were getting smaller.

By 1955 – the year Bill Gates was born – the computer revolution was well under way, drawing the intense interest of thousands of enthusiasts intent on devising ways to develop and widen the use of these powerful machines. It was this loose group of computer professionals and hobbyists that Gates would join in the early 1970s. But before he had finished kindergarten, there were a whole host of advances that set the stage for his upcoming role in the rise of personal computers. Almost all these advances were the result of work funded by the US government and military, and most were the result of teamwork, with individual contributions often hard to identify. Notes Essinger: 'Ever since the late 1950s, this has tended to be the pattern for breakthroughs in computing: they have been the result of collaborative and joint effort by large teams composed of often anonymous people rather than by individual pioneers.'[4]

Some individual pioneers do stand out, most notably Douglas Engelbart, a visionary engineer driven by a desire to develop computers to help solve the urgent problems facing humanity, rather than just as commercial tools enabling people to work faster. With funding from the US Air Force in the early 1960s, Engelbart, along with engineer Bill English, invented some of the key features that we associate with personal computers today, such as the mouse.[5] Up until this point, computers, though immensely powerful, were essentially inaccessible to humans, except to a few initiates possessing sophisticated programming skills. Engelbart and others got around this problem by devising ways for people to interact with these potent machines – through the keyboard, the screen, the mouse, the menu, and other items of what's known as the graphical user interface (GUI) – so that individual users could easily instruct computers to carry out specific tasks.

These devices – absolutely essential in transforming the computer into the ubiquitous machine that is central to the lives of hundreds of millions of people today – were developed by Engelbart and dozens of others, long before Apple Computer (and, later still, Microsoft) simply repackaged them for the mass market. (Before Microsoft developed Windows, it used MS–DOS – short for Microsoft Operating System – a much less user-friendly system in which users typed command words on the keyboard.) In a 1994 interview with *Playboy* magazine, Bill Gates acknowledged that one of the keys to Microsoft's incredible success was 'committing to the graphics interface' – an array of tools developed not by him but by many others, who remain largely obscure and considerably less rich. Engelbart, who has been sadly disappointed by the commercial direction of the computer revolution, held the patent for the mouse, although he never actually received any royalties for it because he allowed it to expire in 1987, on the cusp of the desktop revolution.

So if we were to present the story of the development of the personal computer as a stage play, it would be a rich and complex drama with a long list of characters. From early scenes featuring Joseph Marie Jacquard and his punched-card technology, the play would go on to include starring roles for Charles Babbage, Herman Hollerith, Thomas John Watson, J. Presper Eckert, John Mauchly, Douglas Engelbart and Bill English, with a host of other largely unidentified characters playing crucial supporting roles onstage and off. Toward the end of this rather long drama, there'd be an intriguing subplot about how technological innovator Gary Kildall thought he had a deal with IBM, only to discover his friend Bill Gates had sold IBM an adaptation of Kildall's own operating system for the first mass-market personal computer. It would only be at this point late in the final act that we'd get our first sight of Gates, and he wouldn't come across as a particularly heroic character. Indeed, as the curtain came down at the end of the production, it would be hard to imagine Gates getting a curtain call or receiving the lion's share of the applause, let alone walking away with the entire box office take.

●　　●　　●

Among other things, the story of the personal computer suggests that inventions and innovations are the result of an evolutionary process involving many players, rather than being the product of one brilliant individual. As Isaac Newton famously remarked in a letter to scientific rival Robert Hooke: 'What Descartes did was a good step. You have added much several ways…If I have seen a little further it is by standing on the shoulders of Giants.'

Indeed, an invention typically occurs when the scientific body of evidence has accumulated to the point that the breakthrough is almost apparent – at least to the scientists closely engaged in the field. Political economists Gar Alperovitz and Lew Daly put it this way: 'What commonly happens is that a field of research reaches a certain point in time when "the next step" is obvious to insiders – and because it is obvious, it is also inevitable that somebody, or more likely many somebodies, will take the step. Someone will connect the dots (but only, it is important to note, when the requisite dots have developed to the point where they can be connected).'[6]

This truth is illustrated by the fact that a number of major inventions appear to have been 'invented' by different individuals at virtually the same moment. One striking case is that of Alexander Graham Bell, forever credited with inventing the telephone. Bell did file a patent on 14 February 1876, but that same day, an American electrical engineer named Elisha Gray filed a caveat – a statement of intent to patent – for a similar apparatus. In the log book at the patent office, Bell was no. 5, while Gray was no. 39, which would seem to suggest Bell won the race to develop a telephone, if only by a hair. But two things throw that claim into question. Many of the patents were received by mail, and it's not clear from the patent office logs at what point in the day on 14 February 1876 the submissions by Bell and Gray were received. More importantly, it turned out that the mechanism outlined by Bell in his original patent wouldn't have actually worked – he had to file another patent soon afterward, correcting some of his design problems – while

Gray's original submission would have worked. After years of unsuccessful litigation by Gray, Bell's claim now stands unchallenged in popular history.[7]

But clearly, Alexander Graham Bell was not indispensable to the invention of the telephone. There's even evidence that half a decade before 1876, when Bell and Gray were virtually tied in the race to 'invent' the telephone, Antonio Meucci, an Italian stage technician, had quietly crossed the finish line. Meucci had already essentially developed a telephone, which he called the 'teletrofono'. It appears that he had been able to establish voice transmission between his Staten Island workshop and his nearby home as early as the 1850s. By 1871, Meucci had filed a caveat for his apparatus, but in 1874, unable to afford the $10 renewal fee, he allowed it to lapse. Had he not, Bell would have raced his application to the patent office only to discover that the telephone had already been invented years earlier.[8]

It's also clear that the personal computer would have been invented with or without Bill Gates. Furthermore, it's possible that, without Gates, the revolution in personal computers would have evolved along less commercial lines. A number of the early pioneers were committed to developing personal computer software for the public realm, free from corporate domination. Engelbart, for instance, was deeply motivated by the idea of using the computer primarily as a tool to advance human capacities to cope with the enormous problems facing the world. But despite his brilliant innovations, Engelbart was never able to realize his vision. Nor were dozens of other talented pioneers with aspirations of collectively building computer operating systems freely accessible to all. Their dreams were blocked in part because of the supremacy of Gates. As he achieved greater and greater market dominance, he was able to use his power to squeeze out others relentlessly, prompting years of government antitrust actions that ultimately failed against Microsoft's deep pockets. In the process, Gates took control of the computer revolution, which could have been a vehicle for human empowerment or betterment, and turned it instead into a commercial Shangri-La, where almost every computer user in the world is obliged to contribute to the enlargement of his ever-growing personal jackpot.

Whatever Bill Gates's contribution to the development of the personal computer, it was only possible because of innumerable developments starting well before Jacquard's invention of punched-card technology, including a vast range of scientific and mathematical developments that preceded them for centuries: the invention of everything from geometry and algebra to the printing press, and even the development of human writing, beginning in ancient Mesopotamia. Patent-law expert Alfred Kahn argues that no invention is the work of one individual but is rather 'the aggregate of an almost infinite number of individual units of invention, each of them the contribution of a single person. It is little short of absurdity to call any one of the interrelated units the invention, and its "creator" the inventor.'[9]

It is this enormous knowledge and technological inheritance – which has grown at a particularly breathtaking rate in the last hundred years – that accounts for so much of the wealth we enjoy today. The Nobel Prize-winning economist Robert M. Solow clarified this in a ground-breaking study in 1957, when he identified that the key element in the phenomenal productivity growth between 1909 and 1949 was not the contribution of either capital or labour, as was commonly believed. Instead, Solow attributed the majority of the growth – about 88 per cent – to 'technical change in the broadest sense'.[10] Herbert A. Simon, another Nobel Prize-winning economist, referred to the huge store of knowledge from the past as 'social capital', and argued that access to it was our main source of wealth, responsible for about 90 per cent of national income.[11] Still another Nobel laureate, George Akerlof, points to the economic significance of this technological inheritance in noting that 'our marginal products are not ours alone…[but] are due almost entirely to the cumulative process of learning that has taken us from stone age poverty to twenty-first century affluence'.[12]

Indeed, it's hard to figure out the rationale for the mammoth discrepancies in today's incomes when so much of what any of us are able to accomplish is due to all the learning and knowledge accumulated in the centuries preceding us. As Alperovitz and Daly put it: 'Before anyone is a "talented" entrepreneur or a "menial" laborer, or anything in between, most of the economic gains that get distributed to individuals in a given year or period are derived from what is inherited from the past, not created by them in the present.'[13] All this inevitably raises the question of who should benefit from the wealth made possible by this huge technological inheritance.

As things currently stand, the overwhelming beneficiary is whoever (like Bill Gates) manages to adapt some aspect of our technological inheritance into a marginally new product that gains market dominance – often through a combination of luck, opportunism and ruthlessness. But why should Gates or any other individual take such an extraordinarily large share of the jackpot? Does the technological inheritance that made his marginally new product possible really belong so exclusively to him? If it belongs more properly to all of us, and if this inheritance is the overwhelming source of all wealth today, shouldn't society as a whole enjoy a larger share of the bounty?

This group inheritance is implicitly acknowledged in the tax system, which collects a share of each person's income and deposits it in the national treasury for the general use of society. The question is: does the tax system collect a sufficiently large share of a person's income to compensate for the sheer size of the technological inheritance? In the case of low- and middle-income earners, the answer is probably yes. After all, their incomes are not so large, and they need to be left with sufficient funds to support themselves and their families. But what about the very rich?

A number of important social theorists have argued for greater acknowledgment of the role of society in generating incomes – and greater payback through the tax system. John Stuart Mill, the nineteenth-century British political philosopher best known for his writings in defence of individual liberty, also argued, particularly in his later years, for a recognition of the important role society plays in individual earnings. Mill noted that it was society, not just individual effort or labour, that determined what a person was able to do or create, and that society was morally entitled to receive due compensation for its contribution.

In 1870, for instance, Mill was involved in the founding of the Land Tenure Reform Association, considered an important step in the evolution of modern social welfare philosophy. While arguing that private ownership of land might be desirable to achieve optimal production, Mill, in his draft of the association's programme, insisted that increases in land values caused by the general growth and development of society properly belonged to the community at large.[14] Mill extended this approach to increases in values of all sorts of property that are caused by factors having nothing to do with the contributions of the individual property holder. In a well-known passage from his *Principles of Political Economy*, he explained: 'Suppose there is a kind of income which constantly tends to increase, without any exertion or sacrifice on the part of the owners...it would be no violation of the principles on which private property is grounded, if the state should appropriate this increase of wealth, or part of it, as it arises.'[15] Mill went on to make the case that the failure of society to appropriate its due would result in property holders receiving undue benefit – thereby bestowing on them an 'unearned appendage' to their existing wealth.

Many others have developed arguments along this line. In his 1779 pamphlet *Agrarian Justice,* the renowned American Revolutionary War-era writer Thomas Paine noted that if an individual is separated from society, even given a whole continent to possess, 'he cannot acquire personal property. He cannot be rich.'Thus, continued Paine, 'all accumulation…of personal property, beyond what a man's own hands produce, is derived to him by living in society; and he owes on every principle of justice, of gratitude, and of civilization, a part of that accumulation back again to society from whence the whole came.' British philosopher and reformer Leonard T. Hobhouse, writing in the early 1900s, developed a similar argument. As great fortunes were being amassed through the Industrial Revolution, Hobhouse reminded the prosperous business owner to consider 'what single step he could have taken' if it hadn't been for the 'sum of intelligence which civilization has placed at his disposal' and the 'inventions which he uses as a matter of course and which have been built up by the collective effort of generations'.[16]

Mill, Paine, Hobhouse and others were clearly developing a case for the moral legitimacy of taxation as reimbursement for society's contribution. As Hobhouse argued, taxation should not be seen as 'redistribution' but rather as 'just compensation' – the restoration of the unearned, excess wealth to its proper place in the community's coffers. 'The true function of taxation is to secure to society the element in wealth that is of social origin, or, more broadly, all that does not owe its origin to the efforts of living individuals.' Hobhouse went on to suggest that setting taxes on large incomes too low deprives society of its just share of the rewards, and even amounts to a kind of distorted welfare system in which wealthy individuals unfairly receive the fruits of society's industry.

Certainly, if most of what we are able to create is inherited from the past, it seems reasonable that a significant part of any resulting windfall – which happens to come the way of an individual who is often simply lucky – should go back to society. Jacques Turgot, an eighteenth-century French economist, referred to the techno-logical and cultural heritage of the past as a 'common treasury'.[17] This apt phrase suggests not only that this heritage is something we receive collectively, but also that it is a treasure, a store of riches that should provide benefits for all.

The case for returning a substantial share of large incomes and fortunes to the common purse is based not only on the contribution of the inheritance of the past, but also on the ongoing contribution made by the public treasury. In many cases, inventions are the direct result of substantial government funding of research. So, for instance, in addition to the technological bequest Bill Gates received from Jacquard et al., there was the fact that Gates learned computer programming largely through access to the mainframe computer at the government-funded University of Washington. For that matter, virtually all the early research leading to the development of the personal computer was paid for from the public purse – from Engelbart's Augmenting Human Intellect project, funded by the US Air Force, to a whole range of path-breaking government-sponsored computing projects in the 1940s and '50s, including those at Harvard, MIT, the University of Illinois, the Rand Corporation, the Los Alamos Laboratories, the Stanford Research Institute and the Office of Naval Research.[18]

More broadly, of course, massive government funding of public education makes possible the advanced society we live in, in which people are literate enough to be able to use a computer. And without government funding of police and fire departments as well as roads and the whole urban infrastructure, our sophisticated economy in which citizens can afford to buy personal computers would not exist. Indeed, as noted, government creates the market itself – through laws, regulations, and institutions that govern banking, commerce and international trade, in addition to establishing and enforcing property rights.

Without all this, no one individual could ever make much of a difference – no matter how brilliant, dedicated, motivated or hardworking he or she might be. In the overall picture, one person's contribution would still inevitably be infinitesimally small. If this seems to underestimate the importance of individual greatness, consider some of the most outstanding minds in history and try to imagine how far they would have got without the benefit of society and all the knowledge accumulated before them. Alperovitz and Daly put it well: 'If [Isaac] Newton, in his lifetime, had to learn everything humanity had learned from the time of the caveman to the late seventeenth century – if he had no knowledge inheritance whatsoever to work with – he could not have contributed much more than an insightful caveman could in his lifetime.'[19]

And Bill Gates, stranded on a deserted island, would have his work cut out just figuring how to keep himself warm.

6

why other billionaires are even less deserving

It was late in 2006 when an ageing, little-known economic consultant named Gary Shilling arrived at a well-appointed office in New York's Upper East Side for a meeting with hedge fund manager John Paulson and his team of high-powered analysts. Shilling, who operated out of more modest quarters in suburban New Jersey, may have seemed rather out of place with Paulson and this younger crowd of urbane money traders, but Paulson had sought him out after reading a newsletter Shilling produced. Paulson had been impressed by Shilling's analysis of the nation's economic prospects – and how sharply out of sync it was with the rosy picture painted by others. Just about every other economist and market watcher was adamant that, even after five years of record-breaking growth, US housing prices would continue to surge upward. But Shilling wasn't convinced. As he told his intrigued audience at Paulson & Co., housing prices were about to come crashing down. And that, he said, would trigger a sharp increase in mortgage foreclosures. The scene would not be pretty.

In fact, Paulson and his minions had been watching the housing market intently for the past two years, tracking the explosive growth of risky debt that was obscured by the stunning rise in house prices. He had a gut instinct that Shilling, well into his seventies, was on to something, and it didn't take long for the hedge fund manager to figure out where it could lead.

'Boy, if you're right, the financial system will fall apart,' said Paulson.[1]

Shilling confirmed that he fully expected that to happen.

As the pieces began to fit into place in his mind, Paulson concluded that the global economy was closer to the precipice than anyone seemed to realize.

At last, the moment he had long waited for seemed to have arrived.

• • •

Like a few other savvy Wall Street players, Paulson had been looking for an opportunity to bet that the housing bubble would burst. There was enough information around about the shoddy nature of many of the subprime mortgage deals – with clients who had little in the way of assets, income or employment – that a number of close observers realized a lot of 'homeowners' would soon be in dire straits, unable to meet their monthly payments. In the betting parlours of Wall Street, this represented a chance to make some serious money.

The best vehicle for betting against the housing market, as Paulson and a few other Wall Streeters had figured out, was to take out 'insurance' on packages of mortgages that had been bundled together and sold as a stock. This was an odd concept that twisted the conventional notion of insurance. Typically, for instance, a car owner takes out insurance on his car, paying a small monthly premium to protect himself against the potentially heavy financial loss he would suffer if his car were to be in an accident. In this case, the asset was not a car but a stock. Still, that made sense, since a stock could decline in value, so an investor holding the stock might want to protect himself from the possibility of such a decline. What was unusual here was that the Wall Street types were taking out insurance on something in which they had no personal stake, on something that involved other people's assets. It was like buying insurance on a car owned by a stranger, in the hope of collecting money if the stranger's car crashed. This 'insurance' – known as a credit default swap (CDS) – was simply a bet. The fate of thousands of mortgage holders and their dreams of homeownership had become an opportunity for Wall Street hotshots to roll the dice, in the hope of winning a jackpot.

In some ways, this form of gambling wasn't very risky, because the most the bettor could lose would be the cost of his premiums. (For $1 million a year in CDS premiums, it was possible to insure some $100 million worth of these mortgage stocks.)[2] The problem was that it was impossible to know exactly when the housing market would collapse and cause the mortgage stocks to tumble in value. In the meantime, the cost of paying the premiums would add up. A few bettors had already been badly burned, spending too much on premiums and eventually pulling out of the game, frustrated and bitter that the housing market hadn't yet imploded. Paulson too had been betting on a housing collapse, but he'd assembled a big enough war chest from his wealthy hedge fund clients to keep playing, despite the continued buoyancy of the housing market. After the meeting with Shilling, he was convinced that now was the time to go really big.

One frustration for Paulson was that there just weren't enough of these stocks, known as collateral debt obligations (CDO), to bet against. So he decided to become proactive. He approached a number of investment banks with the request that they create more CDOs to sell to clients, so that he could then take out 'insurance' betting that these would fail. The arrangement Paulson had in mind was rife with potential conflicts of interest. He clearly wanted to help pick the mortgages that would make up the new CDOs. And he would obviously favour particularly risky subprime mortgages, thereby increasing the likelihood that the CDOs would become worthless and he would be able to collect on the 'insurance' he had taken out.

Bear Stearns, the giant investment bank where Paulson had once served as managing director, said no to his scheme. But Goldman Sachs agreed to the arrangement, providing Paulson with his dream opportunity: a chance to bet on toxic CDOs worth about $5 billion. And all went according to plan. The housing bubble burst soon afterward, causing untold misery among homeowners and rendering the $5 billion in CDOs worthless – and allowing Paulson to collect $1 billion in 'insurance'. In fact, that was only a fraction of the money Paulson earned by betting on the collapse of the housing market in 2007. When the winnings from all his bets were counted, he emerged with $3.7 billion, making him the tallest man in that year's US income parade.

• • •

All this turned Paulson into a mini-hero on Wall Street. The financial press celebrated him for his cunning moves in scoring the biggest one-year jackpot ever. *Wall Street Journal* reporter Gregory Zuckerman recounted in stirring detail every step that led to Paulson's winning gamble in a book whose title gives away the author's enthusiasm: *The Greatest Trade Ever.* In the book, Paulson comes across as a sympathetic character, an 'underdog' who overcame obstacles and 'triumphed over the hubris' of Wall Street. 'Paulson was no singles hitter, afraid of risk,' Zuckerman writes breathlessly. 'Anticipating a housing collapse – and all that it meant – was Paulson's chance to hit the ball out of the park and win the acclaim he deserved.'[3]

The acclaim he deserved? Paulson's hit helped trigger the collapse of global financial markets, leaving tens of millions suffering around the world. The activities of Paulson, and others like him on

Wall Street, could surely in no way be construed as socially beneficial. Their actions do nothing to improve the efficient allocation of
capital – the function that financial markets are supposed to perform.
Instead, they amount to little more than gambling, which has no
social utility. Martin Wolf, a columnist for the *Financial Times*, noted
that Paulson's moves served 'absolutely no useful purpose'.[4] By
buying insurance on CDO investments in which he had no ownership stake, Paulson wasn't protecting himself from losses, but rather
was placing a bet that the CDO investments would fail – like buying
insurance on someone else's car, hoping it would crash. But it was
worse than that. Paulson managed to get Goldman Sachs to create
faulty CDOs, so that he would have excellent odds in betting against
them. Paulson was effectively arranging to have a manufacturer build
a car with a faulty brake pedal and then, when the brakes inevitably
failed and the car crashed, collect on the insurance he'd taken out.[5]

In April 2010, the US Securities and Exchange Commission
(SEC) charged Goldman Sachs with fraud for selling CDOs without
telling buyers that they'd been designed with the help of Paulson,
who was betting they would fail. However, no charges were laid
against Paulson, since he hadn't been involved in misrepresenting the
CDOs to buyers. Still, leaving aside the legal issues, he was clearly
instrumental in getting Goldman to create the toxic and destructive
CDOs that lie at the heart of the SEC's fraud case.

Some observers have joked that Wall Street should be regulated,
not by the SEC, but by the Nevada Gaming Commission. In that
spirit, Simon Johnson, a business professor at MIT and former
research director of the International Monetary Fund, says that it
appears as if Paulson and Goldman Sachs were running a 'crooked
roulette table' – something that gets one banned for life from Las
Vegas. Johnson argues that Paulson should be banned for life from
securities markets.[6]

The Paulson–Goldman scheme set off a series of events with
extremely negative repercussions. Investors purchasing the toxic

CDOs lost billions of dollars, unaware that they were buying faulty merchandise. Furthermore, the scheme exacerbated the impact of the housing collapse and the near-bankruptcy of insurance giant AIG, which had sold some $64 billion of CDS 'insurance' on CDOs related to subprime mortgages. AIG was unable to pay out the money it owed to those, like Paulson, who had bought insurance on now-worthless mortgage-related CDOs. (Goldman too had bought such insurance from AIG, which put the firm in the position of both creating the highly risky CDOs and taking out insurance betting they would fail.) But it gets worse. Insisting that AIG's bankruptcy would devastate credit markets, the US government stepped in to prop up the giant insurance conglomerate. In a deal overseen by then Treasury Secretary Henry Paulson,[7] a former Goldman Sachs CEO, Washington bailed out AIG with $170 billion. Out of that huge pool of taxpayer money, AIG paid Goldman $14 billion to make good on the insurance Goldman had bought on its CDOs.[8] Similarly, it paid John Paulson $1 billion.

This means that a billion dollars of taxpayer money went to ensure that Paulson was able to collect his gambling jackpot. By the logic of the marketplace, Paulson should have been left with nothing when the massive bets he'd made, based on faulty products, helped bankrupt the gambling parlour; instead, in the protected comfort of Wall Street's sheltered casino, he walked away with vast amounts of taxpayer dollars bulging from his pockets.

So Paulson not only helped spark the financial collapse – with its ruinous repercussions for tens of millions around the world – but he made off with $1 billion of the public's money for his role in what appears to be a crooked gambling scheme.

While some in the financial world may celebrate him as a home-run hitter, another view was captured in a handwritten sign held by protestors marching on Wall Street right after the crash: 'Jump, you fuckers!'

• • •

If Bill Gates is a poster boy for billionaires, Paulson might be con-sidered the opposite: someone who accumulated great wealth in a way that actively harms society. While Gates could be credited with contributing to the development of the personal computer, Paulson helped trigger a financial meltdown and a worldwide recession.

For that matter, Paulson is hardly the only fabulously wealthy individual whose overall contribution to society veers into nega-tive territory. There's also Joseph Cassano, former head of the financial products division at AIG. Cassano was instrumental in peddling some $500 billion worth of CDOs, including the $64 billion connected to subprime mortgages, leading to the collapse and bailout of AIG. Then there's Angelo Mozilo, former CEO of Countrywide Financial, who made a fortune directly peddling sub-prime mortgages to unsophisticated, would-be homeowners. There's also Sanford I. Weill, former head of Citigroup, whose extensive lobbying efforts helped kill the Glass–Steagall Act, thereby under-mining regulatory supervision of financial markets and allowing Wall Street to turn itself into a giant casino. Indeed, much of Wall Street would fit in one way or another into this non-poster-boy category of billionaires. (And we haven't even mentioned the likes of out-and-out billionaire crooks such as Bernie Madoff, who, in crossing the line into obvious criminality, have lost any claims to deserving their fortunes.)

Of course, if contribution to society were the criterion for determining an individual's compensation, the income parade would look very different. By most people's standards, the giants reaching up into the clouds would be people such as nurses, doc-tors, teachers and social workers, while the bankers and hedge fund managers would find themselves among the dwarves. (In reality, however, the pay of the top twenty-five hedge fund managers in 2009 was the same as that of 658,000 school teachers.)[9] While few would say that our system of rewarding people financially accurately reflects their true social contribution, our society does implicitly subscribe to the view that there is some connection between social contribution and compensation. According to neoclassical economic theory, which has dominated Western thinking for the past century, a person's compensation is a reflection of his marginal product – that is, his contribution to total economic output. So, to make a contribution to society, one doesn't have to be doing social work or directly helping others. By adding to society's economic output, the individual is deemed to have increased the well-being of the community. Under this theory, those who contribute most to economic output receive the largest rewards.

In reality, however, it is hard to make the case that those with the biggest incomes (John Paulson, for instance) have made the biggest contribution to economic output, let alone to any broader goals in society. Supporters of neoclassical theory get around this problem by arguing that a person's contribution to economic output is simply a reflection of what others are willing to pay him for his services. This has a nice simplicity about it; rather than society judging the value of an individual's output, it is left to the market to determine value.

But a problem quickly becomes obvious: under this formulation, a person's contribution is determined by how valued her services are by those who have money and are therefore able to pay for her services. Is a tax lawyer who exploits every ambiguity in the law to benefit her wealthy clients really worth ten to twenty times more than a community clinic lawyer who figures out legal ways to prevent poor families from being evicted from their homes? Is a dentist who performs cosmetic work really worth many times more than a dentist who, responding to pressing community needs, devotes her practice to performing basic dentistry on children? Are politicians who go on to lucrative careers after serving the interests of the rich and powerful really more socially valuable than those who have minimal career prospects after political careers championing the rights of the poor and challenging the status quo? It's hard to see much of a moral principle in a system that rewards people on the basis of how much they're willing or able to pander to the rich.

The flaws in neoclassical economic theory are more evident now than ever, given today's frenzy of pay at the top. Joseph Stiglitz, the Nobel Prize-winning economist, points to the discrepancy between the huge pay of the Wall Street crowd and that of the late agronomist Norman Borlaug, who saved millions of lives by developing methods for improving agricultural productivity: 'If neoclassical theory were correct, Borlaug would have been among the wealthiest men in the world, while our bankers would have been lining up at soup kitchens.' Stiglitz notes that there appears to be no justification for today's top earners receiving so much more than those who performed similar functions in the recent past. He doubts that the difference is a result of any superior skills or talents on the part of the current managerial class. 'Does anyone really believe that America's bank officers suddenly became so much more productive, relative to everyone else in society, that they deserve the huge compensation increases they have received in recent years?'[10]

Clearly, if we just consider social contribution, it is hard to make the case that Paulson deserves his fortune. But there's a fallback argument used to justify large wealth accumulation, often made by the rich themselves. It goes like this: I deserve my money because I earned it. According to this line of argument, as long as John Paulson made his money without breaking any laws – and he has perhaps just got in under the wire on this one – the money is deservedly his.

The notion that a person has 'earned' his income is based, then, merely on staying within the law. But an individual's income is to a large extent simply a product of the particular set of laws that happen to be in place at that time and in that jurisdiction. So, for instance, if financial markets had been more tightly regulated – as they clearly should have been – Paulson wouldn't have made nearly as much money as he did in 2007.

Similarly, Bill Gates's ability to 'earn' his fortune was partly determined by the weak set of laws protecting copyrights in the newly emerging field of computer innovations in the 1980s. Had today's more rigorous legal standards been in force back then, Gary Kildall would have had strong grounds to sue Gates for copyright infringement, according to writer Harold Evans.[11] If Kildall had prevailed in such a lawsuit, Gates would almost certainly not be sitting on a fortune of $53 billion today. Rather, he might be making a comfortable – but unspectacular – living as a software entrepreneur, along with thousands of other individuals with similarly impressive computer skills.

So the notion that a billionaire deserves his fortune because he 'earned' it rests on a rather weak moral foundation. The laws that made his fortune possible are the product of the biases and whims of judges who shape the common law, and of legislators who often succumb to pressure and financial rewards from wealthy interest groups. Indeed, as we see in the Paulson case, the laws that enabled him to get hugely rich were simply the product of the enormous political leverage exercised by powerful players on Wall Street.

• • •

Perhaps the more basic moral question is this: can extreme inequality be justified? The richest 9.5 million people – 0.14 per cent of the world's population – control about one quarter of its assets.[12] What is the moral basis for allowing such a vast amount of the planet's bounty to be held in so few hands? By what right do a mere handful of individuals manage to hoard such a large share of the Earth's resources?

In much earlier times, these sorts of questions didn't really emerge, because people's circumstances in life were considered beyond human control. Medieval nobles enjoyed coddled lives while peasants struggled to survive, but there was little concern about justifying such discrepancies. A person's station in life – and the bounty (or lack of bounty) that went with it – were thought to be determined by birth, as part of God's plan. It was, therefore, everyone's duty, according to medieval thought, simply to submit to God's will and accept one's fate.

All that changed, however, with the transition to the Enlightenment and the modern era. Things that had simply been accepted in earlier times now had to be justified. Inequality was one of those things that seemed to cry out for justification. Why did some people have so much more than others? Since the gap between the pleasurable lives of the rich and the wretched lives of the poor could no longer just be attributed to a plan ordained by the Almighty, rational justification was now required. Enter John Locke, justifier extraordinaire.

Writing in the 1680s, the renowned English philosopher set out arguments that were to become the basis of the modern world's acceptance of inequality. It's worth reviewing them here, partly to highlight some contradictions in them, and also to show how Locke's position has been misrepresented in an attempt to expand and strengthen the case for inequality.

Locke argued that, while land and resources were originally given by God to 'mankind in common', the result of this joint bequest isn't that property is held by all, but rather that it is held by none. However, Locke insists that this can be changed. If an individual applies his own labour to the property, he adds something of value to it, and in so doing develops a legitimate claim to its exclusive ownership: 'It hath by this labour something annexed to it that excludes the common right.'

There is something intuitively appealing about Locke's notion of the transformative power of labour, which perhaps explains why it has resonated so deeply in Western minds for more than three centuries. He is arguing that human labour, or more broadly human effort, is what justifies property ownership. This seems fair and even empowering, since humans have control over their own labour. If they are willing to put forth effort and exert themselves with the sweat of their brows, they can obtain property. What could be fairer? What a wonderful leap forward from the medieval world, where peasants were stuck in their lowly, impoverished station, on God's orders, no matter how hard they were willing to toil!

But Locke had left out society. In focusing exclusively on the rights of the individual, he brushed aside the rights of everyone else. After suggesting that land and resources were given to 'mankind in common', he effectively discards the collective nature of the bequest. To observers today, this may seem reasonable, since we're so used to ignoring the broader rights of society in favour of individual rights. But in the seventeenth century, such an approach involved an intentional denial of the rights of the many. Traditionally, peasants had enjoyed 'common rights' to the land, where they were legally permitted to graze their cattle and forage for wood, peat, berries, and the leftover produce of the harvest. Locke was suggesting wiping out these historic 'common rights' and allowing individuals to claim exclusive rights. Political theorist C. B. Macpherson pointed out that in an earlier period there had been two kinds of property rights: the right to exclude others and the right not to be excluded by others. This latter right established a right of access to property. But under the moral system described by Locke – which became the law in the market economy – only the first right survived. As Macpherson put it: 'The very idea of property was narrowed to cover only the right to exclude others.'[13]

This was a huge change that swept away the rights of countless people – people who were poor and powerless and 'of no importance to anyone but themselves', as historian E. P. Thompson memorably put it. Peasants responded with spontaneous protests and attempts in the dark of night to sabotage the planting of hedges

and building of fences aimed at keeping them off the newly privatized land – protests that continued in various forms over several
centuries. But since peasants don't get to record history or shape
the public debate, their rights were simply eliminated, and have
been largely forgotten in the mists of time. Still, the consequence
of the removal of these rights is worth pausing over. Political
theorist Anatole Anton argues that the 'right of exclusion' that
Locke championed is a right that 'defies moral justification' – or
at the very least requires some serious explaining, which Locke
never really provides. 'Taking something from a group and giving
it to a single person…cries out to the democratic sensibility for
reasons,' writes Anton. 'Private property, from a democratic point
of view, amounts to the surrender of democratic control of social
resources to private individuals. Surrender might be the right
thing to do, but surely some good reasons ought to be given for
so doing.'[14]

In fact, there'd been a lively debate about all this in the decades
before Locke's writing. In addition to peasant protests over the
privatization of the common lands, there had been much popular
argument over the issue, enabled by the growing use of the printing
press. As the English Civil War raged throughout the 1640s, there was
unprecedented freedom of expression, with pamphleteers suddenly
able to reach a broad audience with their dissenting views. Gerrard
Winstanley, leader of a dissident group called the Diggers, attracted
considerable attention with pamphlets championing the cause of
the peasants and calling for their right to cultivate the commons.

Winstanley argued that the civil war shouldn't be just about
ending absolute monarchy, but should go further and usher in a
new age of equality, based on popular rights to the common land.
'Kingly power is like a great tree spread,' he wrote. 'That top bough
is lopped off the tree of tyranny…but alas oppression is a great tree
still, and keeps off the sun and freedom from the poor commons
still.' Winstanley insisted that the next step was for Parliament to

'give consent that those we call Poor should Dig and freely Plant the Waste and Common Land for a livelihood…We claim our freedom in the Commons.'To Winstanley, the private property that the rich were claiming by enclosing the common land for themselves amounted to a kind of theft that permitted them to 'lock up the treasures of the earth from the poor'.

Winstanley won a following among the common folk and the Diggers attempted to set up a string of colonies on the common land – only to be quickly driven off by government forces. As the large landowners and rising merchant class consolidated their power after the civil war, it was John Locke who they turned to for ideas about property rights. While Locke's argument about the transformative power of labour may seem in line with Winstanley's vision of colonies of peasants living off their own labour, Locke went on to include a looser definition of labour that appealed to those who didn't personally labour themselves: 'Thus, the grass my horse has bit, the turfs my servant has cut and the ore I have dug in any place where I have a right to them in common with others, become my property.'

Surely, it's one thing for Locke's prototypical man to make a claim to the ore that he has dug with his own labour, but quite another to claim ownership of the product of his *servant's* labour? Wouldn't that logically belong to the servant? For that matter, how did the servant end up a servant? And how did the horse come to be in this man's possession? If we're supposedly starting from basic principles, examining the legitimacy of the case for private property, how does Locke's prototypical man already happen to own a horse and be in command of the services of a servant? Were these just gifts dropped from the sky, part of a pre-existing entitlement that doesn't need to be accounted for? With this looser notion of one's labour – to include labour done by others inexplicably under one's command – Locke's invoking of the transformative power of labour loses some of its intuitive appeal.

However, Locke's words were a godsend to the newly triumphant capitalist class who were delighted to have an argument to justify endless accumulation. Indeed, Locke's words have become the cornerstone argument in justifying capitalism. By suggesting that human labour is the basis for private property, Locke gave private ownership an apparently compelling moral legitimacy rooted in the human realm, no longer reliant on the authority of God. And the fact that Locke deftly expanded the definition of labour to include work done by one's servant and horse meant that private property accumulations weren't limited to work that one could physically carry out oneself. Without this limitation, the possibilities seemed endless: one could hire a legion of servants (or factory workers) and use dozens of horses (or machines), and then lay claim to the product of the collective sweats of all of their brows! There was no limit to the private fortune one could accumulate – all within the umbrella of moral legitimacy set out by Locke. It was no more than a hop, skip and a jump to the world of Bill Gates.

It's not hard to see why Locke has been celebrated as a seminal thinker in our capitalist societies, while Winstanley can be hard to locate in a library. Yet, in fairness to Locke, it should be noted that he didn't completely ignore the fact that allowing individuals to accumulate private property has repercussions for others and possibly compromises their rights. Locke included a caveat to the effect that someone could claim property as his own – *only provided that there was 'enough and as good' left over for others.*

Needless to say, this changes things significantly; it makes the acquisition of private property conditional on the availability of resources and opportunities for others. What about land and non-renewable resources? Clearly, there eventually wouldn't be 'enough and as good' of these vital resources left over for others; all the available arable land would quickly be claimed, and that eventuality would come all the quicker under the expanded definition of labour, in which an individual could employ a large workforce and machinery to use up a finite resource. If Locke's caveat were to be taken seriously, his justification for private ownership turns out to be rather limited in scope, and does not provide much of a moral basis for the amassing of immense private fortunes. This probably explains why pro-market theorists, citing Locke to justify the legitimacy of large property accumulations, have mostly just ignored the caveat.

• • •

Like Locke, most of the major theorists who have contemplated issues of distributive justice have insisted on caveats when it comes to the rights of individuals to accumulate large fortunes. John Stuart Mill, Thomas Paine, Leonard T. Hobhouse and Jacques Turgot all argued that much of an individual's wealth is actually owed back to the community. John Rawls, the leading theorist of political liberalism, only condones the accumulation of great fortunes if it can be shown that this benefits the poorest members of society. Rawls and other liberal as well as progressive thinkers clearly have some serious reservations about extreme inequality, refusing to accept its moral legitimacy unless it can be shown to provide benefits throughout society, particularly to those most excluded from the bounty. In fact, virtually all the major theorists in the field of distributive justice have been unenthusiastic about large inequalities.

The only exceptions are modern conservatives, or neoliberals, who rose to prominence in the late 1970s. Whereas other theorists from Locke through to liberals and progressives offer only conditional support for extreme inequality, modern conservatives treat wealth accumulation – in unlimited amounts – as a natural human right, essentially free of conditions or qualification. In their formulation, society and its entitlements all but disappear as the individual moves front and centre and is endowed with huge natural entitlement to the fruits of the earth.

The leading theorist of this school is libertarian Robert Nozick, whose influential 1974 book *Anarchy, State, and Utopia* became the intellectual underpinning of the modern conservative movement. Nozick discards the Lockean notion that an individual only becomes entitled to property by applying her labour to it. Nozick's lack of interest in the centrality of labour is striking. For most people, this is the aspect of Locke's concept of property rights that is the most appealing, since it suggests that human toil and effort should be the grounds for entitlement – a principle that seems eminently fair. Instead, Nozick assumes that an individual has some sort of natural right to claim property, as long as no one else has a prior entitlement to it. (This seems to beg the question of where the original entitlement comes from. Nozick simply insists that the property must be fairly acquired. But how so?)

It is in his treatment of the rights of others and the broader society, however, that Nozick and other conservatives really move away from traditional theories of distributive justice. Recall Locke's important caveat that an individual can only appropriate a piece of property if that leaves 'enough and as good' for others. Nozick reduces this standard to insist only that others should not be left worse off by someone gaining title to a piece of property. Of course, even this lesser standard would seem to impose some constraints. If an individual claims a piece of land, for instance, he is clearly leaving others worse off, since they can no longer claim that same piece of land. However, Nozick insists that, except in very unusual circumstances – such as someone owning the only water hole in a desert – an individual's appropriation of property does not leave others worse off. He reaches this odd conclusion by assuming that the property appropriated would otherwise simply remain unused and would attract no interest from others.[15] This assumption is bizarre and seems based on a peculiar conception of human behaviour. Of course, if the goal is to come up with a moral justification for unlimited personal acquisition, it is necessary to assume such acquisition is harmless to others, and that's what Nozick does, even though it obliges him to make some odd assumptions.

Nozick goes on to further justify inequality by arguing that, whatever the gap between the fortunes of those at the top and the bottom, as long as these different holdings are the result of arrangements freely entered into on both sides, without coercion, there isn't a problem. In other words, workers may earn a fraction of what their boss earns, but as long as they freely agreed to that situation – by accepting their jobs – then all is fine. But just because there is no overt coercion doesn't mean there aren't subtle but very real forms of compulsion. For instance, the workers may have had little choice but to accept the jobs offered, because they were hungry and there was no other work available. Or more broadly, they may have had little choice because of the power wielded by employers and the ability this gives employers to shape the economic rules in their favour, such as keeping minimum wages low or placing restrictions on the right to unionize. Similarly, consumers may have no choice but to pay an exorbitantly high price for a product – say, a vital prescription drug – because a company holds an exclusive patent on it. Power, discrimination and monopoly are huge, largely hidden factors that oblige people 'freely' to accept terms that may amount to coercion in all but name.

The modern conservative's intense focus on the right to private property is, in itself, revealing. It allegedly springs from a deep respect for the rights of the individual. But why limit the notion of the individual's natural rights to that of property ownership and economic entitlements in the marketplace? Why not assume the individual also has a natural right to the fulfilment of basic social needs – such as, say, access to a decent education or adequate health services? When it comes to defining natural rights, conservatives seem to care fiercely – but exclusively – about the individual's entitlement to property, and his right to accumulate unlimited amounts of wealth.

● ● ●

Our winner-take-all reward system is based on the idea that there are uniquely gifted or talented individuals whose social contribution is so great that they deserve infinite financial rewards. But this formulation ignores the reality that wealth generation is only possible because of the massive contribution of society, stretching all the way back to the beginning of the Stone Age. Since billionaires are now deemed to have made it on their own, they are also said to owe little back to society. Indeed, the whole notion of responsibility to society has been so denigrated that billionaires are considered deserving of their fortunes when they contribute next to nothing to society – or even when they directly imperil the public interest.

7

bobby moore and the myths about motivation

It was overtime in the final game of the 1966 World Cup match between England and West Germany, with tens of thousands of near-hysterical fans packed into Wembley Stadium. With England leading 3–2 and the clock running out, team captain Bobby Moore placed the perfect pass, enabling team mate Geoff Hurst to drive the ball deep into the German net, putting England's victory beyond doubt. Amid the bedlam, Moore climbed the steps to the Royal Box to receive the coveted trophy, quickly wiping his dirty, grass-stained hands on his shirt and then on some velvet draping before shaking hands with the Queen. Team manager Alf Ramsey called Moore the 'spirit and heartbeat of the team' and insisted that 'without him, England would never have won the World Cup'.

Moore was captain of England in ninety matches. He also skippered West Ham United, leading the team to victory in the European Cup Winners' Cup, winning the FA Cup and being selected Footballer of the Year. He was a legendary player, considered

England's finest football captain. Yet Bobby Moore earned a measly £10,400 a year in 1971 – less than the average UK wage.

Today, England's most celebrated football player is Wayne Rooney, who has been awarded the Professional Footballers' Association Players' Player of the Year and the Football Writers' Association Footballer of the Year, and is widely regarded as the country's best player. Unlike Booby Moore, Rooney is well paid for his efforts. Since the introduction of the Premier League in the 1990s, football pay has gone through the roof, turning players into multi-millionaires and depriving fans of a winning team unless their team happens to be owned by a free-spending billionaire. Rooney now earns £10 million a year – almost a thousand times more than Bobby Moore earned four decades ago. Yet it would be hard to argue that Rooney's performance is a thousand times better, or even that it is much better at all.

It's clear that Bobby Moore was a thoroughly motivated player who achieved spectacular results. That his salary was a mere fraction of what equivalent players earn today suggests that the extra pay may be unnecessary as a motivating factor. In fact, there's little evidence that today's phenomenal pay packages – in sports, entertainment, business and finance – are more effective in motivating today's players, performers or executives than the more modest packages were a few decades ago. For that matter, there's precious little evidence that today's performances are even any better. Can anyone seriously make the case that today's top entertainment superstars – Lady Gaga, Angelina Jolie, Daniel Craig – are noticeably superior (or superior at all) to Vera Lynn, Julie Christie and Alec Guinness?

And when we look at the world of business, the case for today's supersized pay at the top seems even more tenuous, if not preposterous. In 1950, for instance, General Motors paid CEO Charlie Wilson $586,000 (the highest CEO salary at the time, worth about $5 million in today's dollars) for managing what was then a thriving, highly profitable company, widely considered America's leading corporation. In 2007, General Motors paid CEO Rick Wagoner $15.7 million – even as the company he headed suffered a $39 billion loss. So GM paid roughly three times as much in 2007 to get results that were infinitely worse.

Examples like this abound in business and the financial world. Indeed, the 2008 financial meltdown has brought the disconnect between executive performance and executive pay into sharp, tragicomic relief. In the UK, Adam Applegarth collected £10 million over five years as chief executive of Northern Rock, which he transformed into an ultra-aggressive mortgage lender, only to have it collapse in 2007. Joseph Cassano, who headed the credit default swaps team in London for financial giant AIG, received a $35 million bonus – even after it was clear that the swaps had nearly bankrupted AIG in the 2008 crash. Wall Street firms paid out a staggering $18.4 billion in executive bonuses in the early months of 2008, even as many of those firms collapsed in bankruptcy or were only saved by government bailouts. Merrill Lynch, for instance, earned no profit in the 2007 and 2008 financial years, yet paid out $30 billion in bonuses for those years.

The phenomenon of gigantic pay packages at the top has become the norm in a wide range of fields today, in a way that it wasn't a few decades ago. The rationale behind it has been central to the neoliberal case justifying today's extreme inequality: these huge rewards are necessary, we're told, to create the motivation for the most talented individuals to perform at exceptional levels, so that the economy will function at optimal efficiency and we'll all gain.

•　•　•

According to the neoliberals – and indeed to most mainstream economists – high marginal tax rates have the effect of discouraging those in the top income brackets from working harder to earn more income, since this income will be taxed at higher rates. For example, if a corporate lawyer can earn £300 for an extra hour of work, and faces a tax rate of 30 per cent, that will leave her with £200 after tax, making it worth her while to work the extra hour. If the tax rate is instead, say, 60 per cent, leaving her with only £100 after tax, she might well decide to go home and watch TV instead.

It's easy to see how this argument gains traction. At face value, it seems intuitively correct. The lawyer works to earn income; the more she is paid, the more she is motivated to work. If taxes reduce her pay significantly, she is going to be less motivated to work. That's certainly logical. On the other hand, it seems just as likely that high taxes could have exactly the opposite effect. The lawyer works to earn income. If that income is reduced significantly by taxes, she will work longer to make up for the loss, because she wants to maintain an elevated standard of living. Both explanations make sense, and both fit with observations of human behaviour.

And yet it is the first argument – the one that justifies low taxes for high-income earners – that is generally advanced by economists. Indeed, it is considered a truism in our society that cutting taxes will encourage work effort. By this logic, then, a tax cut would inspire the corporate lawyer to work harder. But why? Wouldn't it be equally plausible that she would use the extra money to relax more, take a longer holiday, plan early retirement, or spend more time golfing or Internet dating? In many ways, a windfall as a result of a tax reduction is similar to any other windfall, such as winning the lottery or inheriting money. Do most people respond to winning a lottery or inheriting money by working longer hours?

The truth is human motivation and behaviour are infinitely more complicated, nuanced and variable than the straightforward version presented in economic arguments. In the formulation of standard neoclassical economics, the prototypical human (*homo economicus*) is deeply motivated to satisfy his appetite for material goods. Although he would rather avoid work, he can be enticed into doing it if he is rewarded with income, since that allows him to increase his consumption of material goods.

One can understand why economists have chosen such a one-dimensional, mechanistic character as *homo economicus* as their central player. Clearly, they need to simplify human behaviour into predictable and knowable patterns in order to present economics as a hard science – rather than just another social science, where findings are acknowledged to be somewhat subjective. But while it's understandable that economists want their findings to be treated as authoritative, it's doubtful whether human behaviour really fits into the paradigm they offer. Yes, the human appetite for consumption is real, and potentially huge. But it's clearly not the only thing that motivates humans to do the things they do. Many critics have charged that such a simplistic human prototype as *homo economicus* – which has become the model on which our entire economic system is based – is nothing more than a convenient but fairly meaningless cartoon character.

Evidence in the fields of psychology and other social sciences suggest that the actual motives and behaviour of real-life people are quite different from those of *homo economicus*. Robert E. Lane, a political scientist at Yale University, reviewed more than a thousand studies of human behaviour related to the economy for his book *The Market Experience*. Lane concluded that the way people actually behave bears little resemblance to the greedy, consumption-oriented conduct assumed by standard economic theory. Indeed, a vast array of studies shows that, once people achieve a basic material standard of living, economic factors greatly decline as important sources of happiness and satisfaction and are superseded in importance by factors such as family, friendship, self-esteem, and a sense of personal and intellectual development.[1] Or as economist Robert H. Frank put it in his book *Luxury Fever*: 'Behavioral scientists find that once a threshold level of affluence is reached, the average level of human well-being in a country is almost completely independent of its stock of material consumption goods.'[2]

Before we move on to what really does matter to people who live comfortably above the breadline, it's worth pausing to note briefly what goes on below the breadline. As Frank observes: 'Most careful studies find a clear relationship over time between subjective wellbeing and absolute income at extremely low levels of absolute income.'[3] In other words, while human wants and desires may become more varied and complex once basic needs are secured, until this happens, people are primarily motivated to meet their basic material needs, without which they enjoy little comfort or satisfaction. Perhaps the crude *homo economicus* model, if it has any validity, is most useful as a model of behaviour for those at the bottom of the economic heap. This raises the question of whether the argument about higher pay leading to greater work effort might be most applicable to very low-income workers, who, after all, are typically stuck doing work that is dull, routine, and offers little opportunity for creativity. In such cases, the amount of pay looms particularly large. Such workers don't just badly need money to meet the most basic human needs, but also to compensate for the lack of other job-related satisfactions. For a hotel cleaner earning £7 an hour, for instance, an extra pound an hour would make a significant difference, and might well induce him to give up leisure time in order to spend a particularly profitable extra few hours cleaning up after hotel guests.

Interestingly, however, the argument about higher pay being necessary for greater motivation is primarily used to justify lower taxes on the rich, not on the poor – even though the arguments seem to apply better to the poor. Indeed, in the case of the poor, the opposite argument is often made – that too much income will cause them to slack off. Hence the need to keep welfare and unemployment insurance benefits low, lest those at the lower end be encouraged to remain idle.

But let's get back to the rich. If we follow the logic mentioned above, we could conclude that higher pay might seem least likely to work as a motivator in the case of those with big incomes. First of all, they already have ample income – so ample, in the case of billionaires and near-billionaires, that pay increases or decreases are unlikely to have any effect on how much they consume, since they are already presumably consuming as much as they possibly can (or care to). Secondly, and more importantly, unlike the hotel cleaner, those at the top of their professions enjoy a level of work satisfaction that is, quite simply, immense. Additional pay might induce the hotel cleaner to spend that extra hour cleaning up after others, but there is no shortage of nonmonetary benefits that provide additional motivation for the business executive to work late to close a big deal, or for the rock star to do an encore in front of a stadium full of delirious fans, or for the football player to go all out to score the winning goal.

In fact, the world of work – particularly self-directed, challenging work that one happens to be very good at – offers a stunning array of satisfactions that deliver rewards at the most primal human level. Studies have established that the most basic human psychological needs – for a sense of self, a sense of personal competence and for self-esteem – are very often tied in closely with one's work. 'People's favorable attitudes towards themselves are their most treasured property; in many ways, these are the maximand on which all their other values and motives rest,' observes Lane.[4] Work is a crucial way in which people achieve favourable attitudes about themselves, since it gives them a sense of their own competence and ability to function well in the world. Pay is an important part of this – but primarily as a proxy for these more basic psychological rewards. Notes Lane: 'In the end, all economic behavior is energized and guided by the pursuit of a sense of personal effectiveness, self-esteem and self-consistency' – that is, a sense of an integrated personal identity.

Considering all this, *homo economicus* may amount to a serious misrepresentation, if not an outright distortion, of the human personality. In the *homo economicus* model, work is considered an undesirable activity – a 'disutility', in economic parlance – that humans would rather avoid but perform as a means to earn income so that they can have the pleasure of consuming material goods. This may well be true when the work is cleaning toilets. However, particularly at the upper level, work is often an exceptionally desirable activity in itself – one that offers deeply satisfying rewards that are far more important than consumption.

So it seems unlikely that reducing the pay rewards of the very rich would stifle their desire to work. It's obvious that the most talented individuals in any field are motivated by far more than money. Even billionaires readily admit that money isn't their only or even their primary objective. Leo J. Hindery Jr, the sports cable TV entrepreneur, confided to *The New York Times* that he would have worked just as hard for a much smaller payoff. Wall Street banker Sanford Weill also acknowledged that 'I worked because I loved what I was doing'. Weill said that he didn't even really know how much he'd made until he retired and had 'a chance to sit back and count up what was on the table'. Similarly, Kenneth C. Griffin, who received more than $1 billion in 2006 as CEO of hedge fund Citadel Investment Group, commented that 'wealth is not a particularly satisfying outcome...The money is a byproduct of a passionate endeavour.'[5]

A number of history's most talented individuals, who have made some of the greatest contributions to society, have had little trouble performing without much in the way of financial incentives. Norman Borlaug, who saved millions of lives by developing methods for improving agricultural productivity, spent most of his life living modestly in Third World villages. Vincent van Gogh somehow found the motivation to produce hundreds of works of great art, even though he managed to sell only one of them in his lifetime, receiving a pittance for it just before he died. And William Shakespeare was inspired to produce perhaps the greatest dramas of all time without even the prospect that they'd become Hollywood blockbusters.

•   •   •

None of this is meant to imply that financial incentives don't matter. They clearly do – particularly at the lower levels, where workers need powerful inducements to get them to perform work that is often dreary, repetitive, unpleasant and unrewarding. Financial incentives also matter at the upper levels. While the deep psychological satisfactions of work may matter most, money does act as a proxy for these rewards. Earning an income reinforces an individual's sense of personal competency and self-esteem. Earning a large income greatly reinforces an individual's sense of personal competency and self-esteem, leaving him with very pleasantly favourable attitudes toward himself.

Financial incentives can act as powerful motivators that encourage effort, diligence, creativity, and just plain hard work in people at all levels. The question is: how much is enough to provide the crucial level of motivation? If even some billionaires are willing to acknowledge that they would have worked just as hard for less, it's worth considering whether society could pay them less – or tax back significantly more of what they receive – without diminishing their incentive to work.

And here another important psychological factor comes into play: what seems to matter most to people, once they get above the breadline, isn't how big their compensation is, but how it compares to the compensation of others. Karl Marx observed this human characteristic when he pointed out, 'A house may be large or small; as long as the surrounding houses are equally small, it satisfies all social demands for a dwelling. But if a palace rises beside the little house, the little house shrinks into a hut.'[6] Robert Frank made a similar observation: 'The middle-class professional who lives in Manhattan is unlikely to be burdened by dissatisfaction that her apartment has no room for a Ping-Pong table or wine cellar, and she almost certainly entertains no expectation of having a swimming pool. Yet that same woman living in a Westchester county suburb might not even consider a house that lacked these amenities.' In other words, it's not the absolute size of the material reward that matters, but how that reward stacks up against the material rewards of others – where it puts the individual in the pecking order. As Frank says: 'Evidence from the large scientific literature on the determinants of subjective well-being consistently suggests that we have strong concerns about relative position.'[7]

As early as the fourth century BCE, Aristotle noted that humans are, above all, social animals who naturally seek to relate to and engage with other humans. They feel the need to be part of a larger human community in which they enjoy the acceptance and good opinion of others. Receiving pay for work is a key way that people in our society can establish their place in the community, by proving their competency and worthiness.

So what matters most about a pay package is not its absolute size but how it measures up against others. This perhaps explains why, in the early postwar years, business executives, entertainers and sports stars were motivated to perform very well – indeed just as well as, if not better than, today's much higher-paid equivalents. Although their absolute pay levels were much smaller back then, they were still paid very, very well relative to others at the time. It was this gap between them and others in their world – which gave them an elevated status in their community – that served as the stimulant to high performance.

Of course, now that the gap between the top and the bottom is so much bigger today, isn't the stimulus for high performance all the greater? Probably. But how much stimulus can productively be harnessed? What if Bobby Moore was performing the very best he possibly could when he was the indispensable player in England's 1966 World Cup victory? What would have been gained by topping up his salary to a level a thousand times greater?

Current thinking in our winner-take-all culture would suggest that the added financial incentive would have driven Moore all the harder, so that he might have performed even more spectacularly. Possibly. Or perhaps he'd already gone to the bottom of the well of his capabilities. Who knows? But certainly this raises some questions, such as: is the extra bit of performance – if it could be coaxed out of him through massively higher pay – really worth the extra cost?

The stupendous pay cheques of those at the very top may be creating serious distortions, not just in some people's lives but more broadly in the economy. If Bobby Moore's salary was sufficient to push him to perform spectacularly, what is the effect of making that financial incentive a thousand times larger? It's possible that it makes no difference, that what drives top athletes to spectacular achievement is the thrill of being regarded as the best in the world at something they love – in which case topping up their pay so handsomely is simply a needless and foolish squandering of money. On the other hand, it's possible the increased pay does have an effect, not only in attracting many more participants to compete for a prize that only a few can win, but also in placing ever more pressure on those trying to make it. Could this additional pressure perhaps explain why so many professional athletes, unable to do any better on their own, turn to steroids and other performance-enhancing drugs? Is there really any other way to improve continually upon the performances of the equally talented players who went before them? Are top athletes on a treadmill where they can't possibly go any faster but are willing to try anything – including cheating – to reach new heights, goaded on by the sheer size of the stimulus dangled in front of them?

In the age of winner-take-all compensation, a similar propensity for cheating seems to have infected the upper levels of the business and financial worlds. It's worth considering whether the mindset that led Wall Street types to abandon all sanity and morality – mixing together toxic brews of junk mortgages, car loans and credit card debts and then selling pieces of these sickly concoctions to unknowing 'investors' – is partly the result of the overstimulation of their greed impulses.

When the broader public first became aware of collateral debt obligations and credit default swaps during the financial meltdown in the autumn of 2008, the most common reaction was bewilderment. The hypercharged Wall Street world was so removed from the regular world most people inhabit – where pay bears some relationship to hours worked, effort and results – that it seemed baffling and indecipherable. How did grown men and women make decisions that were not just over-the-top greedy but were so evidently irresponsible and threatening to the well-being of so many others, including themselves? One possibility was that the billion-dollar compensation packages on view all around them had simply stimulated their hypothalamuses to the point of mental, physical and moral overdrive and exhaustion, encouraging them to risk everything for the billion-dollar prize, without which life had become almost meaningless. The point is not to excuse their behaviour, but rather to raise questions about what role excessive financial rewards may have played in encouraging it. If the effect of extreme financial stimulation is to encourage greedy-bordering-on-dysfunctional behaviour, then the large financial rewards of our winner-take-all compensation system may not just be unnecessary, but actually destructive.

•   •   •

It's commonly argued, of course, that companies need to pay high salaries to attract the most talented individuals and keep them from going to competitors. So while it may be true that a lower-paid football player would be just as motivated to go all out for the team, he would probably be enticed by an offer to move to another team that would pay him more. In a competitive free market, then, high pay is necessary to ensure that companies and organizations can attract the best talent so that they can function optimally.

It should immediately be noted that this argument in no way refutes the desirability of imposing high taxes on large incomes. High taxes would not, for instance, prevent teams from attracting the best players by offering gigantic pay packages. Teams could pay as much as they wanted to – and the players could still go to the highest bidder. Only after all this is resolved, and everyone is out playing football, would taxes kick in. The high marginal rates would not interfere at all in the selection process, since they would only apply after the fact and would apply the same to all (this is the beauty of tax rates; they are neutral, applying the same set of rules to everyone).

It should also be noted that while high pay in sports and entertainment may be the result of highly competitive markets, this is less true in the world of business and finance. Of course, businesspeople and financiers make similar arguments – that huge rewards are necessary to attract the best talent. Indeed, this has been the corporate world's main justification for continuing to reward CEOs and top executives lavishly: top talent can command top dollar; that's just the way the free market works.

But on closer examination, it turns out that CEO pay is determined less by the workings of the free market (a misleading concept at the best of times) and more by the power wielded by those at the top of the business and financial world. The corporate elite has used its extraordinary power to push its own rewards to astronomical heights. This has been easily accomplished because executive pay is determined by corporate boards of directors, which are typically made up mostly of other, similarly positioned executives – people who are often friends, colleagues, former classmates from MBA courses, or simply associates who frequent the same golf clubs or art auctions as those whose pay is being judged. As a vehicle for determining pay, these corporate boards are more like cosy clubs than bodies likely to render meaningful, arm's-length market assessments.

Ostensibly, of course, corporate boards represent shareholders. So they theoretically represent a large number of people and interests. In reality, however, shareholder elections are pretty much insider events, particularly in cases where there are large numbers of shareholders who are unlikely to be sufficiently organized to challenge the dominant management group. It's even rare to have a competing slate in a shareholder election. One notable critic of the compensation system is Richard A. Posner, a US Court of Appeals judge and senior lecturer at the University of Chicago Law School. As Posner bluntly puts it: 'Shareholder election of directors resembles the system of voting in the Soviet Union and other totalitarian nations.'[8]

Even leaving aside the actual friendships and close associations between members of the board and those they are assessing, there is an additional potential conflict of interest. 'A board of directors is likely to be dominated by highly paid business executives, including CEOs of other companies,' writes Posner. 'They have a conflict of interest, since they have a financial stake in high corporate salaries, their own salaries being determined in part by the salaries paid to persons in comparable positions in other companies.' Added to that personal conflict of interest is the likelihood that these executives will regard the high level of compensation going to themselves and those they are judging as an appropriate reflection of the intrinsic worthiness of corporate executives.

The problem becomes circular, since the CEO of a company influences the selection of its directors, who then determine the CEO's compensation. If the directors authorize a large compensation package for the CEO who has put them in place, that CEO is likely to appreciate the important contribution the directors are making and support generous directors' fees. The CEO and his team also select the company's auditors, who certify the company's financial statements. If the CEO is pleased by the auditors' report, he might well retain these same auditors to provide consulting services, under which the auditors might steer underwriting contracts to investment banks, whose securities analysts give the company very positive reports. Altogether, Posner suggests that the relationship between the CEO, the members of the board of directors and the firm's auditors typically involves a great deal of 'mutual back-scratching'.[9]

Of course, the cosy nature of corporate boards is nothing new. But in the early postwar years, social disapproval of excessive greed acted as something of a restraint. With that disapproval largely set aside in recent decades – indeed replaced with a culture that reveres 'wealth creators' – there's been nothing to discourage corporate boards from indulging themselves. The problem has been compounded by the tendency of corporate boards to match what other corporate boards are doing. 'We pay our executives not on the basis of performance, but on the basis of peer group,' notes John C. Bogle, former chairman of the Vanguard Group. Bogle says that this creates a 'ghastly ratchet effect' as cosy corporate boards bring up the pay of their CEOs to match what's going on at other similarly cosy boards.[10]

The cosy nature of corporate boards goes a long way towards explaining how executive compensation has climbed skyward – in an era of often lacklustre corporate performance. In the UK, the independent High Pay Commission has highlighted this disconnect between executive pay and corporate results. Commission chair Deborah Hargreaves noted that 'when pay for senior executives is set behind closed doors, it does not reflect company success'.[11] Indeed, despite middling business performance and stagnating wages for ordinary workers, the median compensation of the FTSE 100 CEOs more than quadrupled between 1998 and 2010, and then rose by another 27 per cent by 2011.

Even David Cameron's government felt obliged to acknowledge that soaring corporate pay was not being driven by strong market results. Responding to public outrage over executive pay in autumn 2011, Business Secretary Vince Cable conceded that over the past decade 'we have seen extreme increases in top executive pay which appear to be completely unrelated to the performance of companies'. Launching public consultations on the issue, Cable went on to suggest that this situation was 'undermining the credibility of our markets-based system'. In other words, not only was the excessive pay unconnected to the market, it actually risked destroying the public's trust in the market as a valid system. After a few months of consultations, Cable was even more convinced that executive pay had risen 'despite no clear overall improvement in corporate performance'.

Yet, despite widespread public anger, corporate executives have largely held onto their inflated pay, showing the extent of their power to determine their own compensation levels. While the Cameron government clearly felt the need to mollify the public by criticizing oversized pay cheques in the executive suite, it backed away from taking actual steps that would have risked antagonizing the corporate high-fliers. It largely ignored suggestions from the High Pay Commission, which called for tougher corporate governance laws, including a new national body to monitor executive pay. The government even backed off implementing tougher regulatory measures that had been advanced in its own consultation papers. Overall, despite some grandstanding on the issue, the Cameron government has shown little willingness to take steps to rein in excessive rewards in the corporate world.

All this suggests that the dramatic increase in pay at the top has not been an inevitable development caused by neutral market forces, but rather the product of the diligent efforts of an extraordinarily powerful elite determined to enrich itself.

None of this is surprising, but it contradicts the view typically offered by economists and commentators who insist that today's huge incomes are the product of globalization and technological change. While globalization and technological advances – such as television – may account for the higher incomes of sports and entertainment stars by greatly increasing their audiences and celebrity status, they don't explain the staggering rise in the pay of CEOs. Even if we assume that globalization and technology have made corporations more profitable, this still doesn't explain why such a large share of the profits has drifted to the executive suites.

The technology factor is often cited to explain why so many workers today are earning such low incomes. We're told that skills have become more important than ever in this technological age, leaving unskilled workers highly disadvantaged. This is true. Even so, many highly skilled workers have also experienced minimal income growth. There's been almost no real income growth for the bottom 90 per cent of income earners – a group that includes millions of highly skilled workers and well-educated professionals, including, for instance, teachers and nurses. It is hard to explain this clear pattern of income gravitating higher and higher up the income ladder exclusively by reference to skill or education levels.

And, as noted earlier, the increased concentration of income at the very top is a phenomenon that's been most pronounced in the Anglo-American countries – the United States, Britain, Canada and Australia. But if globalization is a key factor in explaining increasing inequality, why isn't the same trend consistent around the globe, or at least in other countries that are competing successfully in the global economy, such as Germany, France or Japan?

The reason is that technology and globalization are only partly responsible for the huge increase in incomes at the top. Those who are pleased with the current trend toward increased inequality have seized upon these two factors to explain it, perhaps because they appear to be neutral forces beyond human control. If technology and globalization are responsible, then there's no point in trying to do anything about this strange new inequality. The emergence of a new class of billionaires is just the natural outcome of modernity, and attempting to limit it would only hold back the tides of progress, ultimately hurting us all.

Yet while sweeping references to globalization and technology may sound compelling, the explanation for today's exorbitant CEO pay is simpler. Under the pro-corporate dogma of the neoliberal era, those at the top of the business and financial world have largely freed themselves from regulation and supervision, except by cosy boards, opening up immense opportunities for them to direct rewards towards themselves. It's obvious where this leads. If the wages of clerical and cleaning staff were set by boards controlled by clerks and cleaners, would we be surprised to see the salaries of file clerks and floor moppers shoot up?

8

john maynard keynes and the defeat of austerity

Faced with an extremely bleak and deteriorating economy at the end of 2012, the UK government had two choices – admit its controversial austerity measures were taking Britain down the wrong road or suggest that the pain was part of a necessary path to recovery. Nobody was surprised when the Cameron government decided to go with the pain-for-gain argument, adding that reversing course would mean throwing away the hard-won progress already achieved.

'It's a hard road, but we are getting there,' George Osborne told Parliament. 'Britain is on the right track – and turning back now would be a disaster.'

The Chancellor of the Exchequer was clearly grasping at straws. Two and a half years earlier, in June 2010, he had taken a sharp knife to government spending, implementing an austerity plan aimed at eliminating the national deficit in four years. The austerity measures, which cut some government department budgets by up to 30 per cent, sharply applied the brakes to an economy that had slowly been recovering from the 2008 financial crisis and resulting recession. The tough medicine was almost incomprehensibly cruel in its targeting of some of Britain's most vulnerable citizens through massive cuts to the welfare system and tougher requirements for qualifying for housing and disability benefits.

Yet despite the severity of the measures, Osborne was forced to acknowledge in his Autumn Statement to the House of Commons in December 2012 that his government had failed to meet its own deficit targets, and that the nation's debt-to-GDP ratio would continue to climb until 2017–18.

The Chancellor of the Exchequer insisted that the answer lay in staying the austerity course – despite a powerful IMF report in October 2012 showing that austerity measures can have serious adverse effects on economies weakened by recession. As Paul Krugman has explained, the frequently cited comparison to a family reducing its debt by cutting back its expenses doesn't hold true for an entire economy where 'spending and earning go together; my spending is your income; your spending is my income. If everyone tries to slash spending at the same time, incomes will fall – and unemployment will soar.'[1]

Osborne seemed oblivious to the fact that a similar belt-tightening economic orthodoxy had produced similarly disastrous results around the world in the Great Depression some eighty years earlier – until that orthodoxy was challenged and ultimately demolished by a set of ideas developed, above all, in Britain.

• • •

In the grim winter of 1933, only months after the election of Franklin Roosevelt to the White House, the US Senate Finance Committee came up with a plan to try to head off the implementation of the New Deal. With roughly a quarter of the American workforce idle and tens of millions of Americans slipping into desperate poverty, Roosevelt had had little trouble defeating the do-nothing government of Republican incumbent Herbert Hoover. But the conservatives who dominated the Senate Finance Committee were now keen to prevent the new administration from actually proceeding with its radical proposals for national recovery. The senators figured that their committee could provide a forum for the captains of industry and commerce to warn the public of the dangers of Roosevelt's legislative plans. The captains of industry and commerce readily made themselves available.

But the carefully designed plan turned into a fiasco. As the prominent figures – a virtual who's who of the corporate and financial world – got up one after another at the Senate committee hearings, it became painfully obvious that they had no solutions to offer the American people, nor did they even seem terribly concerned about the plight of Americans. Typical was the response of Jackson Reynolds, of the First National Bank of New York, who, asked if he had a solution, simply replied, 'I have not, and I do not believe anybody else has.' This was echoed by Myron C. Taylor, chairman of the US Steel Corp., who commented, 'I have no remedy in mind, except that the government should put its own house in order as an example to the community, balance the budget and live within its income.' There was general agreement that government should do nothing beyond balancing the budget.[2]

Some of the prominent figures went further and suggested the Depression was a refreshing tonic to restore the nation to health. Bernard Baruch, former head of the War Industries Board, portrayed the Depression as a cure for the nation's wayward behaviour: 'Natural forces are at work to cure every evil, but what have we done to aid the cure?…We have set every legislative force against the economics of a cure.' General W. W. Atterbury, president of the Pennsylvania Railroad, painted the Depression as a moral struggle that required pain. 'There is no panacea for a resumption of prosperity except the slow, painful one of hitting the bottom, and then slowly building up with a sane and economical foundation on which to build.'

The same sort of mentality dominated the US government and its central bank, the Federal Reserve.[3] Those running the Fed had concluded that it was better to leave the Depression to work itself out. The strong and the good would survive. As the economy collapsed all around them, the governors of the Fed had maintained high interest rates, convinced that the brutal medicine they were administering would serve the country well in the end. The only answer was austerity. As senior Fed official George W. Norris put it: 'We believe that the correction must come about through reduced production, reduced inventories, the gradual reduction of consumer credit, the liquidation of security loans and the accumulation of savings through the exercise of thrift.'[4] The answer, then, was to shrink the economy, to starve the public body back to health.

Towards the end of the Senate committee hearings, after almost four dozen captains of industry and commerce had paraded their bleak views, a banker from Utah was called to the stand. Unlike the previous witnesses, who were all prominent men, known to the senators on the committee, this man was hardly recognized by anyone in the room, nor was his name – Marriner Eccles – familiar to them. But as Eccles began his testimony, the curiosity in the room turned to utter surprise. Here was a banker who sounded completely different from every other figure from the financial world. The others had all called for government restraint, balanced budgets and learning to do with less. But Eccles stunned the room by calling for a new government activism that would involve massive spending on public works projects and unemployment relief, minimum wage laws and tax reform to redistribute income, as well as changes to the Federal Reserve System that would strip power from the hands of Wall Street. 'We shall either adopt a plan which will meet the problem of unemployment under capitalism,' Eccles told the hushed room of senators, administration officials and reporters, 'or a plan will be adopted for us which will operate without capitalism.'

Eccles's appearance before the committee had largely been an accident. He had been invited because a junior senator on the committee was from Utah, and Eccles was an important banking figure in the state. But no one had had any idea what he was going to say. His testimony was certainly not at all what the senior members of the committee wanted to hear. But it struck a highly responsive chord among the more innovative members of the new administration, who were trying to push Roosevelt into taking dramatic action along the lines that Eccles had just outlined. Here was a banker who was defying Wall Street orthodoxy, who actually had a bold plan to overcome the paralysis of the Depression.

Almost immediately, Eccles was drawn into the inner circle. He quickly became a key architect of the New Deal as well as a close Roosevelt adviser, who helped push the President towards the big-spending initiatives of the early years of his administration.[5] Eccles also had little trouble convincing Roosevelt that it was essential to reform the Federal Reserve System, which he argued concentrated too much power in the hands of Wall Street bankers who were quite content to keep a chokehold on the gasping economy. Roosevelt agreed and decided that Eccles was the man to oversee the reform, in the position of Federal Reserve chairman.

The New York bankers bitterly fought Eccles's confirmation, but failed to block it. Although he was a banker, Eccles was clearly not one of them. Owner of a chain of twenty-eight banks in Utah, Idaho, Wyoming and Oregon, Eccles had little in common with the Wall Street crowd that had dominated the hearings. In the highly stratified world of US banking, there were a small number of extremely powerful banks, mostly located in New York and led by the Morgan financial empire. Beneath this upper tier, there were thousands of smaller regional banks, many of which went down in bankruptcy in the early Depression years. Their demise went unlamented by the Wall Street crowd; these were exactly the kinds of weak, improperly managed enterprises that the Depression was fortunately purging from the American economy.

There was little love lost between the two banking worlds, which were almost totally different in orientation. The New York banks maintained close ties to the sophisticated international banking scene in London, Paris and Vienna, and were focused on squashing inflation. The regional banks, which had played a key role in financing the development of the American west over the previous hundred years, were expansionist, entrepreneurial, even reckless, often relying on the larger banks to bail them out.

Eccles was very much a product of this frontier culture. His father, David Eccles, had emigrated from Scotland with nothing and, in one generation, was living the American dream to the fullest. Through hard work, entrepreneurship and a good deal of luck, he accumulated a considerable frontier fortune in timber, coal mining and construction, building each new business with the savings he had carefully accumulated in his previous endeavours. A Mormon polygamist with two wives, David Eccles left twenty-one children when he died. Marriner, at the age of twenty-two, managed to gain control of a significant part of his father's business ventures and developed it into an even bigger empire, particularly in banking. In the state of Utah, the name Eccles became synonymous with power and wealth. To Marriner, it all seemed to come down to a simple code: work hard, be thrifty, watch out for your own interests, get rich. Had Marriner Eccles been asked to testify at a Senate finance committee hearing only a couple of years earlier, his advice would have been much the same as the Wall Street crowd's.

But the Depression changed everything for Eccles. For three years, he watched the panic and pain spread through the American heartland. Although he had not suffered personally, he had witnessed great suffering. What's more, he had caused great suffering, by ensuring that his banks were aggressive and uncompromising in their collection policies in order to stay afloat. In the end, none of his banks went under. But the experience transformed him. The conservative economic views that he'd absorbed from his father, and that seemed to fit with his own life's experience, now seemed deeply alien and unsatisfying to him. All of a sudden, all around him, he saw hard-working, thrifty people losing their farms and unable to keep up the payments on their business loans. It wasn't that they had changed; rather the world had changed. In the 1920s, the engine of growth had seemed unstoppable on the frontier, bringing new roads, housing construction, public utilities and oil production to the west. Now everything had stopped, and it seemed impossible to get it going again.

The hopelessness of the situation led to a sense of panic that fed on itself, creating an ever-greater paralysis. Eccles witnessed this first-hand in his bank in Ogden, Utah, in the summer of 1931. When another bank in town failed to open one morning, news quickly spread and a line-up of customers, all wanting to take their money out, began to build in Eccles's First National Bank of Ogden. Eccles knew that to close the bank would simply create more panic, so he instructed his tellers to give the people their money, but to do so very, very slowly. Hour after hour, the besieged tellers carried on at an infuriatingly slow pace, as the crowd grew bigger and more restless. Eventually, an armoured truck arrived at the bank, delivering cash from the local Federal Reserve office in Salt Lake City. After ceremoniously ushering the armed guards with their bags of money to the vault, Eccles jumped onto the counter in front of the crowd and tried to seize the moment to quell the panic.

To everyone's surprise, he announced that the bank would actually stay open late, as long as was necessary to deal with anyone who wanted to take his or her money out. 'There is no justification for the excitement or the apparent panicky attitude on the part of some depositors,' said Eccles, projecting a mood of confidence and control that masked his own panic. 'As all of you have seen, we have just had brought up from Salt Lake City a large amount of currency that will take care of all your requirements. There is plenty more where that came from.' While there was indeed plenty more where that came from, Eccles, in fact, wouldn't be able to get any more. But since the crowd didn't know this, most of them were satisfied by his show of bravado and left without withdrawing their money.

In many ways, the Ogden episode was symbolic of the larger Depression drama. There was no shortage of money in the country, but it was locked up in vaults where people couldn't get access to it and where it was doing nothing for the economy. What was needed was a way to unlock these savings and use the money to put the country back to work. Lower interest rates would help, since businesses then could afford to borrow and invest. Under Eccles, the Federal Reserve brought interest rates down and became an active source of assistance in the reconstruction of the shattered economy. Gone were the days when the Fed officials would sit back and watch with indifference – even approval – as the nation's weaker members bobbed helplessly in the water until they were no longer able to keep themselves afloat. The role of the Fed, according to Eccles, was 'to assure that adequate support is available whenever needed for the emergency financing involved in a recovery program'.

But the economy was in such disastrous shape that low interest rates on their own weren't enough. With little prospect of profits, even low interest rates wouldn't prod the private sector to invest. Eccles insisted that, given the severity of the Depression, government had to take some initiative; it had to intervene actively with massive spending programmes. He was particularly inspired by the research work being carried out by a young economist named Lauchlin Currie, the director of research at the Fed and later Eccles's own economic adviser. Currie argued that massive government spending would have secondary benefits of economic stimulation well beyond the amount of the initial spending. This meant that government could 'prime the pump', that is, get things going until the people could continue on their own. If government made the initial outlay of cash, it could revive the economy to the point that business would start spending again. Then government could scale back its own spending and let business carry the can.

As the boldness of the necessary responses became increasingly clear to Eccles, Roosevelt drifted into uncertainty. Rather than getting more radical, Roosevelt seemed to be withdrawing into traditional thinking. In his first few years in office, Roosevelt had defied economic orthodoxy, easing up on credit and, most significantly, experimenting with massive government spending on public works and relief programmes. The results had been encouraging. There were definite signs of improvement in 1935 and 1936. But in 1937, with conservatives winning out over New Dealers inside the administration, Roosevelt drastically cut back the flow of public funds, sending the struggling economy into a tailspin. By the beginning of 1938, the situation seemed bleaker than ever. Somewhere between eight and eleven million Americans – nobody knew exactly how many – were now out of work with little means of support.

It would take the Second World War finally and unequivocally to demonstrate the need to mobilize the economy, no matter what the cost. And it would take John Maynard Keynes to show that what Eccles and Currie were getting at went to the heart of the problem with classical economics.

• • •

Although Keynes had never set foot in Utah and was not the type to jump on a counter to sweet-talk an unruly mob, he and Eccles ended up with roughly the same formula for ending the Depression.

Whereas Eccles was a frontier capitalist who struggled to stave off bankruptcy when his safe, secure world seemed to crumble all around him, Keynes was a highly intellectual academic with a probing, restless mind and a comfortable seat inside England's self-confident elite. Born in 1883, Keynes was the son of a Cambridge don and grew up in a close-knit, high-powered academic community where his father became the chief administrator of the university. Along with the sons of the country's upper class, Keynes went to Eton, where he won prizes for mathematics, classics and English, and later went on to King's College, Cambridge, where he graduated with a first in mathematics and became a prize pupil of the lead-ing economist of the day, Alfred Marshall. But Keynes was more than just a very impressive student. He mixed easily with the elite crowd at Cambridge, becoming a key social and intellectual figure on campus with active involvement in numerous select university societies. Although he had no athletic abilities and considered himself homely, he was deeply involved and accomplished in just about every area of life at the university.

For someone who was to tear down much of the edifice of established thinking in Britain, Keynes was, to an astonishing extent, an insider – both at Cambridge and throughout his life.[6] Although an iconoclast whose ideas often piqued members of the establishment, Keynes moved easily among them, entertaining them, dazzling them, infuriating them. He was at the very centre of the economics establishment, taking on the leading economists and economic wisdom of his day with such vigour and brilliance that his views were sought even by those who disliked them. He was also a successful financier who became independently wealthy from his investments and served as chairman of a large insurance company.

In addition, the lanky, witty Keynes cut a considerable figure in the political world, where he was closely associated at different times with two men who served as Liberal prime ministers, Herbert Asquith and David Lloyd George. Even after years of publicly pil-lorying Winston Churchill for his economic policies as chancellor of the exchequer, he was sufficiently intimate with Churchill to make a private bet with him about the outcome of the 1929 election. Keynes was also associated with some of the leading cultural and literary figures of the day, including Virginia Woolf (whose husband, Leonard, was one of his oldest friends), T. S. Eliot, E. M. Forster, Lytton Strachey and others in the Bloomsbury group. His marriage to ballerina Lydia Lopokova was a widely publicized social event.

It was from these elevated social and political circles that Keynes was to champion a cause dear to the heart of the common people: the fight against unemployment. But Keynes came to this cause by what might be considered a circuitous route – not through union halls or mass demonstrations, but via a crisis of declining religious faith among the philosophical crowd at Cambridge. It was the late Edwardian age and the intellectual elite of England was struggling to deal with the moral vacuum created by the collapse of religious beliefs. The firm moral anchor that Christianity had provided only a generation earlier had given way to a mood of questioning, of moral and spiritual confusion, exemplified by the ultimate challenge posed in Darwin's *The Origin of Species*. For some at Cambridge, this loss of religious moorings had frightening implications, not least of which was the prospect of a breakdown of the social order. Henry Sidgwick, an influential professor of moral philosophy and a contemporary of Keynes at Cambridge, expressed concern that 'the general loss of such a hope [of Christian immortality] from the minds of average human beings as now constituted, would be an evil of which I cannot pretend to measure the extent'.[7]

For Keynes and some of his close friends, however, this demise of religion was liberating. Keynes was, above all, a man of enormous intellectual scope. He was highly rational and logical, with an iconoclastic mind that bristled under the constraints of dogma and refused to bow to established ways of thinking. While the loss of religion did create a void and moral uncertainty, it also created an opening – an opening for the discovery of a new meaning, based on human decency and rationality. Keynes was heavily influenced throughout his life by the thinking of G. E. Moore, another Cambridge professor of moral philosophy, who sought to create a new moral world based on individual reasoning and the achievement of 'good states of mind'. Moore was a powerful teacher who had a dominant influence at Cambridge. He never used notes or seemed to be delivering a prepared lecture. With each class, he appeared to be grappling for the first time with some difficult philosophical dilemma, bringing the students right with him in his search for truth and an understanding of the nature of good.

Running through Moore's thinking, as well as through that of the Bloomsbury group, with which both Moore and Keynes were loosely affiliated, was a cynicism about the narrowness of the Victorian vision. Keynes strongly believed that the social restraints and dogmas of the past could be replaced by a new world of public duty based on human rationality and the desire to achieve good ends. He was deeply impressed, for example, by Sidney and Beatrice Webb, the wealthy anti-poverty activists who jointly founded the journal the *New Statesman* and made a lifetime commitment to fighting for collective human betterment.

Essentially, Keynes sought to bring this aspiration to human betterment to the world of economics, which was dominated by an orthodoxy every bit as rigid as the Christian one but was somehow more adept at surviving in an age of doubt. As the British economy limped from crisis to crisis in the 1920s and '30s, the men supervising the economy seemed no more willing to have the underlying tenets of their economic faith examined than the clergy welcomed scrutiny of the underpinnings of their religious beliefs.

As Keynes watched their efforts through the 1920s, he grew more and more sceptical of their belief that austerity for the working population was the answer. To this end, they were determined to put Britain back on the gold standard, the international trading system that linked national currencies to the value of gold. While ostensibly just about enabling trade, the gold standard had a significant impact on the domestic economy, and a punishing impact on workers. If Britain experienced a trade deficit, Britain's central bank had to raise interest rates, attracting foreign capital into the country, and thereby maintaining the pound's required value under the gold standard.

But the higher interest rates slowed the economy, depressing prices, and pushing down wages. And there was no point in workers turning to government for relief. Under the gold standard, governments were obliged to keep their budgets balanced, since deficits were considered potentially inflationary, and inflation threatened to erode the external value of the currency.

The gold standard had been abandoned during the First World War, but the British financial elite was determined to restore it after the war. After all, London had served as the capital of the world financial system, which was anchored by gold. Foreign governments, central banks and international firms held significant deposits in London and looked to London for financial leadership. The gold standard was seen as the centrepiece of the world trading system, which Britain had dominated in the nineteenth century. Restoring it seemed synonymous with restoring Britain's dominion over its glorious empire. To some, it was practically synonymous with Britain's honour.

And yet, through the early 1920s, Britain remained off gold. It was clear that, given Britain's trade deficits, returning to the gold standard would involve higher interest rates, pushing the country into recession. (This was less of a problem for the US, which was running trade surpluses.) Times were already hard enough in Britain. After years of wartime deprivation, the working population was hungry for better conditions, not more hardship.

With British unions flexing their muscles, the financial elite increasingly came to regard the gold standard as not just essential for international trade, but as a powerful vehicle for holding the masses at bay. The disciplinary effect of the gold standard – and its appeal to the moneyed classes – became clear at hearings set up under Sir Austen Chamberlain in 1924. Prominent figures from the business and financial worlds noted that one of the key benefits of returning to gold would be limiting the growing power of the unions. They also insisted that it would prevent governments from being pushed into delivering costly programmes or reducing interest rates. The hopes and dreams of millions of people wouldn't rest in the hands of politicians who might feel the need to respond to the electorate, but rather with an international requirement that the value of the British pound would be precisely 3 pounds, 17 shillings, 9 pennies per ounce of 11/12 fine gold.

The anti-democratic power of the gold standard was perhaps captured best by Lord Bradbury, an influential senior official in the Treasury department. Bradbury testified before the Chamberlain Committee that the gold standard was 'knave-proof'.[8] The knaves he had in mind were clearly the ordinary people of Britain, who were increasingly demanding a say over whether they'd be able to find employment or could count on receiving a public pension. Such knavish behaviour was regarded as a threat to the propertied class, who felt no qualms trying to squelch it.

Britain returned to the gold standard in April 1925, forcing the already-tightened belts of British workers to be tightened another few notches. As the pound rose to its old pre-war level, British coal became uncompetitive on world markets, and mine owners demanded a 10 per cent wage cut. The miners dug in their heels, and the standoff led in 1926 to a nationwide general strike, organized by the giant Trades Union Congress. The strike lasted twelve days but ended in defeat for the workers. With the stock market crash in New York in 1929, conditions grew even bleaker for ordinary Britons. By 1931, when the UK finally went off the gold standard again, some 2.6 million Britons were out of work.

Yet British authorities still clung to classical economic theory, insisting that austerity and deprivation were the path towards recovery: once wages came down enough, employers would start hiring again.

One of the few powerful dissenting voices was that of Keynes, who was appalled at the level of unemployment and human misery, and at how much this approach favoured owners over workers. But apart from considerations of fairness, he had a more fundamental objection to the theory: it didn't work. As he told a startled audience at the Institute of Bankers in 1922, the strategy was 'almost hopeless' as a method of restoring economic health.

To begin with, the strategy was based on a misunderstanding of the problem, according to Keynes. The reason employers weren't hiring was not because the price of labour was too high, but because there was no demand for their products. No one was investing in any kind of productive enterprise and for good reason: with so much unemployment and the economy so flat, there was little prospect of making a profit. So the problem was circular. As long as the economy was flat, investors wouldn't invest, and as long as they wouldn't invest, the economy stayed flat. And so the slump continued, and even became worse.

If this analysis sounded fairly straightforward, in fact it was an attack on one of the most basic premises of classical economics: the belief that the economy was self-correcting. Classical theory held that the economy would naturally achieve full employment. Once wages dropped low enough, employers would start hiring again. Keynes disputed this, arguing that as long as there was no demand for their products, employers wouldn't start hiring, no matter how low wages fell. The classical theory failed to account for a crucial element: human psychology, particularly human reticence and fear.

The nature of capitalism involved people taking risks with their money. But, at times like this, it made little sense to put one's money at risk, rather than, say, putting it in a bank account or buying a bond with a fixed rate of interest. Capitalism only worked well – and employed large numbers of people – when those with money were able to overcome their fears, suspend their natural caution and, boldly invest their money in some risky venture, out of an enthusiastic expectation of large future profits. But this involved some reason to believe, some hope. When things slowed down and everything was stalled all around them, where would this hope come from? Rather than seeing depression and high rates of unemployment as an aberration, Keynes saw them as a natural and recurring state of affairs. Capitalism, left on its own, was far from self-correcting. On the contrary, said Keynes, it was inherently unstable.

Something else was needed. When humans were nervous and uncertain, as they are during a recession, it wasn't enough to rely on the unpredictable 'invisible hand' of supply-and-demand forces in the marketplace. A strong, highly visible hand was needed, one that would be seen injecting money directly into the economy, into the pockets of consumers and business owners. But whose hand would this be? Individual entrepreneurs were understandably obsessed with their own financial survival and were unlikely to be able to rise above their fears. What was needed, then, was government, with its ability to draw on the collective resources of the community and to operate in the collective interest. There were times when the steady bureaucratic hand was preferable to the more exotic invisible one.

Classical economics, by failing to see the inherent weakness in capitalism, failed also to see this solution. Instead, the classical school offered up a mixture of remedies that only made things worse. It emphasized cutting wages, encouraging lower expectations, and doing without. It considered suffering and self-restraint essential. The similarity to Christianity was striking; both suggested that redemption would come from virtuous living and virtuous living alone.

Keynes regarded the piousness and self-denial of classical economics with the same contempt that he regarded religious dogma; both were confining and limiting, imprisoning people in a world of false faith. The dogma of classical economics was particularly lethal during a depression, when what people most needed was to overcome their fears and their natural tendency towards caution. It was not puritanical living that was needed, but exuberant living, the unleashing of the 'animal spirits' that lurked inside the human personality. Keynes particularly bristled at the notion that human society thrives on abstinence, on learning to do with less. The 'saver' is the hero in classical economics, but in Keynesian economics, the 'saver' is portrayed as a hoarder and miser, a killer of hopes and dreams. As long as people simply hoard their money, nothing will get built, needs will remain unsatisfied, people will remain idle. It is the consumer, the doer, the entrepreneur who makes the economy go around. As Keynes put it: 'It has been usual to think of the accumulated wealth of the world as having been painfully built up out of the voluntary abstinence of individuals from the immediate enjoyment of consumption which we call thrift. But it should be obvious that mere abstinence is not enough by itself to build cities or drain fens…It is enterprise which builds the world's possessions.'[9]

In the Keynesian view, it is essential to get the world expanding, not shrinking, to harness the life force of human activity towards the goal of satisfying human needs. Keynes is at his best unleashing his fury against the abstinence imposed by the authorities in some misguided attempt to restore government balance sheets, while ignoring the more basic problem of putting people back to work. In a wonderful, rarely quoted commentary, Keynes attacks these death-mongering purveyors of gloom:

> Negation, restriction, inactivity – these are the government's watch-words. Under their leadership we have been forced to button up our waistcoats and compress our lungs. Fears and doubts and hypochon-driac precautions are keeping us muffled up indoors. But we are not tottering to our graves. We are healthy children. We need the breath of life. There is nothing to be afraid of. On the contrary. The future

holds in store for us far more wealth and economic freedom and possibilities of personal life than the past has ever offered.

There is no reason why we should not feel ourselves free to be bold, to be open, to experiment, to take action, to try the possibilities of things. And over against us, standing in the path, there is nothing but a few old gentlemen tightly buttoned-up in their frock coats, who only need to be treated with a little friendly disrespect and bowled over like ninepins.[10]

• • •

But how does an economy recapture boldness when it is short of funds? How would all this exuberant living be paid for? Government spending might offer immediate relief, but wouldn't it have to be paid for in the future, as the country is left with mounting debt and inflation? The classical position was clear: there was no such thing as a free lunch, just as there was no easy way into heaven. Sacrifice and good living were the only answers, in economics as in spiritual matters.

But here Keynes had another insight. The answer to the apparently baffling question of how to pay for the government intervention was staring everyone in the face. The new investment would be paid for not by some cache of gold found on a pirate ship but from the idle resources themselves – the unemployed workers and idle plants, mills and factories. By putting them back to work, productive capacity would be created, which was the source of wealth. 'When we have unemployed men and unemployed plant and more savings than we are using at home, it is utterly imbecile to say that we cannot afford these things,' wrote Keynes. 'For it is with the unemployed men and the unemployed plant, and with nothing else, that these things are done.'

The assumption that things were unaffordable was based on the notion that not doing them was costless. '[T]he Treasury will reject something on the ground that it will cost money regardless of what they could hope to save on the "dole" or from increased revenue,' Keynes noted. In other words, the increased tax revenue collected from a revitalized economy and the decreased spending on public relief would ultimately become the source of the funds to pay for the revitalization. Furthermore, there was a kind of loaves-and-fishes effect from government injecting money into a depressed economy: the benefits multiplied. First, there was the direct benefit, as the government money employed someone. Then that person would turn around and spend his or her payment on something, which would feed into someone else being employed. '[I]magine that initial sum of money passing from hand to hand, perhaps twenty times in the course of a year, in exchange for the production of goods and services, which would have gone otherwise without a buyer. Each recipient in turn can become a purchaser and create fresh employment,' Keynes wrote enthusiastically in a letter to his mother.

This 'multiplier effect', which was similar to the pump-priming idea of Lauchlin Currie, would become key to the Keynesian system. It showed how an injection of seed money from government could have a ripple effect far beyond its initial value, bringing a revived private sector back into play.

And all this could be accomplished without setting off inflation, according to Keynes. It was a basic tenet of classical thinking that pumping extra money into the economy would simply set off inflation, leaving no one further ahead in the long run. Keynes agreed that that was true – under conditions of full employment. But he argued that when so many resources were idle, there was little prospect of inflation; the extra money circulating would not push prices up but would mostly have the effect of creating more employment. So, according to Keynes, one of the key concerns of classical economics – that government deficits would set off inflation – did not apply during a recession, when there was substantial idle capacity to absorb the extra money pumped into the economy. Keynes had deftly turned the classical theory on its head: not only was a large outlay of government funds affordable in a recession, but the outlay would actually pay for itself, without setting off inflation. In some circumstances, there was a free lunch after all.[11]

With the publication of his *General Theory of Employment, Interest and Money* in 1936, Keynes had thrown down the gauntlet to the established order. In hundreds of pages of mostly technical argument, Keynes took aim at the underpinnings of classical economic thought with a sharpness and logic that the orthodox school found more and more difficult to brush aside. Although there was still plenty of resistance, Keynes was becoming an international superstar whose influence was spreading throughout the academic and policy-making world. In the United States, the impressiveness of the Keynesian assault on classical thinking was breathing new life into the flagging spirits of New Deal reformers. At Harvard, long a bastion of classical economics, a new crop of young economists was transforming the university into a hotbed of Keynesian activism. That new crop included many who would go on to be senior policy advisers and prominent commentators in the postwar years – John Kenneth Galbraith, Paul Samuelson, James Tobin and Robert Solow. Galbraith recalled that while classical economics continued to be taught in Harvard classes by day, 'in the evening and almost every evening from 1936 onwards almost everyone in the Harvard community discussed Keynes'.[12]

The ideas were even reaching a popular audience. There was an enormous popular appeal in the way Keynes put the problem of unemployment front and centre, whereas the classical school treated employment as a mere byproduct of achieving good economic fundamentals, a reward for good clean living. Implicitly, Keynes was turning the equation around, demanding that the economy serve the interests of the people, rather than demanding that the people fit into some economist's conception of how an economy should function.

This deeply radical notion meshed with Keynes's desire to replace dogma with a world governed by human rationality. For Keynes, the ultimate goal remained a variation of G. E. Moore's aspiration of attainment of 'good states of mind'. But he increasingly came to believe there could be no good states of mind in a society that was in a state of collapse. Thus, society had to be restored, and a key part of this restoration involved overcoming the enormous social ill of mass unemployment. Achieving this was a prerequisite for moving on to meet the higher goal – a more rational, decent, enlightened human society. One of Keynes's biographers, Robert Skidelsky, notes: 'Today the main object of business activity is to make a quick profit, the quicker the better. The main object of contemporary statecraft is to make societies even richer. To what end, and with what effect on individual and social virtue, we no longer ask, and scarcely dare think about. Keynes was the last great economist to hold economics in some sort of relation with the "good life".'[13]

Keynes's search for a new moral order had led him to mount a devastating attack on the elite's cherished economic theory and replace it with a scheme that would address some of the deepest grievances of the common people. Although he was born into a privileged world and lived all his life among the elite, Keynes had produced a vision of a world where the economy would be made responsive to popular needs and desires.

The vehicle for this was government. If economic conditions could be managed by government, and government was elected by the people, then the economy could be managed not in the interests of the elite, but in the interests of the majority. The theory Keynes had provided was sweeping in scope. Never before had ordinary people come so close to holding the reins of power.

9
triumph of the welfare state

What is perhaps most striking today, looking back on the intro-duction of the expansive welfare state in Britain right after the Second World War, was how bold wartime planners were in their thinking, how unshaken they were in their resolve – despite the sheer costs of the project. There was really no precedent in Britain for the scale of what they had in mind. Previous government social support had mostly been piecemeal and typically came with a stigma that was reminiscent of the punitive, means-tested Poor Laws. Yet, as the war came to an end, plans were being drawn up with the aim of seizing the moment to ensure that victory would be accompanied by a vast extension of economic rights to the entire British population.

From the point of view of public finance, it is hard to imagine a less favourable moment to be envisioning such ambitious changes. The UK national debt, as a percentage of GDP, was higher than it had ever been, reaching 225 per cent of GDP, eclipsing even the post-First World War high of 180 per cent of GDP reached in 1933, which had been considered calamitous at the time. To put this into perspective, the UK national debt was 75 per cent of GDP in 2010.

But while today's debt level is invoked as evidence that government spending must be sharply curtailed, the much higher debt levels of the 1940s weren't considered a sufficient impediment to truly far-reaching plans for a postwar welfare state that included a national public health care system and a universal social insurance scheme aimed at providing citizens with a minimum income.

Of course, the war had changed British society in profound ways, making the possibility of ambitious reform seem plausible, even inevitable. The war had provided a sense of cohesiveness and common purpose, breaking down deeply ingrained social barriers as Britons huddled together in air raid shelters, opened their homes to more than a million evacuees from elsewhere in the country, and headed off to battle united against a hated common foe. The resulting breakdown of traditional British formality was nicely captured in a 1941 comment by Lord Marley, who noted that it had become quite common during the war 'to see Englishmen speaking to each other in public, although they had never been formally introduced'.[1]

Certainly, the war had illustrated Keynes's point about the power of collective action, and the positive role that government could play as the agent of that collective action. The notion that it was impossible to defeat social ills such as unemployment and poverty seemed less convincing now that government was on the cusp of defeating nothing less than one of the most powerful armies in history. Weary, devastated and broke though they were, the British people also felt strangely empowered by the sheer scale of what they'd collectively accomplished, and there was a widely shared determination never to return to the despair and hopelessness of the pre-war period.

The end of the war, therefore, presented an opportunity to tap into this collectivist impulse to create a better peacetime world – something that Sir William Beveridge well understood, as he went about planning the broad strokes of the British welfare state.

Like Keynes, Beveridge was a man of many talents, with a commitment to advancing the common good. Born into privilege as the son of a British judge in India in 1879, he was educated at Oxford and became close to a number of influential thinkers. Among his close associates were Keynes, R. H. Tawney, and the prominent social reformers Sidney and Beatrice Webb, who were also key figures in the Fabian Society, which in the 1880s developed and actively promoted the case for state intervention in the interests of 'Collective Welfare'. From an early age, Beveridge showed a concern about poverty, developing an academic interest in the subject, and also working among the poor in London's East End.

As a young journalist in his mid-twenties, Beveridge caught the attention of Winston Churchill, then a Liberal cabinet minister. In 1908, Churchill brought Beveridge into the civil service, where he became involved in the development of a social insurance scheme that was influenced by Fabian ideas and also by the social insurance schemes that had been in place in Germany since the 1880s.

The social insurance scheme that was introduced by the Liberals in 1911 was modest compared to the German version. It covered only a fraction of the workforce and offered limited benefits. But it was the first attempt at providing some form of minimal unemployment and health care coverage to British workers, paid for out of compulsory contributions by workers, employers and the government. This bare-bones forerunner of the welfare state – dubbed the 'ambulance state' – was as far as things would go for the next thirty years, as progress was stalled by the First World War and after that by the obsession with reinstating the gold standard and by the Depression. By the early 1940s, however, with the end of the Second World War dimly in sight, Beveridge, almost by chance, was in a position to push things considerably further.

Beveridge had spent the inter-war years as director of the London School of Economics, but in 1941 he was asked to head a committee to co-ordinate the government's meagre social assistance

185

programmes. This hardly seemed like a top priority in the midst of the all-out war effort, and Beveridge was initially disappointed and even insulted that he wasn't being tapped for something more important and war-related. But swallowing his pride and accepting the position anyway, Beveridge soon spotted the chance to turn the modest mandate of the committee into an opportunity to devise a sweeping postwar welfare scheme that was in no way on the government's radar.

The report Beveridge produced in December 1942 called for a stunning reshaping of the harsh and austere world Britons had experienced in the 1920s and '30s. Although his report bore the dull title *Social Insurance and Allied Services*, Beveridge used it to set out a strikingly bold agenda that proposed giving Britons a guarantee of work, income and access to health care as a matter of their rights as citizens. He noted that 'a revolutionary moment in the world's history is a time for revolutions, not patching'. War was a chance for meaningful change, he argued, insisting that 'the purpose of victory is to live in a better world than the old world'. He described five giants that needed slaying: Want, Disease, Ignorance, Squalor and Idleness. The task would require collective efforts, and co-operation between citizens and government. The key elements of his plan were: universal family allowances, a national public health service and a government commitment to maintaining full employment.

Given that unemployment had hovered above a million – at times reaching three million – for most of the previous twenty years, the notion of a government commitment to full employment was nothing short of audacious. In devising his scheme, Beveridge had consulted extensively with Keynes, who supported it and whose theories were central to the notion that it was affordable. But, apart from Keynes, Beveridge had worked largely on his own, with little input or consultation with bureaucrats or members of cabinet, some of whom distrusted Beveridge as unduly independent-minded. Now, as Beveridge tantalized the public with talk of his sweeping reform proposals, he was effectively throwing down the gauntlet to a government coalition headed by a Conservative prime minister, Winston Churchill, whose focus was almost exclusively on war.

Using radio broadcasts to tout his ideas in what amounted to a surprisingly modern media campaign, Beveridge ensured that his report was highly anticipated. The night before its scheduled release, people actually lined up to be sure to get a copy. And so it was that *Social Insurance and Allied Services* became an instant hit, indeed a runaway bestseller. Some one hundred thousand copies were sold in the first month, with sales eventually topping six hundred thousand. And the people apparently liked what they read. A public opinion survey taken shortly after its release found 86 per cent supported it.[2]

Whatever reservations the government had, it spotted an opportunity to inspire hope in the war-weary population. It distributed copies to British troops, even dropping copies from planes into parts of occupied Europe. The BBC broadcast details of the report in twenty-two languages. Improbably, the somewhat stiff, upper class–sounding Beveridge almost instantly became a national icon, holding forth on the radio and in packed hallways. Riding a wave of public adulation, he easily put down critics who argued that strong social supports would leave Britain's population pampered and lacking in moral fibre. When one American critic suggested a Beveridge-type social system would never have produced the likes of Sir Francis Drake or Sir Walter Raleigh, Beveridge duly noted: 'Adventure came not from the half-starved, but from those who were well fed enough to feel ambition.'[3]

With the public uniting behind Beveridge's plan, there was less open resistance than one would have expected from members of the elite, given their past fierce adherence to conservative economic doctrine. Sir Kingsley Wood, Chancellor of the Exchequer, was strongly opposed, insisting the welfare state envisioned by Beveridge was unaffordable, without driving up taxes substantially. Wood particularly objected to the untargeted way in which it would deliver benefits – not just to the needy, but to everyone, including the rich. There was also, of course, opposition from elements within the business community. For the most part, however, resistance was surprisingly muted, with many employers indicating support, perhaps reflecting the degree to which the war and Keynesian economic ideas had changed public opinion, even among the elite. The same public opinion survey (cited above) that found strong support among the general public also reported that 73 per cent of employers backed the Beveridge plan, as did 76 per cent of those in upper income groups.

Within the Conservative Party, however, the Beveridge plan quickly became a divisive issue. Historian Richard Cockett insists that the notion of a wartime consensus in favour of Beveridge has been exaggerated; that some 90 per cent of those considering themselves Conservatives opposed the report.[4] However, there was undoubtedly a significant faction of Conservative MPs who were prepared to abandon the party's traditional economic positions, and chafed at the way the coalition government appeared to be stonewalling on plans to implement it. Calling themselves the Tory Reform Committee, members of this dissenting faction had quiet support from some prominent Conservatives, including Rab Butler and future prime minister Harold Macmillan.

The reformers insisted that the Beveridge plan was in many ways a conservative document. While it provided what amounted to a minimum income, workers were required to pay into the plan, making it an insurance programme rather than a government handout. (This aspect of it was popular with unions and workers as well.) It also provided fairly minimal benefits – less generous than similar European schemes – which conservatives considered a plus. More importantly, from a conservative viewpoint, the Beveridge plan provided a means of preserving capitalism, by softening its harsh effects.

This was to become a key selling point. Quintin Hogg, one of the Tory reformers, captured the idea perfectly in noting that Beveridge provided for 'publicly organized social services, privately owned industry'.[5] In other words, it involved a trade-off that was to become central to the postwar era: there would be free-market capitalism, but the brutal reality of capitalism would be mitigated by government provision of social services. This was a compromise, then, that offered something for conservatives as well as progressives. A wide range of new social benefits would ensure popular support for capitalism – something that couldn't be taken for granted, given the tumultuous times, the potential appeal of Communism, and the painful, not-so-distant memories of pre-war capitalism. Highlighting the ultimately conservative nature of the Beveridge scheme, Hogg (later Lord Hailsham of St Marylebone) introduced a motion in Parliament calling for the immediate creation of a Ministry of Social Security, which won the support of more than forty Conservative MPs, sending shock waves through Parliament.[6]

Churchill himself seemed torn. He had been among those who disliked Beveridge's attempt to single-handedly reshape Britain, and had resisted being pressured into implementing the report. But he appears to have been at least somewhat sympathetic to the ideas in the report, and to Keynesian economics. His key economic advisor, Lord Cherwell, had become a Keynesian who believed full employment was a worthy and achievable goal, to be maintained through government spending when necessary.[7] After the mini-revolt by the Tory Reform Committee, Churchill began publicly to endorse key aspects of Beveridge's plan. In a radio address in March 1943, the Prime Minister adopted some of Beveridge's ideas in discussing the postwar world. Without mentioning Beveridge by name, Churchill pledged to use government action to control unemployment and promised 'national compulsory insurance for all classes for all purposes from cradle to grave' – a phrase, used for the first time here by a Conservative prime minister, that was to become permanently attached to the welfare state.

Yet the British public was apparently not confident in Churchill's commitment to reform. With the end of the war, it became clear that the public had more confidence in the Labour Party to make good on the dreams for a better life as envisaged by Beveridge. Despite Churchill's wartime heroics, he found himself booed in the 1945 election campaign by a crowd of twenty-five thousand in Walthamstow, in east London, demanding jobs and housing.[8] The stunning landslide victory of the Labour Party, winning its first-ever majority government, reflected the extent of the popular hunger for a serious modification of the terms of capitalism.

•   •   •

The Beveridge report became the blueprint for far-reaching reforms that transformed British society after the war. While the concept of civil and political rights had evolved in Britain in previous centuries, the establishment of the postwar welfare state effectively created what T. H. Marshall called 'social rights'. These social rights entitled all individuals to a certain level of well-being – not on the basis of neediness, but rather as an inherent right of citizenship.[9]

On a practical level, the changes in people's lives were considerable. In 1946, family allowances were launched, giving families with children a small weekly stipend. In 1948, after a bitter two-year battle with doctors and the British Medical Association, Health Minister Aneurin Bevan, a fiery ex-miner, brought in National Health Insurance, making Britain the first Western nation to offer free medical care to its entire population. Labour also made good on Beveridge's promise of a state-run social insurance scheme – paid for jointly by workers, employers and government – that provided unemployment and sickness benefits, as well as allowances for dependents and pensions for retirement.

While the Labour government was responsible for initiating most of the reforms, the welfare state remained essentially intact in the early postwar period under Conservative governments as well. In fact, even before the war had ended, Rab Butler, a Conservative who served as education minister in the coalition government, pushed forward the reform agenda with legislation dismantling the worst aspects of the deeply class-ridden education system. To a striking extent, a pro-welfare state consensus prevailed into the early 1970s, with both Labour and Conservative governments maintaining and expanding on the broad outlines of the plan proposed by Beveridge. The consensus became known as Butskellism – the conflation of Butler's name with Labour Chancellor of the Exchequer Hugh Gaitskell. While there were perennial attacks from the right over the growing cost of the welfare state and attacks from the left over the inadequacy of the programmes, the consensus largely held. The welfare state became accepted, for the most part, as simply a reality of postwar Britain.

And it proved to be, by any reasonable measure, a success. Although it failed to eliminate poverty, as had originally been anticipated, it did greatly improve the lives of ordinary Britons. As Nicholas Timmins notes: 'at the end of the sixties and a quarter-century on from the Beveridge report, the welfare state's condition can only be described as one of mature flowering. The services it provided were bigger, better and more comprehensive than anything that had gone before'.[10] At the same time, Britain enjoyed sustained economic growth, with a Keynesian approach by government maintaining a high level of employment and rising living standards. Average earnings (after inflation) rose by 2.7 per cent a year between 1951 and 1961, while profit rates averaged a healthy 15.5 per cent.[11] From 1951 to 1964, the number of cars on the British roads rose from 2.5 million to six million, and there was similarly impressive growth in the number of households owning refrigerators (from 5 to 37 per cent) and washing machines (from 11 to 52 per cent).[12] In 1959, the Conservatives, portraying themselves as the trusted managers of the welfare state, were re-elected with the campaign slogan: 'You've never had it so good.'

• • •

Analysts often credit the war – and the enormous manpower demands it created – with ending the Depression of the 1930s. And this is undoubtedly true. The war effort required exactly what Keynes had long advocated – pumping huge amounts of government money into the economy. As virtually the entire adult male population was conscripted into the armed forces or hired to work in factories churning out weaponry, the unemployment problem that had plagued Britain for two decades quickly disappeared. By 1943, unemployment had dropped from well over a million before the war to a mere sixty-two thousand, with most of these 'unemployed' workers simply between jobs.[13]

But what accounts for the tremendous economic boom that occurred during the decades following the war? Why didn't demobilization plunge Britain back into economic stagnation? That was what had happened after the First World War. Back in 1918, there had been a brief economic boom when the war ended and wartime controls were lifted. But after that boomlet, the economy slipped into recession – a recession that was intensified with deep spending cuts in 1922, and that essentially gripped Britain for the next twenty years.

Why didn't the same scenario unfold after 1945? There were widespread fears that it would. But it didn't. Instead, the opposite happened. The end of the Second World War ushered in an era often described as the 'Golden Age of Capitalism'; economic growth rates in Britain were among the highest in British history. What explains this apparent contradiction – a period of sustained economic growth in the face of an apparently crippling level of debt, a combination that seems impossible to imagine today?

The postwar boom is typically attributed to market-related forces unleashed by the end of the war, with its pent-up demand. Here's how British political economist Colin Leys explains the strong postwar economic growth: 'This was fundamentally due to the "long boom", the worldwide upturn in the accumulation cycle which lasted from the 1940s until the late 1960s.'[14] But why were things so different after the Second World War compared to after the First World War? Why was there an upturn in the 'accumulation cycle' after 1945 and not after 1918, when four years of war-related deprivation also unleashed an enormous desire to accumulate?

Of course, a number of factors account for the difference between the periods that followed the two wars. But one that has perhaps not been adequately highlighted is the difference in the level of income inequality in the two periods. As discussed, the period following the First World War was one of widespread deprivation, with a small wealthy elite at the top. After years of hardship on the battlefields, the returning troops no doubt craved the many new consumer items available – cars, refrigerators, radios – not to mention sufficient food and adequate housing. But the brute austerity of the period, reinforced by the gold standard and by the economic orthodoxy of the day, ensured a highly unequal distribution of income. As Keynes noted, it was this lack of resources in the hands of working people that kept the wealthy from investing in the economy, and ensured that factories remained idle.

The opposite happened after the Second World War. While the gold standard had kept money largely confined to the wealthy, out of the hands of the broader public, the welfare state distributed it more broadly throughout society. Family allowances and a comprehensive social insurance scheme lifted millions out of poverty, with higher taxes keeping a lid on the growth of top incomes. The result was a significant redistribution from the top to middle- and lower-income Britons. In 1937, the share of income captured by the top 1 per cent of British society had been huge – almost 17 per cent. Throughout the 1950s and '60s, the share of this top group dropped to 9 per cent, then 8 per cent, and, by the late 1970s, to as low as 6 per cent. This meant that a significantly larger share of the national income was in the hands of the rest of the population – people who, unlike the rich, were likely to spend virtually all of their incomes. Thus, the British welfare state ensured that more money was in the hands of those who would spend it on goods and services, thereby creating incentives for business to invest in producing those goods and services.

•   •   •

It is striking the extent to which the same pattern of rising income equality – and greater prosperity – is evident in the twentieth-century history of the United States. As in Britain, there was a high level of income inequality after the First World War (although the gold standard was less of a factor, since the US was a creditor nation with few trade deficit problems).

The United States had already evolved into a top-heavy society dominated by an incredibly wealthy class of industrial and banking interests, led by oil magnate John D. Rockefeller and banking magnate J. P. Morgan, who between them controlled just about every corner of the US economy. Unionization efforts had been fiercely opposed, with strikes ruthlessly suppressed, often with state support. Americans returning from the First World War battlefields came home to high unemployment and stagnant or falling wages. So although the 1920s proved to be a decade of significant techno-logical advances, workers were in such a weak bargaining position that they were unable to demand a meaningful share of the gains, leaving them largely sidelined and left out of the rambunctious economic growth of the 'Roaring Twenties'. As John Kenneth

Galbraith observed: '[T]he rich were getting richer much faster than the poor were getting less poor.'[15]

With the buying power of workers severely constrained, wealthy Americans happily turned their capital over to Wall Street for lucrative financial speculation. In 1926, Republican Treasury Secretary Andrew Mellon, the fifth richest man in the US, introduced an enormous tax cut for the rich. This provided the elite with a massive windfall that quickly flowed to Wall Street, inflating the stock market bubble. When that bubble burst in an orgy of unregulated financial speculation three years later, the resulting crash plunged the American economy into a deep depression with unemployment levels rivalling those in 1930s Britain.

But, as in Britain, the harsh experience of the 1930s in America prompted a demand for significant changes that led to greater equality. America didn't go as far as Britain in embracing the welfare state, but it did make some important moves in that direction under Franklin Roosevelt's Democratic administration. In 1936 – at the height of the brutal Depression – FDR introduced a social security system that provided benefits for the elderly, the unemployed and the sick (and which remains extremely popular today – as virtually the only US social programme). Furthermore, FDR's New Deal used the resources of the state to put people back to work. Crucially, starting in the 1930s, the New Deal also strengthened the rights of unions, thereby enabling them to push up wages for their members, with positive ripple effects on wages across the economy.

Roosevelt would have likely pushed the US even further towards economic equality had he lived to implement the economic 'bill of rights' he called for in his January 1944 State of the Union address. Addressing the nation by radio, he outlined a set of economic rights for Americans that he called 'self-evident' for the postwar world, including the right to a job, adequate food and clothing, a decent home, adequate medical care, and freedom from domination by monopolies. 'We have come to a clear realization,' he said, 'of the fact that true individual freedom cannot exist without economic security and independence.'

Roosevelt died in April 1945, and his economic 'bill of rights' effectively died with him. But his New Deal reforms created an upward pressure on wages that grew stronger after the war, and helped deliver a growing share of US national income into the hands of ordinary Americans. This played a crucial role in the creation of a strong middle class in the early postwar period. Whereas the top-earning 1 per cent of Americans had captured fully 24 per cent of the national income in 1928, by the mid-1950s, their share had dropped dramatically to just below 10 per cent. With money much more widely diffused throughout the US economy in the postwar years, middle-class America had considerable buying power. As a result, corporations had plenty of incentive to invest in making products to sell to eager consumers.

Recent research has shown that, in addition to generating strong consumer buying power, a high degree of equality creates social and cultural conditions that are beneficial to economic growth. David Madland, director of the American Worker Project at the Center for American Progress, has noted that more equal societies, in which there is a strong middle class, have been shown to have higher levels of trust among citizens. Higher trust translates into economic gains because it reduces the amount of resources necessary for monitoring and policing transactions, and also makes people more optimistic, more likely to innovate and to experiment with new technologies and methods.[16] Similarly, strong middle-class societies seem to value education and to produce better systems of governance, with broader political engagement and better functioning bureaucracies. A 2008 study by US political scientist Frederick Solt showed that high levels of wealth concentration actually lead to wasteful government spending, as the wealthy are able to use their influence to win policies that are favourable to themselves but economically inefficient.[17]

This evidence reinforces the case that increased income equality was probably a key factor in the higher economic growth in the period following the Second World War in Britain and the United States. With the emergence of strong middle classes, both countries maintained robust consumer demand, as well as generating social and cultural attitudes that lead to higher economic growth. The period after the Second World War – with the influence of Keynesian economics and a commitment to wider sharing of economic gains – stands as a compelling example of the economic benefits of greater income equality.

A couple of additional points are worth highlighting here, because they run counter to the conventional wisdom.

First, as noted, this sustained period of growth after the Second World War happened at a time of unprecedented debt levels. Both in the US and Britain, national debt as a percentage of GDP was higher than it has ever been, before or since. There were prominent business voices on both sides of the Atlantic who insisted that this alone made additional government spending unwise, and likely to worsen the economic situation. Yet, refreshingly, those voices were ignored back then, as a new consensus – led by Keynes and the positive experience of activist wartime government – resulted in policies that substantially reshaped British and American society.

So what happened to that towering mountain of debt? In both countries, the debt remained intact, with neither government trying to repay it. But the debt was eventually dwarfed by the rapidly growing economies, shrinking as a percentage of rising GDP in both countries. The particularly strong economic position of the United States, which emerged as the dominant world power after the war, allowed the US to finance postwar reconstruction in Britain as well as throughout much of Europe. That aid, through the Marshall Plan, was classic Keynesian strategy, injecting government resources into a stagnant economy when the private sector wasn't willing or able to step up to the plate.

The second point worth highlighting is the existence of very progressive income tax systems in both Britain and the US throughout the postwar period. In the US, the top marginal tax rate was 70 per cent or higher throughout the postwar period; in the 1950s (during the administration of Republican Dwight Eisenhower) it actually rose to 91 per cent. Similarly in Britain, the top marginal rate was 75 per cent or higher throughout the postwar period, and hovered around 90 per cent during the 1950s and '60s.

Needless to say, these high marginal rates are out of whack with today's top rates – 35 per cent in the US and 45 per cent in Britain. According to today's conventional wisdom, high marginal tax rates hurt economic growth, by depriving high-income people (often, mistakenly, considered to be uniquely creative and productive) of sufficient incentive to work. If this were true, we would therefore expect the early postwar period to have been an era of poor performance among the elite. However, there is no evidence of this. The corporate managers and professionals in the postwar period seemed to perform as well or better than their counterparts today. Certainly, there was no demonstrable negative impact from the high taxes on economic growth. As noted, economic growth rates were strong in both the US and Britain throughout the high-tax 1950s, '60s and '70s.

Another common misconception is that the higher marginal tax rates that prevailed in the postwar period were largely theoretical, and that a vast array of loopholes and deductions allowed the rich to avoid actually paying them. This is simply not true. In fact, there were fewer loopholes and deductions in the postwar years, when the tax avoidance industry was still in its infancy compared to what it has developed into today. We will discuss this further in the final chapter.

By the 1970s, the rose of the postwar economic boom was beginning to wither in the face of strong bouts of inflation. It was not hard to identify the cause – sharp spikes in world oil and food prices precipitated inflationary bursts in the 1973–5 and 1978–80 periods.[18] However, for the first time, Keynesian economics no longer seemed to have a ready answer, especially when inflation became combined with stubbornly high unemployment. The return of such uncertainty had long been awaited by those who had never accepted Keynes and the social egalitarianism of the welfare state. When that uncertainty finally materialized, they were ready.

•   •   •

Ironically, it appears that Beveridge inadvertently helped undermine the welfare state when he offered a position at the London School of Economics in 1931 to an up-and-coming Austrian economist named Friedrich von Hayek.[19] At the time, Hayek was a bright young contributor to the so-called Austrian school, known for its advocacy of free markets and private property, and its fierce opposition to collectivism and state intervention. While Hayek's views were known in academic circles, it is unlikely that Beveridge, then the LSE director, would have had any idea of the key role Hayek would go on to play in Britain in undercutting support for the welfare state that Beveridge put such effort into creating.

At the LSE, Hayek provided a strong counter to the pro-welfare state positions advocated by prominent figures such as Richard Titmuss and T. H. Marshall.[20] A dedicated opponent of Keynesian economics, Hayek was entering the public debate just as the once-radical Keynesian school had become the new orthodoxy, leaving Hayek outside the mainstream.

Hayek was a central figure in a small international group of anti-Keynesian economists who met in Paris in 1938 in an attempt to revive the largely discredited school of pro-market economic liberalism. Those efforts were put on hold by the war, as successful wartime state planning left their free-market theories even further out of favour with the public. With the stunning wartime popularity of the Beveridge report, Hayek was going against the tide in 1944 when he published *The Road to Serfdom*, arguing, provocatively, that the overgrown British state would ultimately lead to German-style totalitarianism. The book sparked considerable controversy and public interest, even winning qualified praise from Keynes, and brought Hayek intellectual acclaim. But its fervent market-oriented ideas were out of sync with the times. Still, the book became a bible of the libertarian movement, keeping the flame of pro-market economics alive in an era dominated by Keynesian thought.

The Road to Serfdom also aroused interest among the economic conservatives at the University of Chicago, which published it and brought Hayek on a tour of the United States in April 1945. Energized by the support he received in the US, particularly in Chicago, Hayek decided to revive the anti-Keynesian efforts launched at the 1938 meeting in Paris by organizing an international forum of scholars committed to advancing free-market economics. While the ideas may have been out of vogue, free-market economics remained a cause dear to the hearts of the wealthy, and Hayek easily lined up ample financial support from Swiss industrialist Albert Hunold and members of the Swiss banking elite.[21]

Flush with cash, Hayek held the inaugural meeting of his forum at the spectacular Swiss mountain retreat of Mont Pelerin in the spring of 1947, attracting the major free-market theorists, including Milton Friedman of the University of Chicago and leading members of the Austrian school Ludwig von Mises and Karl Popper. After a decade of growing support for Keynesianism in official circles and among the public, Hayek was cautious about the prospects for reviving interest in anti-collectivist ideas. He made this clear at the Mont Pelerin Society's inaugural meeting, pointing out that there were no quick victories ahead. Instead, he set out his vision for a long, slow struggle to discredit Keynesianism and the welfare state. Key to this goal was to enlist the best minds – such as had come together at the Swiss retreat – for a marathon, twenty-year effort 'concerned not so much with what would be immediately practicable, but with the beliefs which must regain ascendance'.[22]

While the struggle ahead was indeed a long one, it wasn't lacking in financial support. Even during the war years, business funded a number of groups aimed at opposing industrial nationalizations and the drift towards the welfare state, including the Progress Trust, the National League of Freedom, and the Aims of Industry. Also important was an organization called the British United Industrialists, which was established towards the end of the war by Sir William Goodenough, chairman of Barclays Bank, and industrialist Robert Renwick (later Lord Renwick). So while the Mont Pelerin Society was focused on long-term efforts to change the intellectual mindset, these business organizations offered more direct, practical efforts to shape public views and lobby for pro-market choices. Probably most important of all was the network of think-tanks established by British farming entrepreneur Antony Fisher, whom Milton Friedman later credited with being 'the single most important person in the development of Thatcherism'.[23]

Inspired by Hayek's ideas after reading a *Reader's Digest* condensation of *The Road to Serfdom*, Fisher had considered going into politics to promote the free-market cause. But Hayek talked him out of it, explaining, Fisher later recalled, 'that the decisive influence in the battle of ideas and policy was wielded by intellectuals whom he characterized as the "second-hand dealers in ideas".' Hayek urged Fisher instead to form an academic research organization 'to supply intellectuals in universities, schools, journalism and broadcasting with authoritative studies of the economic theory of markets and its application to practical affairs'.[24]

Fisher followed Hayek's advice, establishing the Institute of Economic Affairs (IEA), which was to become hugely influential in shaping British public attitudes as the years went on. The IEA set out to spread the gospel developed by Hayek and other doyens of the Mont Pelerin Society. It focused on destroying the power of trade unions, a favourite theme of Hayek's. Another key focus for the IEA was promoting Milton Friedman's doctrine of monetarism, a variation of the old monetarist theories from the 1920s that gave priority to controlling inflation over maintaining employment, as the gold standard had done. The IEA also paid tribute to entrepreneurs, and their role in wealth creation. It's not hard to see why the IEA was able to attract substantial funding. In addition to financing from Fisher, who had become rich developing a broiler chicken business, there were more than three hundred donors who were keen to advance its pro-business agenda. Although Hayek moved to the US where he worked alongside Friedman at the University of Chicago throughout the 1950s, the IEA kept the ideas of both men alive and increasingly prominent in British academic and journalistic circles.

The IEA attracted support from key members of both the British Liberal and Conservative Parties, including a young Margaret Thatcher. By the early 1960s, when she held a junior ministerial post in the Ministry of Pensions, she was introduced to Ralph Harris and Arthur Seldon, who jointly ran the IEA, and who spotted potential in her uncompromising pro-market views. As a rising star in the Conservative Party in the late 1960s, Thatcher readily absorbed the detailed economic arguments developed by the IEA, which seemed to provide analytical support for her views and even push them further to the right. Ralph Harris (later Lord Harris of High Cross) introduced her to Friedman over an intimate dinner, during which they had an animated exchange, leaving them both enthused about the encounter. The IEA was also instrumental in introducing her to Hayek in 1975, shortly after she'd become Leader of the Opposition. After their half-hour meeting in the IEA boardroom, he is reported to have said simply: 'She's so beautiful.'[25]

The extent of Hayek's impact on Thatcher is perhaps best illustrated by her meeting with the Conservative Party research department around the same time. At the meeting, one of the researchers presented a paper making the case for the party to avoid the extremes of right and left. This was not at all what the new Conservative leader wanted to hear from the party's research staff. She signalled that clearly by interrupting the presentation, pulling a copy of Hayek's book *The Constitution of Liberty* from her briefcase, holding it up for all to see and then slamming it forcefully down on the table saying: 'This is what we believe!' She then proceeded to harangue the Conservative research staff on what was right for the British economy.[26]

As the IEA proved increasingly successful in establishing an intellectual infrastructure for conservative economics in Britain, Fisher embarked on a campaign to develop a wider network of think-tanks modelled on the IEA. He became involved, particularly on the fundraising side, in establishing the Fraser Institute in Vancouver, Canada. From there, he moved on to New York in 1977 to create the International Center for Economic Policy Studies (later renamed the Manhattan Institute), then to San Francisco in 1979 to establish the Pacific Institute for Public Policy. At the same time, Fisher helped develop the Centre for Independent Studies in Australia. He established the ATLAS Foundation to co-ordinate his international efforts, teaming up with another Mont Pelerin-inspired organization called the Institute of Humane Studies. By 1990, the ATLAS Foundation had grown to more than sixty think-tanks. Its director, John Blundell, described its mission thus: 'to litter the world with free-market think-tanks.'[27]

•   •   •

Meanwhile, in the US, a similar story was unfolding. In the wake of the 1929 Wall Street crash, business and financial interests had lost the prestige and influence they had previously enjoyed. To an extent that is hard to imagine happening today, the power of the business elite was at least partially curtailed during the 1930–70 period, as Keynesianism and the programmes of Roosevelt's New Deal won widespread support. Business attempts to challenge the new orthodoxy were largely unsuccessful. The American Liberty League, orchestrated and funded by the wealthy du Pont brothers in the 1930s, threw its support behind Republican Alf Landon in the 1936 presidential election, while Roosevelt openly attacked business interests as 'agents of organized greed'. After Roosevelt won one of the biggest landslides in US history, the American Liberty League quietly disbanded, and business largely retreated to the political sidelines.

The reticence of the business elite in fighting the profound changes ushered in by the New Deal was rebuked by Barry Goldwater (later the Republican presidential candidate) when he complained of 'scared-e-cat' businessmen in a 1939 editorial in the *Phoenix Gazette*: 'There isn't a businessman in this country today that does not fear the future status of our rising tax figure, yet he confines his suggestions for correcting the situation to his intimates who will agree with him.'[28] Even the Republican Party largely went along. Republican President Dwight D. Eisenhower, in a personal letter to his brother in 1954, reveals his own acceptance of the broad terms of the New Deal: 'Should any political party attempt to abolish social security, unemployment insurance, and eliminate labor laws and farm programs, you would not hear from that party again in our political history. There is a tiny splinter group, of course, that believes you can do these things. Among them are H. L. Hunt (you possibly know his background), a few other Texas millionaires, and an occasional politician or businessman from other areas. Their number is negligible and they are stupid.'[29]

But a group that Eisenhower regarded as negligible and stupid was soon to start reasserting itself. The Great Society reforms brought in by Lyndon Johnson in the 1960s – particularly the expansion of social security to include Medicare for the elderly – convinced a growing number of business leaders that the state was becoming far too involved in ensuring the well-being of the citizenry. They also felt they were losing ground to a broader movement that came out of the mass student protests against US involvement in Vietnam and 'corporate power'. The threat felt by business leaders is captured well in an eight-page memo written in 1971 for the US Chamber of Commerce by Lewis Powell, a prominent Virginia attorney who served on a number of corporate boards (and later on the US Supreme Court). The memo, which was to become highly influential in business circles, expressed a feeling of being under siege. It amounted to a manifesto warning business that 'The American economic system is under broad attack' and the assault was gaining influence 'from the college campus, the pulpit, the media, the intellectual community...and from politicians'. Powell echoed Goldwater's earlier condemnation of 'scared-e-cat' businessmen, urging them to 'stop suffering in impotent silence, and launch a counter-attack'.

Powell laid out a comprehensive plan for a counter-attack that bears an almost uncanny resemblance to what actually happened. He pointed out that business largely owned, funded or had influence over the key media, religious and academic institutions in society, and should use its leverage to counter what he perceived as the liberal, anti-business bias of these institutions. He advocated explicit business intervention in the political sphere, where he said the American businessman had become 'truly the forgotten man'. This had to be countered with concrete steps – expanding the 'role of lobbyist for the business point of view' – in order to regain political clout with governments. It was time, wrote Powell, for business to learn that 'political power is necessary; it must be used aggressively and with determination – without embarrassment and without reluctance which has been so characteristic of American business.'

Powell's manifesto reverberated powerfully within business circles, especially after it received national attention when it was leaked to syndicated liberal columnist Jack Anderson. The memo clearly touched a nerve, stirring some of the wealthiest interests in the country to re-engage politically. As historian Kim Phillips-Fein notes: 'Not all businessmen shared Powell's passions. But those who did began to act as a vanguard, organizing the giants of American industry.'[30] Along with Charles and David Koch, who inherited the massive Koch Industries oil empire, a number of America's biggest corporate dynasties came forward to inject massive funds into the cause of pushing the country sharply to the right.

The Olin family, owner of a giant chemical and munitions business, provided tens of millions of dollars to think-tanks, organizations and programmes at major universities aimed at inculcating right-wing ideas and policy solutions. Huge financial support for libertarian and conservative causes (and later the attempt to impeach Bill Clinton) also came from Richard Mellon Scaife, heir to the massive Mellon banking, aluminium and oil fortune. Joseph Coors, who had inherited the brewery fortune, described how he was 'stirred up' by reading the Powell memo and wondered why businessmen were 'ignoring a crisis'.[31] Coors was a key figure in establishing the Heritage Foundation, which was to become an influential promoter of radical pro-capitalist ideas as well as 'the Judaeo-Christian moral order'. It quickly attracted major corporate funding from Dow Chemical, General Motors, Pfizer Mobil, and the Chase Manhattan Bank.[32] The du Ponts, who had failed so notably with the Liberty League in the 1930s, were back in the game. Du Pont CEO Charles McCoy became one of the instigators of the Business Roundtable, an exclusive group of CEOs of leading US companies, who planned to use their economic clout to gain access to top government and congressional leaders.

The ample funds from wealthy families and corporations provided the seed money for a huge new infrastructure of organizations, think-tanks, publications and 'astro-turf' campaigns funded by the wealthy but designed to appear as grass-roots movements. With this massive effort to reshape the discourse and politics of America, the wealthy elite was investing in a deliberate long-term strategy – exactly what Powell had called for. Just as Hayek and the IEA had done in Britain, US conservative planners, with their ample war chests, were mapping out a slow, methodical and ultimately highly effective strategy to retake control of the American public debate.

• • •

In this thumbnail sketch of the counter-revolution against Keynesianism and the welfare state, we've highlighted the role of big money. Certainly, in both Britain and the United States, the forces that worked steadily and relentlessly to roll back the welfare state and the egalitarian gains of the early postwar period were well funded by wealthy interests who went on to benefit enormously from the adoption of more market-oriented policies after 1980. But, of course, these wealthy interests – and the economists who champion their agenda – never acknowledge self-interest as a factor in the formulation of conservative economic views. Rather, the case for embracing the marketplace and eschewing state-run social programmes is presented as intimately tied up with liberty. Hayek became the high priest of the conservative movement back in 1944 when he built the case that adopting the welfare state was nothing less than the 'road to serfdom'.

But it's difficult to avoid the suspicion that deep-down conservatives are actually just self-interested in arguing for the unleashing of market forces. As Galbraith memorably put it: 'The modern conservative is engaged in one of man's oldest exercises in moral philosophy; that is, the search for a superior moral justification for selfishness.' Certainly, it's not hard to imagine this in the case of immensely wealthy individuals, such as the multi-billionaire Koch brothers, whose oil interests have benefited from the campaigns they've funded to dismantle environmental controls and block action on climate change. It's perhaps harder to imagine pure self-interest being the dominant factor in the case of a scholar such as Hayek, who presumably could have made a name for himself in the academic world on either side of the ideological spectrum.

That said, it's fascinating to look at a recently discovered exchange of letters between Charles Koch and Hayek dealing with the subject of the US social security system. We might expect this 1973 correspondence – unearthed by investigative reporter Yasha Levine at the Hayek archive at Stanford University – to give us insight into the nature of their objection to this key programme of the US social safety net. Instead, we find them matter-of-factly discussing how Hayek could use the US social security system – so that the medical costs related to his gall bladder surgery would be covered – making it more financially attractive for him to accept a post at a Koch-funded think-tank in California.[33]

Nowhere do the two men reveal any embarrassment, awkwardness or even a slight sense of irony at the thought that they are planning to take advantage of a system that they have gone to great lengths to depict as the very antithesis of freedom. In his 1960 book *The Constitution of Liberty* – the one Margaret Thatcher slammed down on the table – Hayek devotes a whole chapter, entitled 'Social Security', to denouncing the moral and economic impact of this centrepiece of the modern welfare state. But, as we learn in his exchange with Charles Koch, Hayek had in fact chosen to pay into the US social security system while he was teaching at the University of Chicago in the 1950s.

This doesn't faze Koch, a committed libertarian who, along with his brother David, has for decades waged a campaign to dismantle America's social safety net (and who in recent years has been a key funder of the Tea Party movement). Upon discovering Hayek had paid into the US social security system, Koch – rather than being crestfallen at the moral failings of this guiding figure of the libertarian movement – is cheered by the thought that this will allow Hayek to cash in on the benefits of the modern welfare state: 'You may be interested in the information that we uncovered on the insurance and other benefits that would be available to you in this country,' writes Koch. 'Since you paid into the United States Social Security Program for a full forty quarters, you are entitled to Social Security payments while living anywhere in the Free World. Also, at any time you are in the United States, you are automatically entitled to hospital coverage.' Koch even helpfully enclosed a government pamphlet on how to apply for social security benefits. A government bureaucrat could hardly have been more helpful.

On one level, the letters could be read as simply a useful summary of the many excellent features of a social security system, and what a sensible and beneficial addition it is to the Free World. But since we know the identity of the correspondents, the question inevitably arises: why have these two men been so keen to dismantle a system that they clearly understand works well, helping millions of Americans with far fewer resources than they themselves have? The simple answer appears to be that they just don't care about anyone but themselves.

While it's a bit of a digression here, it's worth pondering the implications of this by considering the careful analysis of Harry G. Frankfurt, the distinguished chair of the Yale University philosophy department. In a thoughtful essay in *Harper's* magazine entitled 'Reflections on Bullshit', Frankfurt sought to develop a philosophical theory to distinguish between truth-tellers, liars and bullshitters.[34] In a nutshell, his argument, as it might apply here, is that those who assert that social security is a threat to freedom while enthusiastically taking advantage of its benefits, are not necessarily lying, they're simply disregarding the truth in order to advance their agenda.

Liars are people who deliberately tell untruths. Bullshitters, on the other hand, don't really care about the truthfulness of their assertions. When Koch discovered Hayek could qualify for social security, he wasn't horrified by the implications of this for Hayek's personal liberty, nor was he worried that this godfather of laissez-faire capitalism would end up on some private road to serfdom. It's hard not to conclude that the right's claims about the freedom-depriving nature of social security are nothing more than empty statements meant to advance a larger agenda. Neoliberals and libertarians seem to be simply pretending to be concerned about the political and economic effects they allege. In reality, they don't appear to care about these things at all.

When business interests insist that the path to freedom is through the elimination of social security – or that low tax rates on investors will lead to economic growth for all – they don't take these positions because they are misguided, uninformed, or even because they believe them to be true. They take them because – to put it in philosophical terms – they are greedy, manipulative bullshitters who are only concerned about maximizing their own wealth and power, or those whose interests they serve.

10
revamping the ovarian lottery

So triumphant have the rich been in recent decades that it's easy to lose sight of the fact that they weren't always so dominant. In the post-Depression era, from 1940 to 1980, their supremacy was greatly diminished because of progressive taxation, government regulation and labour empowerment. The result was a far more equal distribution of economic gains in the early postwar era, with a dramatic improvement in the financial security and well-being of ordinary citizens. But while the European countries (particularly the Nordic nations) have retained and even further developed this egalitarian model, the Anglo-American countries have largely discarded it, leaving tens of millions of their citizens economically vulnerable and with fewer prospects in life than their parents.

The economic equality achieved in that postwar era (and in the Nordic countries today) was an extraordinary accomplishment – unparalleled in modern Western history. In many ways, it can be seen as the culmination of centuries of political battles for a better deal for the common people, dating back to the Diggers and other early social movements that we looked at in Chapter Six. It also illustrates something that is often lost in the current debate – that the dominance of the rich isn't a law of nature. American author Sam Pizzigati, highlighting this obvious but routinely overlooked fact, documents the popular triumph over plutocracy in postwar America in a book appropriately entitled *The Rich Don't Always Win*.

What is striking is how little interest there is among politicians, economists and commentators in the remarkable advance in economic equality in the postwar era, and the possibility of replicating that achievement today. This lack of interest is particularly notable because, as discussed earlier, the 1940–80 period was also an era of sustained prosperity, suggesting that high taxes and government regulations are compatible with (even supportive of) economic growth. This potent combination of high levels of equality and high levels of economic growth are why the era is sometimes referred to as the 'Golden Age of Capitalism'. Why, then, do those shaping our economy show so little interest in reproducing a system that provided such significant benefits to such a large swathe of the population? Their answer would undoubtedly be that globalization has fundamentally changed things, that the postwar egalitarian society wouldn't be able to compete in the global economy. But then, once again, the Nordic countries expose the fallacy in such an argument.

This lack of interest – or even basic curiosity – is particularly remarkable in the case of economists. After all, they are professionals who presumably study the economy. Yet mainstream economists, while presenting themselves as committed to value-free science, have increasingly lined up with wealthy interests in recent decades. They have done this, Norbert Haring and Niall Douglas argue, by removing the consideration of power from the study of economics. In *Economists and the Powerful*, Haring and Douglas examine 'how we got from an economic science that treated relative economic power as an important variable and regarded the resulting income distribution as a core issue of the discipline, to a science that de-emphasizes power and does not want explicitly to deal with distributional issues'.[1] Indeed, mainstream economics today largely ignores the issue of power and scorns efforts to reduce inequality, confining itself instead to economic models focusing on consumer preferences within a laissez-faire economic system. As a result, economists, who enjoy great influence in public debate and the formation of policy, not only fail to examine how we might achieve a more equal society, they actually further the notion that such a goal is inappropriate.

But, as we've argued in this book, such a goal is both appropriate and urgently needed. Having command over economic resources is a vital element in freedom and empowerment in our society. The rich know this, which is why they guard their ample income and wealth so zealously. Through aggressive efforts in recent years, they have managed to put in place policies that have diverted an increasingly large share of national income towards themselves. This has had a negative impact on the lives of millions of other citizens, depriving them of basic material well-being and therefore the ability to participate fully in society. Even worse, it has led to a revival of plutocracy, undermining the broader public's ability to protect its own interests including even the viability of the Earth's ecosystems.

Fortunately, the tools for achieving a more equal society are available – through the tax system. The rich understand what a powerful instrument the tax system is in a democracy, and have therefore worked tirelessly to denigrate and vilify all taxes. By obscuring and distorting the issues around taxation, they have attempted to make the public regard taxes as the enemy. In particular, with the assistance of the economics profession, the wealthy have worked diligently to convince the public that raising taxes on the rich would somehow harm the public interest – even though the evidence powerfully suggests otherwise. Reclaiming the tax system as a powerful tool is thus a crucial first step towards reclaiming democracy and greater equality.

• • •

On the surface, it seems obvious that people would hate taxes. After all, taxes require people to hand over money. But then, there doesn't appear to be similar antipathy towards other things that require people to hand over money – such as grocery bills or the bill that arrives at the end of a restaurant meal. Of course, in these situations people are paying for goods and services that they receive. But taxes also pay for goods and services that people receive, and that are at least as essential to their well-being: an education, health care, pensions, police and fire protection, national security, roads, bridges, canals, libraries, museums, parks, sewer systems, refuse collection, food inspection, disease control, and so on. The success of the anti-tax lobby lies in its ability to separate taxes in the public's mind from these many services and necessities that taxes pay for, and which the public truly values.

These efforts, exemplified by Tax Freedom Day, simply omit the reality that citizens get things in return for taxes, and instead focus exclusively on the amount of taxes citizens pay. Tax Freedom Day – developed in the United States by the business-funded Tax Foundation and promoted in the UK by the Adam Smith Institute – is designated as the day of the year when the average family has earned enough to pay off its annual tax bill. Only then is the family considered to have stopped 'working for the government'. Does it follow, then, that for the rest of the year Britons will be working for Tesco, Debenhams, Amazon, Marks & Spencer and other places where they'll spend money?

Of course, it should be acknowledged that there is an important difference – people choose to shop at those stores while taxes are not optional. But the attempt by anti-tax lobbyists to present taxes as coercive obscures their essentially democratic nature. Taxes result from decisions made through the democratic system, in which we all have an opportunity to participate. Through the democratic process, we have decided to pay collectively for certain goods and services because we consider them important, and because if we paid for them individually on the open market, they'd cost a lot more and be much more difficult to provide. Rather than seeing taxes as a denial of freedom, we should regard them as an essential part of citizenship in a free and democratic society. Indeed, raising money collectively through taxation and then making collective decisions about spending it constitute the very basis of democracy. These are functions that are central to popular self-government.

It could be added here that the growing reliance of our public institutions on philanthropy – rather than on funding through the tax system – has had the effect of undermining popular self-government and democracy. Philanthropy has become increasingly important as tax revenues from the rich have declined, leaving hospitals, universities, museums, libraries and other vital public institutions strapped for cash and reliant on charitable donations from the rich. But collecting money from the rich through philanthropy is very different to collecting it from them in taxes. When money is collected through the tax system, it is the public who decides collectively how to spend it. When the rich donate money, it is they who make the crucial decisions about how and where the money will be spent, which institutions and causes will be helped and which will be neglected. Among other things, this has meant that causes primarily aimed at helping the poor and destitute have been neglected. Wealthy patrons have shown far less interest in building community centres, swimming pools or drug rehabilitation clinics in poor parts of town than in contributing to their alma maters or to hospitals or concert halls, where their names are often prominently emblazoned on buildings where they'll be seen by their peers.

Philanthropy also gives the wealthy considerable influence over the actual institutions they fund, further diminishing democratic control in society. This is particularly a problem with academic institutions, which have a central role to play in democracies as centres of critical thought where prevailing orthodoxies and power structures can be scrutinized and questioned.

The challenge to academic freedom – as tax revenues decline and public universities become more dependent on philanthropy – underlines the important role that taxes play in a democracy. This role, so little acknowledged today, was widely understood in earlier times, when taxes were regarded as a cornerstone of liberty and democracy. In the United States, the slogan 'no taxation without representation' became the rallying cry of the Revolutionary War, reflecting the connection the colonial rebels made between taxation and democracy. Similarly, Adam Smith, the eighteenth-century Scottish philosopher and founder of the classical school of economics, rejected suggestions put forward by some in his day that taxes were 'badges of slavery'. As he wrote in *The Wealth of Nations*: 'Every tax…is to the person who pays it a badge, not of slavery, but of liberty. It denotes that he is subject to government, indeed, but that, as he has some property, he cannot himself be the property of a master.'[2]

• • •

Key to the development and promotion of today's fierce anti-tax ideology was the emergence of a school of thought known as 'public choice theory'.

In essence, public choice theorists, borrowing from modern economic thought, take as their central premise that humans are motivated exclusively by personal self-interest, greed and material acquisitiveness. These theorists basically extend the assumptions of modern economic theory to the political sphere, insisting that all participants in the political process (voters, politicians, civil servants) are only interested in and capable of acting on their own self-interest. As critics Hugh Stretton and Lionel Orchard note, the public choice theorists have attempted 'to persuade people that material greed is, and will inescapably remain the single, natural dominant motive of their political, economic and social behavior'.[3] So the notion that a government could represent some sort of broad 'public interest' is deemed to be naive, even fraudulent. According to the public choice theorists, there is no overarching public interest, just a collection of individual desires and preferences.

With the notion of a broader public interest set aside like this, public choice theorists turn simply to maximizing the rights of the individual and limiting the power of government to interfere with the individual, particularly through taxation. They argue that government shouldn't be allowed to use the tax system for redistribution, since this enables the majority to pursue its own self-interest unfairly at the expense of the wealthy few. To prevent this, some public choice theorists in the US have argued for actual constitutional protections against majority rule in the field of taxation. Needless to say, many in the elite see much merit in this idea of effectively outlawing the masses from exercising their democratic power in this crucial area.

The impact of the public choice theorists has been significant. Although their writings are largely technical and remain obscure outside the academic world, they have provided apparent intellectual backing to bolster the conservative case for smaller government and lower taxes.

However, human needs are more complex and varied than public choice theory implies. Specifically, the theory fails to take into account our intensely social nature – an aspect of human behaviour that has been identified in decades of research in the social sciences, particularly psychology, anthropology and sociology. This highly social nature explains the tendency of humans to measure their success against others, to be acutely conscious of their status and rank in the social hierarchy. It also suggests that humans have a deep need for community. They naturally seek to relate to and be accepted by other people. They desire to belong to a larger community – whether family, clan, gang, club, social network or society at large – and as part of the group, will generally participate and contribute willingly.

The late economic historian and anthropologist Karl Polanyi argued that this social aspect is the most consistent feature of human behaviour and is clearly visible across continents and through time. By emphasizing the social aspect, Polanyi did not mean that people are unselfish. Humans are primarily concerned with their own welfare, just not exclusively so. But this focus on their own welfare doesn't mean that their motivation is mainly materialistic. On the contrary, Polanyi argued that the welfare of individual humans depends largely on their social relationships, and on the preservation and viability of their communities. This suggests that sustaining and strengthening those communities – by improving their social cohesion, maintaining their physical infrastructures, and protecting them against threats that can only be addressed collectively (such as global warming and other environmental disasters) – is ultimately as important to humans as their individual material accumulations.

Under the neoliberal dogma that has dominated Anglo-American society for several decades, these social and collective needs have been given short shrift, forced to take a backseat to the supposed dictates of the marketplace and the facilitation of individual wealth accumulation. But if social needs and the desire for viable communities are as deeply ingrained in humans as Polanyi and others suggest, this intense focus on personal material acquisitiveness may not be the great liberator it's purported to be. On the contrary, it may well be depriving humans of something very basic to their hard wiring as social beings.

While focusing on material acquisition seems utterly natural and normal to us, Polanyi noted that earlier societies throughout history typically gave top priority to other goals, such as worshipping religious figures, celebrating cultural icons, or honouring bravery on the battlefield. Until the emergence of capitalism in parts of the Western world in the early sixteenth century, the so-called 'economic motive' of material acquisition was simply one of many aspects of community life, and not one singled out for special attention. Indeed, until the eighteenth century, there wasn't even a separate word for 'the economy'; the material well-being of the community was treated simply as part of its overall well-being.

In traditional societies, the bonds of the community involved some sense of responsibility to others, a willingness to share to prevent members of the group from going hungry. While there were frequent periods of scarcity – caused by external threats such as war, pestilence or drought – the principle that everyone in the community should be free from hunger prevailed in traditional societies, according to Polanyi, 'under almost every and any type of social organization'.[4] Even in feudal societies, where peasants toiled on vast estates controlled by wealthy nobles, the peasants were entitled to certain 'common rights' that gave them access to sufficient land and resources to cover their basic needs (albeit at a very modest level).

This suggests that co-operation and sharing of resources – something that can be accomplished efficiently through a tax system – may be a natural tendency in humans, connected to our nature as social animals. Polanyi argues that, with the emergence of capitalism, there was a deliberate attempt to eliminate the long-established social practices of sharing and replace them with behaviour based on personal acquisitiveness. Whereas traditional and feudal societies had discouraged greed and materialism among the people on the grounds that they posed a threat to the common good, capitalism actively encouraged these traits, massaging them and cheering them on, indeed elevating them to the centrepiece and guiding principle of society. At the same time, the new capitalist system abandoned the traditional imperative of the social bond, to the point of actually allowing members of the community to go hungry. In fact, the threat of hunger became a deliberate strategy under capitalism, a means to prod peasants to work even under the horrific conditions in the new mines and factories (today we might call that a 'work incentive'). Breaking with centuries of history, capitalism introduced the concept of using scarcity and deprivation as a deliberate tool of social engineering and control.

Of course, capitalism is generally regarded in the West today as key to our evolution as a species toward a more advanced way of life. But Polanyi reminds us that capitalism, which was developed by the rising merchant class in seventeenth-century England, was especially brutal in its early stages and was not appreciated nor widely accepted for a long time. On the contrary, it was so dev-astating and disruptive to the lives of the vast majority of people that they attempted to resist it with whatever means they could, often tearing down hedges around the newly enclosed fields with pitchforks and hoes.

Resistance to unbridled capitalism went on in various forms for centuries, and still continues. Without this resistance, in which members of the public seek 'the protection of society', there would have been nothing to stop the most appalling abuses of the early days of capitalism, when young children were obliged to work all night in factories and mines or were stuffed up blackened chimneys to serve as human cleaning utensils. Polanyi describes the process that's taken place over the last few centuries as a 'double movement' in which each step implementing capitalism was countered by a determined effort by large numbers of people to protect themselves from the damaging effects of these changes.

While their actions didn't stop the entrenchment of capital-ism, their resistance did lead ultimately to the development of the modern welfare state, with its labour and social protections. This has certainly helped moderate capitalism's worst excesses, with some countries opting for more moderation than others. The progressive tax system has been a central feature of this welfare state, funding its programmes and distributing income in a more equitable manner than the market systems installed under capitalism typically allow. The welfare state and progressive taxation have gone a long way toward restoring the social dimension that raw capitalism shunts aside.

It is this bulwark of progressive taxation and welfare state protections that the neoliberals have moved aggressively to tear down. But their case rests on a flimsy premise: that human behaviour boils down to individual greed and acquisitiveness. Such a formulation flies in the face of the overwhelming evidence that humans are intensely social animals. As such, their desire to protect themselves and their communities from the full force of unleashed greed is at least as natural – and historically evident in the resistance to unbridled capitalism – as their endless desire to accumulate material possessions. Rather than elevating greed to a hallowed, iconic stature, as the neoliberal movement does, it would seem more in keeping with human needs to treat the impulse toward material acquisitiveness as simply one aspect of human behaviour – one that can release useful energy but that, unchecked, can cause great damage to the social fabric upon which so much human well-being relies. As the late British historian R. H. Tawney eloquently put it: 'So merciless is the tyranny of economic appetites, so prone to self-aggrandizement the empire of economic interest, that a doctrine which confines them to their proper sphere, as the servant, not the master of civilization may reasonably be regarded as…a permanent element in any sane philosophy.'[5]

●   ●   ●

Perhaps the most potent argument put forward by the anti-tax movement in recent years has been the notion that taxes are unduly coercive, that they amount to an assault on freedom.

Yet it was the lack of coercion involved in taxation that led the late Henry Simons, a founder of the Chicago School of Economics, to endorse the progressive income tax system. Simons' arguments on the subject have largely been ignored in recent years, but they are worth considering briefly here. Simons, who considered himself a libertarian and is still revered by many conservatives, defended progressive taxation as part of his strong belief in the merits of capitalism. He recognized that capitalism could only survive in a democracy if the general public benefited from it, and this involved redistributing its bounty, which otherwise ends up concentrated in the hands of the few.

Simons argued that progressive taxation was the best way to achieve the necessary redistribution – since it involved the least amount of government intrusion in the market. Taxes, after all, don't interfere with the market's ability to determine prices and to allocate resources through the price mechanism – key features of the market economy. They don't involve a government bureaucrat imposing measures that interfere with the basic elements of supply and demand. 'No fundamental disturbance of the whole system is involved,' noted Simons in his classic 1938 text *Personal Income Taxation*.[6] He elaborated on this theme later, in *Economic Policy for a Free Society*, emphasizing how progressive taxation achieves redistribution without impinging on freedom: 'What is important for libertarians is that we preserve the basic processes of free exchange and that egalitarian measures be superimposed on those processes, effecting redistribution afterward and not in the immediate course of production and commercial transactions.'[7]

It could be added here that taxation – and even heavy taxation of the rich – was supported by no less a conservative heavyweight than Adam Smith. This might come as a surprise since Smith's legacy has been largely appropriated in recent years by neoliberals. While they've managed to tear snippets out of context to present his *The Wealth of Nations* as a manifesto for unbridled capitalism, in fact

Smith was a philosopher who was wary of the social consequences of the emerging industrial capitalist system, and in particular the dangers of inequality. Throughout *The Wealth of Nations*, Smith consistently championed the rights of workers against the rights of merchants and industrialists. And he showed his cynicism toward business interests when he famously noted that 'people in the same trade seldom meet together, even for merriment and diversion, but that conversation ends in a conspiracy against the public'.

Far from rejecting the legitimacy of taxing earnings, Smith devoted much of *The Wealth of Nations* to a discussion of the best means of collecting taxes, and he repeatedly indicated a preference for shifting the burden off the poor and on to the rich. He strenuously objected, for instance, to a particular tax – common in his day – that was based on the number of windows in a house. 'The principal objection to all such taxes is their inequality, and inequality of the worst kind, as they must frequently fall much heavier upon the poor than upon the rich. A house of ten pounds rent in a country town may sometimes have more windows than a house of five hundred pounds rent in London; and though the inhabitant of the former is likely to be a much poorer man than that of the latter.'[8] Smith called for heavier highway tolls on luxury carriages than on freight wagons so that 'the indolence and vanity of the rich [can be] made to contribute in a very easy manner to the relief of the poor'. Indeed, although he wrote before the introduction of income taxes, Smith clearly anticipated and supported the idea of progressive taxation: 'It is not very unreasonable that the rich should contribute to the publick expence, not only in proportion to their revenues, but something more than in proportion.'[9]

●　　●　　●

Given the success of the conservative movement in directing public anger against taxes in recent years, it will only be possible to rebuild a properly progressive tax system once the self-serving arguments of the anti-tax zealots have been exposed, and an appreciation of the importance of taxation in a democracy is restored. The Occupy Wall Street movement and UK Uncut have begun this task.

It involves not so much creating a new way of thinking as reviving long-established notions of justice and democracy. While these notions have come under attack in recent years, they were originally championed by some of the leading thinkers of the modern age – including Adam Smith, John Stuart Mill and Oliver Wendell Holmes Jr – and were widely accepted in the Anglo-American countries throughout the early postwar years. In essence, taxes are about collectively creating things of value in a democracy. As Holmes, a former US Supreme Court justice, memorably put it: 'Taxes are the price we pay for civilization.' It could be added that they are also the price we pay for membership in the community and for citizenship in a democracy.

So those who try to cheat their way out of paying them should be treated with disdain, as antisocial members of the community. In recent decades, tax avoidance and even evasion have become socially acceptable. There's been a growing industry of tax professionals who push the envelope, coming up with ever more creative ways for clients to get around or subvert the law, including hiding assets offshore. What's striking is the lack of public outrage (until recently, at least) over this blossoming industry and its participants – both the professionals and the clients – who defraud the community of badly needed revenues.

While we're considering the need to change social attitudes, here's another attitude badly in need of change: the acceptance of excessive greed. Part of the credo implanted by the conservative business revolution of the last few decades has been a tolerance for, indeed an encouragement of, unlimited personal acquisitiveness. Rather than seeing extreme selfishness as boorish and antisocial, there's been a tendency to treat the most acquisitive among us as heroes and leaders, people to be featured admiringly in the media and celebrated on who's who lists of the rich and famous. This approval of greed has given corporate boards the green light to award ever larger bonuses to executives, and it has encouraged legislators to provide ever more generous tax savings at the upper end, with the idea that the tax system should reward these high-fliers.

And yet, such encouragement of greed – supposedly based on Adam Smith's notion that the pursuit of individual self-interest benefits all – is in fact a gross distortion of the broader vision of Smith, who was forceful in his indictment of the rich and the powerful. As Smith wrote in *The Theory of Moral Sentiments*: 'This disposition to admire, and almost to worship, the rich and the powerful, and to despise, or, at least, to neglect persons of poor and mean condition…is…the great and most universal cause of the corruption of our moral sentiments.'[10] Reviving a healthy contempt for excessive greed and extreme inequality – along the lines of Smith's critique – would help restore a saner approach to unwarranted wealth concentration, and provide an important social restraint on corporate boards and legislators.

While conservatives have done their best to erase the notion of society as a community, and taxes as a badge of citizenship, it is essential that we revive these potent ideas. Here, for instance, are two personal commentaries – one from a successful American businessman and one from billionaire author J. K. Rowling – that reframe the issue of taxation in a compelling way.

Martin Rosenberg, a New York-based software entrepreneur, explains why he is a supporter of the campaign to preserve the US estate tax:

> My wealth is not only a product of my own hard work. It also resulted from a strong economy and lots of public investment, both in others and in me.

225

I received a good education, and used free libraries and museums paid for by others. I went to college under the GI bill. I went to graduate school to study computers and language on a complete government scholarship, paid for by others. While teaching at Syracuse University for 25 years, my research was supported by numerous government grants – again paid for by others.

My university research provided the basis for Syracuse Language Systems, a company I founded in 1991 with some graduate students and my son Larry. I sold the company in 1998 and then started a new company, Glottal Enterprises. These companies have benefited from the technology-driven expansion – a boom fueled by continual public and private investment…

I was able to provide well for my family. Upon my death, I hope taxes on my estate will help fund the kind of programs that benefited me and others from humble backgrounds: a good education, money for research and targeted investments in poor communities. I'd like all Americans to have the same opportunities I did.[11]

And here's J. K. Rowling, who came from modest roots, explaining why she hasn't left Britain:

I chose to remain a domiciled taxpayer for a couple of reasons. The main one was that I wanted my children to grow up where I grew up, to have proper roots in a culture as old and magnificent as Britain's; to be citizens, with everything that implies, of a real country, not free-floating ex-pats, living in the limbo of some tax haven and associating only with the children of similarly greedy tax exiles.

A second reason, however, was that I am indebted to the British welfare state; the very one that Cameron would like to replace with charity handouts. When my life hit rock bottom, that safety net, threadbare though it had become under John Major's government, was there to break the fall. I cannot help feeling, therefore, that it would have been contemptible to scarper for the West Indies at the first sniff of a seven-figure royalty cheque. This, if you like, is my notion of patriotism.[12]

To these powerful commentaries, let's add a third. Here's John C. Bogle, founder of the Vanguard Group, nicely capturing the pointlessness of excessive greed:

> At a party given by a billionaire on Shelter Island, the late Kurt Vonnegut informs his pal, the author Joseph Heller, that their host, a hedge fund manager, had made more money in a single day than Heller had earned from his wildly popular novel *Catch 22* over its whole history. Heller responds: 'Yes, but I have something he will never have…Enough.'[13]

• • •

Here, then, are some key tax reforms that could go a long way to addressing the egregious overconcentration of income, wealth and power in the hands of the few.

The income tax should be made more progressive

We propose that a new rate of 60 per cent be applied to incomes above £300,000 and a new top rate of 70 per cent to incomes above £1 million. We are not dogmatic about these precise rates and thresholds. Our point is that the tax system is an appropriate instrument for achieving a more equitable distribution of income, and a more equal and just society. It is also an important tool for raising revenue. To achieve these goals, high marginal income tax rates should be applied to very high incomes.

Our proposed higher rates are clearly much higher than the present top rate of 45 per cent that kicks in at £150,000. We believe that this rate should be increased back up to 50 per cent, where it was when it was introduced by the Labour government in 2010. In addition, we propose adding the two additional rates (60 and 70 per cent, mentioned above) to very high income levels. These additional rates might seem unrealistic in view of the fact that there has been a huge political battle over whether the present top rate of 45 per cent should be abolished altogether. But, taking a longer view over the past seventy years, it is a top rate in the range of 40 to 50 per cent – not our suggested top rate of 70 per cent – that is anomalous.

Before Prime Minister Thatcher began the assault on progressive taxation in the 1980s, the top rate had been 70 per cent (or higher) for over four decades. Indeed, during the Second World War, the top rate rose above 95 per cent, and it remained around 90 per cent throughout the 1950s and '60s. When Thatcher came to power in 1979, her government's first budget reduced the top rate from 83 to 60 per cent. Then, in 1988, Thatcher largely gutted the progressive income tax by cutting the number of rates to just two – a basic rate of 25 per cent and a top rate of 40 per cent. Hence, from 1988 onwards, taxpayers paid 40 per cent tax on the next pound they earned, whether their income was £19,300 (in 1988) or £1 million.

The richest taxpayers won spectacular tax cuts under Thatcher. Now that Thatcherism has been largely discredited for the harm it inflicted on the typical family, there is no reason why low rates on the rich should be regarded as the baseline for serious discussion of the appropriate tax rates. Indeed, we are simply suggesting moving closer to the tax rates that prevailed during the 'Golden Age of Capitalism', that early postwar period of widely shared economic prosperity. And now, as then, the higher rates would only apply to a relatively small number of very high-income individuals, who can easily afford to bear a heavier tax burden. In 1975, for instance, when the top rate was 83 per cent, it applied to incomes over £20,000 (about £190,000 in today's pounds), substantially lower than the threshold to which we are suggesting a 60 per cent rate should be applied. We also note that our proposed higher rates are consistent with the recommendations of a committee of leading UK public finance scholars and tax practitioners who argued that 'tax schedules should never be set so as to cause such marginal rates of tax to exceed, say, 70 per cent'.[14]

It might seem curious to be arguing for a 70 per cent top rate when the government has recently contended that even the additional 50 per cent rate raised almost no revenue and for that reason the top rate was reduced to 45 per cent. The 50 per cent rate was originally expected to bring in about £2.5 billion a year in extra revenue. But a government study, produced under the Conservative-led coalition, found that the extra revenue actually collected was much smaller. The study concluded that reducing the additional rate from 50 to 45 per cent would only reduce the extra revenue by about £100 million a year.[15]

But the study, prepared by HM Revenue and Customs, appears to have been prepared to provide support for the government decision to reduce the rate to 45 per cent. It was based on incomplete data, and made lengthy arguments about the harmful effects of high taxes on economic growth. In fact, what the study really showed is that when individuals are given advance notice of a pending tax increase, they will arrange their affairs in order to receive as much of their income as possible before the increase comes into effect.

Indeed, as the study noted, there were just six thousand British taxpayers reporting incomes above £1 million when the higher tax came into effect – compared to sixteen thousand the year before. Much was made of this by the government and media commentators, who claimed it proved two-thirds of British millionaires had left Britain to avoid the higher tax rate.[16] In fact, what it showed was that rich taxpayers had shifted about £18 billion of their income to the earlier tax year, in order to avoid the higher rate. But avoiding tax by this kind of shifting is a strategy that only works once. In subsequent years, if the higher tax had been maintained, those taxpayers would have been unable to shift their income to a lower tax year. However, the Cameron government stepped in after only one year of the new additional tax, and reduced it from 50 to 45 per cent.

It has been estimated that reducing the additional rate to 45 per cent saves those earning over £1 million on average about £107,500 a year. This is a huge gift to the richest members of society, and one that seems particularly perverse at a time when the government is cutting benefits to low-income earners, disabled people, pensioners and families with children.

It's often argued that higher tax rates increase the incentive for individuals to engage in tax avoidance strategies. However, the evidence suggests that many people try to avoid taxes no matter what the rate. Indeed, the tax avoidance industry and the behaviour it promotes have grown much larger over the past thirty years, even as tax rates have fallen significantly. Surely, if tax avoidance is a concern, the rational response is tougher legislation to close tax loopholes and avoidance opportunities.

It's also argued that individuals might respond to higher tax rates by changing their real behaviour, such as by reducing their work effort or passing up on entrepreneurial opportunities. Here the research clearly suggests little connection.[17] There is no evidence that professional athletes put forth less effort when they were paid a fraction of what they're paid today. Nor is there evidence of stifled entrepreneurship during the decades when the top marginal tax rate reached 90 per cent. It bears repeating that during the four-decade period in recent UK history when the top rate was above 70 per cent, Britain experienced not only much greater income equality but also some of its highest rates of economic growth and lowest rates of unemployment.

It's also frequently argued that higher tax rates will cause high-income earners to migrate. But moving to another country is a significant decision that affects one's ability to maintain close relationships with family, friends and communities. Many people develop strong attachments to the country in which they and their family members were born, raised and prospered. It reflects an utterly impoverished view of human nature to imagine that people – other than a few zealots – make decisions about something as important as where they will live purely on the basis of the amount of taxes they might save. Besides, as discussed earlier, there's no evidence that the departure of wealthy individuals actually harms the overall community.

In proposing higher tax rates on the rich, we are not simply focused on maximizing revenue – although the evidence suggests that our proposed rates would raise a good deal of badly needed revenue.[18] More importantly, we are concerned with making the tax system an effective instrument for achieving a more equal and just society, and for avoiding plutocracy.

Furthermore, in proposing a higher tax rate for those earning above £300,000 and another for those earning above £1 million, we might make the obvious point that these are enormous incomes. Frankly, it is hard to imagine a person making £1 million a year deriving anything other than perverse satisfaction from receiving an additional pound. In feeling the need to cater to this overindulged class, government officials seem to have lost all sense of proportion.

Finally, even if these high rates only affect a small number of people, they make an important moral statement. They send a message that we are all essentially alike. While there are differences that are often interesting, no one is so special, or so obviously superior that he or she should have vastly more economic resources than everyone else. High tax rates on the rich also communicate that society regards extreme inequality as a danger to the public good, as something that, in the words of Henry Simons, is inherently 'unlovely'.[19]

Close the loopholes and remove the tax reliefs and allowances that now riddle the income tax system and almost exclusively benefit the rich

Imposing income taxes on high-income individuals can be especially challenging. They tend to have multiple sources of income and the resources to arrange their affairs to exploit every ambiguity in the law through sophisticated tax avoidance strategies. It's not surprising, then, that they are able to reduce their tax bills considerably. Figures from HM Revenue and Customs reveal that high-income earners often have very low effective tax rates – that is, the percentage of their incomes that they actually pay in tax. Of the ten thousand UK taxpayers who earned between £1 million and £5 million in 2010–11, three hundred paid less than 10 per cent of their income in tax; of the four hundred taxpayers earning between £5 million and £10 million, sixteen individuals paid less than 10 per cent in tax; and of those earning over £10 million, twelve people paid less than 10 per cent of their income in tax.[20]

In response to media reports of multi-millionaires paying lower rates of tax than their gardeners, the coalition government proposed in 2012 to cap the benefits of tax relief measures for high-income individuals. The proposed cap would limit the total saving individuals could receive from various tax relief measures to £50,000 or 25 per cent of their annual income, whichever is higher. But a better solution would be simply to abolish many of these tax breaks. Most of them don't serve any pressing national priority, and those that do would be better achieved through direct government payments or grants, which are more visible to the public.

One tax break commonly used by the rich is the deduction for charitable contributions. Although it was originally to be included in the proposed cap, the government quickly backed down in the face of intense pressure from wealthy individuals and charities. The charitable deduction may appear to be in the public interest, but it includes some remarkably inequitable features. Oddly, it provides no benefit to almost 90 per cent of charitable donors, who have low incomes and pay the basic tax rate of 20 per cent. Instead of providing a tax rebate directly to these donors, the government rebates the 20 per cent tax they paid directly to the charity. Donations by high-income taxpayers also attract this 20 per cent rebate for the charity, but in addition high-income taxpayers can claim a personal deduction from the higher tax rates.

This means that when basic-rate taxpayers donate to charity, their total donation is comprised of, in effect, 80 per cent of their own money and 20 per cent of the government's money. However, when donations are made by those earning £150,000 or more, the donation is comprised of, in effect, only 55 per cent of their own money and 45 per cent of the government's money. Why should a donation from a high-income individual attract more government funds than a donation from a low-income individual?

The tax deduction for charitable contributions allows wealthy individuals, in effect, to decide how the public's money is spent, since they get to direct where the money they are saving in taxes will go, whether it will, for instance, be directed to their alma mater or their favourite hospital, museum or concert hall. This allows the wealthy to direct the spending of hundreds of millions of pounds of other people's money, over which the government has no control, and for which there is no public accountability or transparency. In addition, high-income donors receive enormous public recognition and adulation for their charitable donations, often in the form of having important public buildings named after them, which gives legitimacy to their concentrated economic power. Repealing the tax deduction for charitable contributions would not prevent the rich from giving to charities. It would simply mean they would have to give their own money, instead of using some of the public's.

Many of the tax breaks are for investments and various forms of income from capital. For example, there are tax concessions for venture capital trusts, enterprise investment schemes, individual savings accounts and capital gains.

As a result, income from capital – which is received disproportionately by the rich – is taxed at lower rates than income from labour. Interestingly, this was not the case for most of the history of the British income tax system. On the contrary, capital was traditionally taxed more heavily than income from labour (or 'earned income'). Indeed, until Margaret Thatcher abolished it in 1984, there was a 15 per cent surtax on income from capital. This was justified on a number of grounds, including that earned income is generally more precarious than investment income and that it involves the sacrifice of leisure time. Above all, the favoured treatment for earned income was seen as a recognition of the dignity of work.

That respect for the dignity of work is no longer reflected in the tax system. While earned income is taxed at a basic rate of 20 per cent and a top rate of 45 per cent, capital gains are taxed at the lower rate of 18 per cent (for taxpayers paying the basic rate) and 28 per cent (for higher-income taxpayers).

This favourable tax treatment leads high-income taxpayers to try to convert their earned income into capital gains. Those who have been most successful at this ploy are private equity, venture capital and hedge fund managers. Typically, the managers of these funds are paid an annual management fee of 2 per cent of the fund's net assets, plus a 20 per cent performance fee based on the fund's profits for the year. This performance fee, or 'carried interest' as it is sometimes called, can amount to millions of pounds. The managers of these funds have persuaded the government to allow them to classify this performance fee as a capital gain, even though it is simply income earned for a job performed and should be taxed as regular earned income.

The ostensible purpose of the lower capital gains rate is to compensate investors for the risk they take in investing their capital. But private equity and hedge fund managers aren't investing their own capital. They're investing other people's capital. They're simply money managers, being paid for the service of handling other people's money. If their fund loses money, they don't suffer losses, as investors do.

The fund managers insist that their compensation is still very risky; while some deals may lead to huge profits, others prove disastrous. True. But risk is hardly confined to fund managers. Politicians can find themselves out of work after an election; a TV anchor can get fired if ratings plunge; a Hollywood star can find work dries up as he ages. At lower income levels, the risks are far larger. Indeed, vast swathes of the economy could be designated as risky for those needing to earn a living. The sort of stable, lifelong jobs that were common a generation ago have been largely replaced by contract or part-time work, with little or no security. A lay-off can mean the loss of the family home or health benefits, or even destitution – far more serious plights than anything likely to befall a hedge fund manager. (For that matter, no one ever seems to argue for special low tax rates for the real risk-takers among us – miners, oil rig workers, acrobats, fire fighters, and window washers working on tall buildings.)

There's a larger question of whether capital gains – even real ones – should ever be taxed at lower rates. On the face of things, the lower rate seems patently unfair. Why should someone earning income by investing her fortune be taxed at a substantially lower rate than those earning income from the sweat of their brows or from using skills they've spent years acquiring?

The fairness argument has essentially been set aside, however, as business has relentlessly promoted the notion that such preferential treatment is necessary to coax those with capital to invest it. But do investors really need coaxing? Billionaire Warren E. Buffett, one of the world's savviest investors, doesn't think so. 'I have worked with investors for sixty years and I have yet to see anyone – not even when capital gains rates were 39.9 per cent in 1976–77 [in the US] – shy away from a sensible investment because of the tax rate on the potential gain,' Buffett argues. 'People invest to make money, and potential taxes have never scared them off.'[21]

Of course, a higher tax rate might discourage investors from making foolish investments in unpromising enterprises. Alan S. Blinder, economics professor at Princeton University and former vice chair of the US Federal Reserve, points out that the lower capital gains rate actually encourages people to make investments that they might not otherwise make without tax incentives. 'The government thus induces people to make bad investments, which is a good way to run an economy into the ground,' says Blinder. 'Come to think of it, that's just what the old Soviet Union did. It invested copiously, but badly.'[22]

Our business culture tends to portray investors as modern-day heroes who put their hard-earned capital into worthy high-risk ventures that lead to ground-breaking discoveries that enrich the lives of all of us. Sadly, the vast majority of investments don't fit into this category (and those that do qualify for additional tax incentives). Rather, as former mutual fund manager John C. Bogle notes, 'most capital gains are made from gambling in the stock market.'[23] So the ultimate function of the special low rate on capital gains is to save our wealthiest citizens billions of dollars a year on their winnings in the City casino.

Of course, reducing the special deductions that permeate the tax system won't prevent the well-to-do from avoiding tax. The small army of lawyers and accountants who make their living advising wealthy clients will come up with new tax avoidance strategies.

In response to public outrage over several high-profile cases of tax avoidance, the government proposed new legislation in 2012 to prevent tax avoidance transactions. However, the new rules were poorly designed and likely to be ineffective. In particular, they called for the government to appoint a panel of experts to provide advice to the courts in considering tax avoidance cases. The advisory panel would almost certainly consist of private-sector tax lawyers, accountants and business people – the very people who devise and promote tax avoidance schemes. It is outrageous to suggest that the courts should be required to listen to advice from this self-serving group.

Finally, there are no penalties in the proposed legislation for those who engage in aggressive tax avoidance, other than having their schemes set aside and having to pay the appropriate tax. There should be strict penalties for those who deliberately understate their income to avoid tax, as well as penalties for those who promote aggressive avoidance schemes. The tax avoidance profession, whose activities do great harm to the public good, should be treated more like the rogue industry that it is.

Support international efforts to clamp down on tax havens; begin by reforming the laws and practices that make the UK one of the world's most notorious tax havens

When all other arguments fail, the fallback position argued by people opposed to higher taxes on the rich is simply this: they will move their assets offshore to a low-tax or no-tax jurisdiction. With this threat, they take control of the chessboard.

Or do they?

An estimated fifty to sixty countries, by providing a shroud of secrecy over all banking activities, have deliberately structured their tax and banking laws to provide a safe haven for the rich and their wealth. Among the better known are the Cayman Islands, Bermuda, Panama, and the Channel Islands of Jersey and Guernsey, as well as Switzerland and Liechtenstein. Although many are small, exotic islands that conjure up sunny images of the good life, tax havens actually inflict incalculable harm on the world.[24]

By depositing their assets in tax haven banks, the world's wealthy are able to hide their assets from tax authorities in their own country.

Tax havens thus facilitate a wide range of clearly objectionable outcomes – including drug and human trafficking and other forms of organized crime, embezzlement and bribery. In addition, tax havens help terrorists move untraceable funds around the world; they allow individuals to escape from professional, parental and other legal obligations; they distort world trade and investment flows; and they exacerbate financial crises by making much of the global financial system invisible. Over the past few decades, the use of tax havens has been the common denominator in almost every large money laundering operation, Ponzi scheme, financial crisis, mega commercial fraud, and large accounting and business scandal.

And, of course, they facilitate tax evasion by wealthy individuals and multinational corporations. This evasion is particularly catastrophic for poor countries, where corrupt politicians and local ruling elites make off with billions of dollars of desperately needed revenue and assets. While there are no precise figures for this confiscation, it is conservatively estimated that the annual loss to low-income countries as a result of tax havens amounts to about £77.5 billion – more than the worldwide foreign aid these countries receive. As John Christensen, a founder of the Tax Justice Network, bluntly put it: 'the time has come for the world to wake up and do something about the fact that tax avoidance, tax competition and tax havens cause poverty.'[25]

Even in developed countries, the effect of tax havens is highly destructive. The tax evasion they facilitate dramatically reduces revenues for public services. In economic downturns, this leads to deficits and austerity measures, which hit the poor the hardest. The Euro crisis is in part due to tax evasion by wealthy elites in Italy, Spain and Greece. George Papandreou, the former Greek Prime Minister, claimed that tax havens contributed greatly to Greece's dire financial situation: 'I know this, Greece is suffering from this [the flow of money to tax havens]. Had this alone been tackled, Greece would have most likely never have needed a bailout. Yet

Europe, the G8, G20, the banking system despite my pleas as prime minister, despite token reference in our council of G20 decisions, have done nothing to change this.'[26]

In all countries, tax havens relentlessly shift the tax burden from dishonest to honest taxpayers; from capital to labour; from large multinationals to small local businesses, and from wealthy citizens to those in the middle- and low-income range.

It is estimated that a third of the world's GDP is channelled through tax havens and more than half of the money passed around the globe each day moves through accounts in secrecy jurisdictions. About three million global corporations with no identifiable owner are located in secrecy jurisdictions.

In 2012, the Tax Justice Network, an independent organization that promotes transparency in international finance, published what is widely regarded as the definitive report on the amount of the world's unreported private financial wealth held through tax havens, *The Price of Offshore Revisited*. Written by James Henry, former chief economist of McKinsey & Company, the report estimates that at least £13 trillion and perhaps up to £20 trillion is held in tax havens. According to Henry's calculations, £6.1 trillion of the wealth held offshore is owned by only ninety-two thousand people, or 0.001 per cent of the world's population. Those in the top 0.14 per cent, who essentially make up the global elite, hold almost half their wealth (about £12.5 trillion) in tax havens. If that wealth were subject to taxation, it would generate revenues of at least £120–£175 billion a year.

Among other things, assets hidden in secrecy jurisdictions are not taken into account in the official statistics on inequality. As a result, the statistics (including those used in this book) inevitably understate the degree of inequality and wealth concentration at the top. Since the use of tax havens has grown explosively over the past thirty years, the rise in inequality in recent decades is actually even more dramatic than the official statistics suggest.

Given the damage inflicted by tax havens, it's worth asking why the world's richest nations have tolerated them. The answer, of course, is that many of their own wealthy, powerful citizens benefit from them, and have used their considerable influence to prevent any clampdowns. Furthermore, a number of rich nations have attempted to profit from the inflow of illicit capital – and no country has done so more than the United Kingdom.

Indeed, among the rich countries, the UK is by far the most tolerant of tax havens. Wealthy and influential members of Britain's economic elite have a long history of exploiting tax havens to dodge British tax laws. The Prime Minister's own fortune is in part attributable to tax havens. As the *Guardian* reported, 'David Cameron's father ran a network of offshore investment funds to help build the family fortune that paid for the prime minister's inheritance.'[27] The UK's top twenty companies have more than a thousand subsidiaries in offshore tax havens.[28] An investigation of the use of tax havens found that sixty-eight MPs and peers were either directors or had a controlling interest in businesses with links to tax havens.[29] These Parliamentarians have influence over tax and financial regulations in relation to tax havens. Conservative Party treasurer Lord Fink admitted that, when the Tories were in opposition, he lobbied to make domestic tax laws even more like those of offshore tax havens so that British hedge funds and other businesses would not have to set up offshore operations in order to avoid tax.[30]

Over the past few years, the UK corporate tax rules have been continually changed to reduce the taxes paid by multinationals. Yet the government has failed to enforce even these looser corporate tax laws. The multinational giant Starbucks, for instance, has avoided taxes in the UK by paying large royalties to a subsidiary located in a tax haven. So, despite racking up sales of more than £3 billion at seven hundred stores in the UK, the coffee mega-giant has paid a meagre £8.6 million in UK corporate income tax since 1998.[31]

Furthermore, the UK's tax rules for 'non-domiciled' individuals actually encourage the use of tax havens by the world's wealthiest citizens. Indeed, the rules effectively turn the UK itself into a tax haven. Most countries tax their residents on all income they receive, whether from sources inside or outside the country. But the UK's 'non-dom' law permits foreigners to reside in Britain (while maintaining an official domicile elsewhere) and not pay tax on income generated from assets held outside the country. This means that wealthy foreigners can place all their assets in a corporation or trust in an offshore tax haven, and legally avoid tax entirely on the income generated. In recent years, the UK government has imposed an annual fee on those claiming 'non-dom' status. But at the annual rate of £50,000, the fee amounts to mere pocket change to the global billionaires residing in Belgravia, Mayfair, Knightsbridge, Notting Hill and Chelsea. The 'non-dom' law allows Saudi princes, Greek shipping magnates, Russian oligarchs, Indian steel tycoons and billionaires of all kinds to live in London and pay almost no tax.

The UK has also been deeply implicated in tax haven activity worldwide through its close connection with well-known tax haven jurisdictions. Britain's Crown Dependencies, the Channel Islands of Jersey and Guernsey and the Isle of Man, are well-known secrecy jurisdictions. Many of its Overseas Territories, remnants of the British Empire, such as the Cayman Islands and the British Virgin Islands, are notorious tax havens.

Two UK-based independent organizations, Christian Aid and the Tax Justice Network, have published a Financial Secrecy Index that ranks countries on the basis of their accommodation of tax evaders through secrecy provisions. In the most recent ranking, the UK itself was in thirteenth position among seventy-three countries, but the authors note that if the entire British network were considered, it would easily be ranked as the world's number one secrecy jurisdiction. In his book *Treasure Islands: Tax Havens and the Men Who Stole the World*,[32] Nicholas Shaxson tells the story of how the UK became the centre of a web of tax havens in the 1950s in a deliberate attempt to funnel illicit funds from the crumbling British Empire to the City of London.

While it's impossible to estimate accurately the revenue loss from granting non-domicile status to the super-rich living in London, it probably amounts to billions of pounds a year[33] – an unconscionable loss at a time when ordinary UK citizens are being subjected to austerity measures to reduce the deficit. Presumably, the policy has been maintained because of the political influence of the fantastically wealthy non-doms, who have reportedly contributed millions of pounds to political parties. Notoriously, the billionaire Lord Ashcroft, deputy chair of the Conservative Party and one of its large donors, was obliged to admit that he filed his tax returns as a non-domicile.[34]

The good news is that there is growing interest, even inside governments, in clamping down on tax havens. In 2010, the US Congress passed a sweeping law (the Foreign Account Tax Compliance Act or FATCA) that will force all foreign financial institutions to report all assets held by their US clients to US tax authorities.

The law, which is scheduled to come into effect in 2014, is a bold step towards undermining tax havens. But what is needed is a global system in which all financial institutions would be obliged to know the real owner of the money they are handling, and would be required to report that information to relevant tax authorities. This idea of imposing financial disclosure requirements on banks worldwide was pioneered by US tax scholar Michael J. McIntyre and has been promoted internationally by the Tax Justice Network.

Here's how it would work: all financial institutions, whenever they make any sort of payment to a client, would be required to report that payment to the tax authorities of the country where the client resides. The report would be automatic, in electronic form, and would include a unique number to identify the client.

That way, governments around the world would be notified of all payments made to their wealthy citizens and be able to tax them accordingly – in the same way that governments receive notification from their domestic banks about payments to citizens within the country and use that information to verify the tax returns of those citizens. Indeed, the proposal is simply to extend to the international arena a system that has long worked well domestically in many countries. The international system could be enforced by an existing body such as the World Trade Organization, the Bank for International Settlements or the International Monetary Fund.

The scheme may sound ambitious, but it is in fact no more complicated than the international system of passports, which works well and with few compliance problems. Each passport has a unique identification number. Every time a person crosses a border, her number is swiped into a computer, which instantly discloses information about her. Transmitting an electronic record of all payments made by all banks would be no more complicated than that.

It turns out that, among the benefits of the computer age, are not only video games, but also the easy tracking and taxation of the gigantic fortunes of the world's billionaires. People wanting to conceal income from authorities would then find it no easier to move money undetected around the world than to travel without a passport.

Checkmate.

Support the international implementation of a Financial Transaction Tax, sometimes referred to as the 'Robin Hood Tax' or the 'Tobin Tax'

The idea of curbing financial speculation by imposing a tax on financial transactions was first proposed by John Maynard Keynes in 1936 during the Great Depression. His purpose wasn't raising revenue, but rather deterring financial speculation; as he put it:

'mitigating the predominance of speculation over enterprise'.[35] A variation of Keynes's idea was proposed in 1972 by Nobel Prize-winning economist James Tobin.

The financial speculation that Keynes and Tobin were trying to curb was small stuff compared to the immense, high-tech free-for-all of financial speculation that exists today, with its power to quickly destabilize the world economy. The rise of the computer over the past two decades has enabled lightening-speed, high-volume trans-actions largely to replace the traditional trading between individual buyers and sellers haggling in person over price on the floor of stock exchanges. Now powerful computers send out millions of orders per second. In this world of 'High Frequency Trading' (HFT), time is measured in milliseconds – that is, one-thousandth of a second. Accordingly, trading houses have paid to relocate their computers next to stock exchanges in order to reduce the time of electronic transmission. Hedge funds based in France have moved their computers to London, while Goldman Sachs in New York moved its computers next to the NASDAQ. 'It's become a technological arms race, and what separates winners and losers is how fast they can move,' noted Joseph M. Mecane, executive vice president of Euronext, which operates the New York Stock Exchange.[36]

This computer-driven trading, which was mostly unknown even a decade ago, has fundamentally altered the nature of finan-cial markets. The rapid-fire computer systems are able to scan vast market data to detect the slightest fluctuations in price. They can spot trends, change course and issue new orders all in a matter of milliseconds, allowing them to gain a slightly more favourable price than those trading a split-second later. Although the advantage may be only a cent or two, the compounded advantage over millions of trades can add up to multi-million-dollar profits.

This high-speed computer trading favours financial speculation and limits the ability of actual investors to participate in any mean-ingful way. Indeed, it is impossible for humans to keep up or even see what's going on. The computers are often programmed further to confound human competitors by issuing millions of orders at once and then almost simultaneously cancelling large numbers of them, thereby flooding the market with 'toxic' quotes aimed at disguising the true strategy behind the orders.

It's not hard to see how this HFT encourages market volatility, exchange rate and stock price distortions, and excessive risk-taking – all things that destabilize markets, contributing to financial crashes like the one in 2008.[37] But HFT has already become deeply entrenched and largely beyond the reach of regulators. One promising option for curbing it would be a Financial Transaction Tax (FTT), which would constantly cut into its small profit margins.

The FTT is a very tiny tax – as little as a 0.01 per cent or 0.1 per cent – per transaction. This would have no impact on serious long-term investment, but would eat into the profitability of rapid, high-volume trading. For instance, an investor buying £1 million worth of stocks as a serious long-term investment would be undeterred by paying a one-time $100 FTT on such a large investment that might well be held for a number of years. But a hedge fund buying the same amount of stock, and holding it for less than a second, would face the identical $100 cost, and would face it again on every new transaction with that money, with potentially multiple transactions every second. Ross P. Buckley, a professor of international finance law at the University of New South Wales in Australia, argues that an FTT would make 'the ultra-short-term trade, and much high frequency trading, unprofitable'[38]

Furthermore, it would be easy to administer, since the tax could be collected electronically as part of the computer transaction. The same computer revolution that makes possible the reckless speculative world of HFT also makes possible the easy collection of an FTT. The International Monetary Fund reported in August 2011 that an FTT 'is no more difficult and, in some respects easier, to administer than other taxes'.[39]

Certainly, the idea of an FTT is brilliant and appealing: impose a tax so small that it would have little or no impact on serious investors but would amount to a million pinpricks in the hides of those using computer-driven trading techniques, which have helped turn financial markets into wildly gyrating, high-risk casinos. Some critics of the FTT have argued that the tax would end up falling on ordinary people. Buckley disputes this. He insists that, on the contrary, ordinary people would benefit from the greater stability and efficiency that an FTT would bring to markets. The real victims of the tax would be the big financial players. 'Most short-term trades are initiated by hedge funds, and hedge-fund-like proprietary trading desks of the major banks,' writes Buckley. 'Accordingly, this tax will impact the profits of hedge funds and many of the major banks.'

In doing so, it would take a bite out of the financial sector – something that is long overdue. As the respected US tax commentator Lee A. Sheppard observes, an FTT would hit those in the financial sector who were bailed out after the financial crash with taxpayer money. 'Some of it should be clawed back,' she argues, pointing to the FTT as an effective instrument. Sheppard insists that an FTT would drive up the cost of derivatives trading, thereby acting as a proxy for regulation in this largely unregulated domain. As a result, an FTT would likely help shrink the bloated financial sector, which has increasingly been drawing capital and talent away from productive enterprises. Indeed, a recent study by two economists at the Bank for International Settlements, the self-regulating arm of the banking industry, concluded that a large financial sector can act as a drag on a country's economic growth.[40]

And then, of course, there's the benefit of the revenue raised by an FTT – potentially billions of dollars worldwide a year, even if the tax has the desired effect of discouraging a lot of speculative trading. Indeed, although the main goal of the tax is to discourage financial speculation, most estimates suggest that the tax would also generate considerable revenues. It has been estimated, for instance, that a US financial transaction tax could raise up to $175 billion a year – even if the total number of trading transactions was cut in half.[41]

It's hard not to love the FTT: it could raise billions of dollars a year from financial speculators, hampering their ability to destabilize markets, while leaving genuine investors unharmed – like a miracle drug that targets cancerous cells while leaving the healthy surrounding tissue undamaged.

The spectacular potential of the FTT makes it a huge crowdpleaser among the public. Not surprisingly, however, it has prompted fierce resistance from the financial community, which exerts great influence over government policy. This no doubt explains the strong opposition to the tax from governments in countries with powerful financial sectors, notably the UK and the US. The UK's opposition was sufficient to derail an ambitious plan, which gained traction in early 2012, to implement an FTT throughout the twenty-seven-state European Union. However, by the autumn of 2012, ten EU nations – including France, Germany, Italy and Spain – were taking steps towards proceeding with the idea on their own, in the hope that other nations would join later. If applied across the EU, an FTT would bring in an estimated £46 billion a year, thereby obliging the banking sector to make a far more significant contribution to public treasuries.

There is even some high-level support for the tax in the United States. In the spring of 2010, Obama himself is reported to have said during a high-level discussion of the tax, 'We are going to do this!' However, Lawrence Summers, director of Obama's National Economic Council, apparently convinced Obama otherwise.[42] Treasury Secretary Tim Geithner, with his close ties to Wall Street, has been a strong opponent. But by the autumn of 2012, there was growing support among influential Americans for taxing financial transactions, with the idea endorsed by Bill Gates and John C. Bogle, by Nobel Prize-winning economists Paul Krugman and Joseph Stiglitz, as well as by mainstream editorial boards at *The New York Times*, *Boston Globe* and *USA Today*.

There is certainly a compelling case for an FTT – a case that has virtually universal appeal outside the financial community, particularly in the wake of the 2008 financial disaster and the ongoing recession and austerity. 'This tax is an idea that has come of age,' wrote a thousand economists in a letter to the G20 finance ministers in April 2011. 'The financial crisis has shown us the dangers of unregulated finance, and the link between the financial sector and society has been broken. It is time to fix this link and for the financial sector to give something back to society...Given the automation of payments, this tax is technically feasible. It is morally right.'[43]

Repeal the inheritance tax, and replace it with a genuine, progressive inheritance tax

An effective inheritance tax is a crucial tool in limiting the dynastic power of enormously rich families.

As unequal as the distribution of income is in the UK, the distribution of wealth is even more unequal. Whereas the top 1 per cent capture about 14 per cent of all income, they hold fully 28 per cent of total personal wealth. And the concentration of wealth has been increasing in recent years, almost doubling since 1988, when the top 1 per cent held just 17 per cent of total wealth.

The UK has a long history of taxing the transfer of property at death. Since 1694, Britain has levied taxes in various forms on the value of a deceased's estate. The current tax, put in place by the Conservative government in 1986, is known as an inheritance tax, but, like its predecessors, it is calculated on the estate of the deceased. We propose moving to a genuine inheritance tax, providing a larger exemption for small inheritances and imposing higher rates on very large inheritances.

The current tax is so poorly designed that, for the very rich, it is essentially a voluntary tax. Theoretically, the tax is levied on all estates above the threshold of £325,000 at a flat 40 per cent rate. However, as long as a person passes her wealth to the next generation seven years before death, the tax can be completely avoided. Moreover, one can obtain relief from the tax by investing in certain kinds of assets, such as family and private business, or agricultural and forestry land, as well as by setting up trusts. As a result of these exemptions, wealthy people are largely able to avoid paying the inheritance tax.

Indeed, most of the revenue collected under the tax is paid by moderately well-to-do people who are hit by the relatively low threshold and tend to be less financially flexible and less sophisticated in their tax avoidance strategies. This has provided the very rich with a large constituency of political allies in their ongoing battle against the tax.

The case for taxing inheritances is similar to the case for a more progressive income tax, except even stronger. As we've argued, the way the market distributes income is quite arbitrary. But at least income received in the marketplace is in some way connected to the individual's effort, labour and skill. This is not true with inherited wealth, which allows individuals to become incredibly rich by doing nothing more than being born into the right family.

The circumstances of one's birth are always a key determinant of a person's financial well-being. Warren E. Buffett has dubbed this the 'Ovarian Lottery'. Here's how he describes it:

> Imagine there are two identical twins in the womb, both equally bright and energetic. And the genie says to them, 'One of you is going to be born in the United States, and one of you is going to be born in Bangladesh. And if you wind up in Bangladesh, you will pay

no taxes. What percentage of your income would you bid to be the one that is born in the United States?'...The people who say, 'I did it all myself,' and think of themselves as Horatio Alger – believe me, they'd bid more to be in the United States than in Bangladesh. That's the Ovarian Lottery.[44]

Buffett also notes that if he had been born in some different epoch of human history, he (and, for that matter, Bill Gates) might well have ended up as some other animal's lunch, because both he and Gates have poor vision and can't climb trees well. Buffett also observes that his particular talent – knowing how best to allocate capital – would have been useless in many other eras and geographical locations. His point is that people lucky enough to be born with appropriate talents for their time and place are winners in the Ovarian Lottery.

But those who inherit wealth are particularly big winners in the Ovarian Lottery. The circumstances of their birth mean that they don't have to do anything at all to thrive materially. The money just falls into their hands. It is surely perverse to spare them paying tax the way they would if they'd earned the money, like other citizens, by actually working for a living.

So taxing large inheritances is vital to any plan seeking to diminish the power and influence of extraordinarily wealthy families and to prevent their entrenchment as a kind of permanent aristocracy – something that surely sits uneasily with the notion of 'equality of opportunity'.

We think, however, that this can be better accomplished through a properly designed inheritance tax than an estate tax. The key difference is to whom the tax applies. In the case of the estate tax, the levy is imposed on the estate of someone who's just died. This allows opponents to label it a 'death tax' – a levy that appears to punish someone for dying or at least is associated with the sad fact of someone's demise. An inheritance tax, on the other hand, imposes the levy on the heirs. It's logical to impose it on them, because they are in fact the beneficiaries, and to them it is not a tax on assets long held, but rather on newfound gains – some lucky bounty that will enhance their financial situation through no effort of their own. In this sense, it becomes, in the words of New York University law professor Lily L. Batchelder, not a tax on death but a tax on 'privilege'.[45]

Privilege is the very negation of the idea that everyone starts out with an equal chance in life. The notion of privilege acknowledges that some people start the race ten metres ahead of the rest, or in some cases almost at the finish line. Applying a tax on this special status seems not only intrinsically fair, but appears far more likely to resonate with the public.

In both the UK and the US, there have been proposals for an inheritance tax that would require individuals to keep a lifetime record of the gifts and inheritances they received. In the US, such a tax has been advocated over the years by several prominent tax scholars, including Lily L. Batchelder.[46] In the UK, support has come from several public finance scholars as well as the widely respected 1978 report of the tax committee chaired by James Meade, *The Structure and Reform of Direct Taxation*.[47] More recently, a variation of the tax was recommended by the Fabian Society's Commission on Taxation and Citizenship in its report *Paying for Progress*.[48]

This is not the place to elaborate on the precise design features of such a tax, except to note that it should be designed so that it achieves its primary goal of breaking up large concentrations of wealth. Hence, a personal lifetime exemption could be set reasonably high, say £500,000, before any tax is applied. This means that for the few who are lucky enough to inherit money at all, the vast majority would be spared paying any tax whatsoever on their inheritance. For those exceptionally fortunate individuals who receive lifetime gifts and inheritances above £500,000, the tax would be applied at progressive rates, starting with a relatively low rate. A top rate of 70 per cent would apply to inheritances over £10 million. While 70 per cent might seem like a high percentage, let's not lose sight of the fact that we are talking about applying it to amounts in excess of, say, £10 million – an amount far greater than most individuals, no matter how wildly extravagant, could reasonably dream of spending in a lifetime. There need be no fear that privilege would disappear in the UK.

With the extra money raised from this more progressive inheritance tax, educational trust funds could be established for every child in the UK

Let's just pause for a moment to savour this idea, and what it would mean to the lives of millions of young people, and how it would change the very nature of British society. The inheritance tax could easily be designed so that the revenue collected from it would be sufficient to create individual trust funds so that all children, on their sixteenth birthday, would receive a fixed amount of, say, £15,000. The money would be deposited into an individual trust, which could be used exclusively to cover costs of education or training. This would amount to a direct transfer of wealth, taking from the most privileged families and giving improved educational opportunities to all young people as they prepare to enter adulthood.

There would clearly be many benefits. Improving the education and skills of the next generation would greatly enhance their future work prospects, contributing to their own development and, ultimately, to the nation's productivity. It would also enhance the democratic nature of the country by taking concrete steps toward realizing the widely supported goal of 'equal opportunity'. This would send a powerful signal to young people, many of whom have become withdrawn and cynical, that their country is serious about democracy and about their participation in it.

This would be Robin Hood in grand style, achieving in one swoop a transfer of wealth from the very richest families to the next generation, helping them in the most fundamental way. And it would in no way interfere with the push for other urgently needed reforms – such as enhancing assistance to the poor, improving public health care, strengthening retirement security – which are funded out of other revenues. This proposal involves additional revenues generated by the new, more rigorous inheritance tax, and the revenues would be handled separately. Such a clear relationship between the new tax and the new education trust funds would allow the public to see a direct connection, establishing a strong moral case for the inheritance tax as a vehicle for greatly enhancing the prospects of young people and creating a more democratic and egalitarian society.

It strikes us that this proposal fits very well with the values of UK citizens, who respect hard work and effort and support the notion that individuals should earn their own way. Large inheritances are clearly unearned income – a gift that only a very few individuals, as a result of their lucky draw in the Ovarian Lottery, will ever be fortunate enough to receive. So, imposing a limit to how much of this unearned income remains tax-free, seems well in keeping with the moral principles and sense of fairness held by most citizens.

The idea of using revenues from taxes on the rich to finance broad-based programmes has been proposed over the years by numerous commentators and commissions. The Commission on Taxation and Citizenship proposed a similar plan that would provide a capital grant to young people at age eighteen.[49] Two Yale University law professors, Bruce Ackerman and Anne Alstott, proposed an ambitious scheme to provide a large grant of $80,000 to every American upon reaching adulthood, and financing it with an annual wealth tax of 2 per cent.[50]

Ackerman and Alstott make a lovely point when they note that the idea of taxing wealth in order to provide benefits for all is really a way of ensuring that inheritance is something in which we all share as part of our democracy, not just a privilege enjoyed by the rich: 'The time has come to create a world in which inheritance is not merely a function of family but of citizenship – where all members of the commonwealth have a right to inherit a fair share of the material endowment created by previous generations and are not merely forced to rely on the luck of inheriting wealth from a rich family.'[51]

This is certainly an idea we endorse. The fortunes amassed by the rich represent an enormous legacy from humanity's past. As we've argued in this book, the vast sums that the rich have been accumulating, particularly in recent decades, are based on the technological, scientific and cultural advances achieved over many centuries due to the work of countless scientists, innovators and thinkers (and those who helped them, taught them and nurtured them). The contribution of any one innovator or entrepreneur to the overall development of today's products is actually minuscule in the grand scheme of things. Furthermore, it is only because of property laws governing copyright and licensing – part of our manmade system of laws – that these individuals have been able to lay claim to such a large proportion of the benefits of this legacy.

It seems utterly appropriate, then, to use another man-made system of laws – the tax system – to ensure that the benefits are distributed much more widely, so that this vast inheritance ends up, not in the hands of a privileged few, but in the hands of many. Equality of opportunity – a concept that is almost universally admired and celebrated – has sadly become more myth than reality in recent years. As it risks fading further into mythology, educational trust funds could put real heft behind the notion that society is a community and that all in the community should have a chance to live their dreams.

notes

1 Return of the Plutocrats

1 This was noted by Michael Meacher, Labour MP for Oldham West and Royton.

2 Heather Stewart, 'George Osborne's austerity is costing UK an extra £76 billion, says IMF', *The Observer*, 13 October 2012. See also Aditya Chakrabortty, 'The graph that shows how far David Cameron wants to shrink the state,' *The Guardian*, 15 October 2012.

3 http://www.guardian.co.uk/society/2013/jan/19/super-rich-fight-poverty-oxfam.

4 Richard Murphy, 'In wooing French tax exiles, Cameron makes a mockery of democracy', *guardian.co.uk.*, 19 June 2012.

5 C. G. Fiegehen & W. B. Reddaway, *Companies, Incentives and Senior Managers* (Oxford: Oxford University Press, 1981), p. 92.

6 'Cheques with Balances', Final Report of the High Pay Commission, London, 2011, p. 9.

7 Heather Stewart, '£13tn hoard hidden from taxman by global elite', *The Observer*, 21 July 2012.

8 W. D. Rubinstein, *Men of Property* (London: The Social Affairs Unit, 2006), p. 288.

9   Matthew Whittaker & Lee Savage, *Missing Out* (London: Resolution Foundation, 2011), summary.

10   Data are from The World Top Incomes Database. Breaks in 1961, 1980 and 2008 are smoothed over with the average of the year before and the year after. Estimates of income share were based on tax units until 1989 and adults afterwards.

11   David Cay Johnston, '9 Things the Rich Don't Want You to Know about Taxes', Association of Alternative Newsmedia, 14 April 2011. Johnston's calculations, using pre-tax, inflation-adjusted 2008 dollars, are based on data compiled by economists Emmanuel Saez and Thomas Piketty, the leading scholars in the field of income inequality data. See also A. B. Atkinson & T. Piketty (eds) *Top Incomes: A Global Perspective* (Oxford: Oxford University Press, 2010).

12   One of the best-known attempts to reconstruct the distribution of income in pre-industrial societies relates to England and Wales in 1688. Prepared by seventeenth-century English civil servant Gregory King, it was based on confidential government information. Recently, economic historians, led by Peter Lindert, have revised King's data and used additional data to provide a fuller picture of income distribution in the seventeenth, eighteenth and early nineteenth centuries. See Peter Lindert, 'Revising England's Social Tables 1688–1812', *Explorations in Economic History* 19, no. 4 (October 1982): p.385.

13   Interestingly, people confined to lunatic asylums had somewhat better incomes (averaging £30 a year in 1801) than household servants and common labourers.

14   Average income is the total income of all the individuals in a group, divided by the number of individuals. Median income, on the other hand, is the income of the person exactly in the middle of all the income earners, with half earning more than the middle person and half earning less.

15   Becky Barrow & Rob Davies, 'Bob's Barclays bonanza', *MailOnline*, 4 July 2012. See also Jill Treanor, 'Ex-Barclays boss Bob Diamond under pressure to hand £2m payoff to charity', *The Guardian*, 10 July 2012.

16   The allegations were made in a lawsuit brought against the Royal Bank of Scotland by fired former bank trader Tan Chi Min. See Andrea Tan & Jesse Westbrook, 'Brevan Howard Asked RBS to Change Libor, Lawsuit Says', Bloomberg.com, 30 March 2012.

17   Jon Bakija, Adam Cole & Bradley Heim, 'Jobs and Growth of Top Earners and

the Causes of Changing Income Inequality: Evidence from US Tax Return Data',
Working Paper, November 2012, table 1, p. 49.

18 John C. Bogle, *The Battle for the Soul of Capitalism* (New Haven, CT: Yale University
Press, 2005), p. xx (Introduction).

19 Final Report of the High Pay Commission, p. 8–11.

20 Quoted in Andrew Clark, 'Top hedge funds boom despite recession', *The Guardian*,
25 March 2009.

21 Mike Brewer, Luke Sibieta & Liam Wren-Lewis, 'Racing away? Income inequality
and the evolution of high incomes', Institute for Fiscal Studies (London: 2007),
table 4, p. 34.

2 Why Pornography Is the Only True Free Market

1 John Arlidge, 'I'm Doing "God's Work". Meet Mr Goldman Sachs', *Sunday Times*,
8 November 2009. See also Helia Ebrahimi, 'Goldman Sachs Teams Could Quit
the City over Taxes and Regulations', *The Telegraph*, 4 January 2010.

2 The top marginal rate was later cut back to 45 per cent by the Conservative–
Liberal Democrat government in the winter of 2012. (A marginal tax rate is the
rate applied to any income received above a certain income threshold. By raising
the top marginal rate, the government is raising the rate of tax to be collected on
income above a specified high income threshold.)

3 Iain Martin, 'Britain Is Going to Need Far More People Like Sir Michael Caine',
The Telegraph, 27 April 2009.

4 Liam Murphy & Thomas Nagel, *The Myth of Ownership: Taxes and Justice* (Oxford:
Oxford University Press, 2002), p. 17.

5 For an excellent discussion of the theories of Robert Hale, see Barbara H. Fried,
*The Progressive Assault on Laissez-Faire: Robert Hale and the First Law and Economics
Movement* (Cambridge, MA: Harvard University Press, 1998).

6 Philip Augar, *The Death of Gentlemanly Capitalism* (London: Penguin, 2005), p.
313.

7 See Dean Baker, 'The Reform of Intellectual Property', *Post-Autistic Economics
Review* 32 (5 July 2005). See also Michele Boldrin & David K. Levine, *Against
Intellectual Monopoly* (Cambridge: Cambridge University Press, 2008), chapter 2.

8 Murphy & Nagel, *The Myth of Ownership*.

9   Hindery, Frankfort and Weill are all quoted in Louis Uchitelle & Amanda Cox, 'The Richest of the Rich, Proud of a New Gilded Age', *The New York Times*, 15 July 2007.

3 Paying for a Civilized Society

1   Paul Krugman, *End This Depression Now* (New York: W. W. Norton & Company, 2012).

2   OECD data for the late 2000s. Poverty rate refers to the percentage of households with income after taxes and transfers below 50 per cent of median income. Child poverty rate refers to the share of all children living in households with an equivalized disposable income of less than 50 per cent of the median for the total population.

3   All tax data used in this chapter are from the OECD.

4   We exclude the poorest countries in the OECD since their economies are less likely to be comparable and we also exclude the small OECD countries of Luxembourg and Iceland. We also leave out Japan, since it is an anomaly. It has low taxes, but still achieves a high level of equality, mostly due to cultural traditions favouring equality in its workplace. In other words, Japan starts out with a high degree of equality and therefore doesn't need high taxes to finance social transfers and programmes aimed at reducing inequality.

The common way of comparing tax levels across countries is to express the total amount of taxes collected in a country as a percentage of the size of that country's economy. A country's gross domestic product (GDP) is the common measure of the total value of the goods and services produced by that country's economy. Over the past twenty years, taxes collected in the average OECD country have been around 35 per cent of GDP. Over this period, the taxes collected in the UK as a percentage of its GDP has always been about the OECD average, slightly above in a few years and slightly below in a couple of others. Tax levels vary at least slightly from year to year; therefore, a five-year average from 2000 to 2010 was used in this study. This period immediately precedes the year or years in which most of the social and economic indicators that we examine apply.

5   In 2006, one of the co-authors, Neil Brooks, along with Thaddeus Hwong, carried out a comprehensive study comparing low- and high-tax countries, 'The Social

Benefits and Economic Costs of Taxation', published by the Canadian Centre for Policy Alternatives. The study revealed that high-tax countries have been much more successful at achieving their social objectives than low-tax countries and that they have been able to do so with no economic penalty. The study examined fifty indicators that are commonly used to measure a country's social progress. On over half of these indicators (twenty-nine), the outcomes in high-tax Nordic countries were significantly better than those in low-tax Anglo-American countries, and on most of the remaining indicators (thirteen), social outcomes were somewhat better in Nordic countries. Low-tax Anglo-American countries ranked higher than Nordic countries on only seven of the fifty social indicators. In each case, it is a trivial difference that could be easily due to chance. With respect to the pursuit of economic goals, of the thirty-three economic indicators examined, the Nordic countries lead on nineteen indicators and the Anglo-American countries on fourteen. The results of this study suggest a trade-off does not have to be made between social equity and material prosperity. Some of the text in this chapter is drawn from this study.

6 Poverty data from the OECD around 2008.

7 The data are from the OECD. The average tax ratio of 2002-6 explains about 49 per cent of the variation of child poverty rates from around 2008. The relationship is statistically significant at one-per cent level. The child poverty rate refers to the share of all children living in households with a disposable income equivalent to less than 50 per cent of the median for the total population. The relationship remains statistically significant at one-per cent level if the analysis excludes the US. In that case, the tax ratio explains about 40 per cent of the variation of the child poverty rates.

8 The average tax ratio of 2006–10 explains about 41 per cent of the variations of the 2011 Gender Inequality Index of the United Nations Development Program. The relationship is statistically significant at one-per cent level. The relationship remains statistically significant at five-per cent level if the analysis excludes the US. In that case, the tax ratio explains about 31 per cent of the variations of the index.

9 The average tax ratio in 1996–2000 explains about 60 per cent of the variations of ILO's Economic Security Index published in 2005. The index is based on data

from early to mid-2000s. The relationship is statistically significant at one-per cent level.

10 For its most recent report see Lars Osberg & Andrew Sharpe, 'Moving from a GDP-Based to a Well-being Based Metric of Economic Performance and Social Progress: Results from the Index of Economic Well-being for OECD countries 1980–2009', CSLS Research Report 2011–12 (September 2011).

11 The average tax ratio of 2003–7 explains about 52 per cent of the variations of the Index of Economic Security of 2008. The relationship is statistically significant at one-per cent level.

12 The average tax ratio in 2002–6 explains about 21 per cent of the variations of infant mortality rates in the late 2000s from OECD. The relationship is statistically significant at five-per cent level, mainly due to the high infant mortality rate of the United States among the OECD-20.

13 The average tax ratio of 2006–10 explains about 43 per cent of the variations of the Social Justice Index of 2012. The relationship is statistically significant at one-per cent level.

14 The average tax ratio in 2006–10 explains about 20 per cent of the variations of the Environmental Performance Index of 2012. The relationship is statistically significant at five-per cent level. The relationship became stronger if the analysis excludes Switzerland, with the tax level explaining about 56 per cent of the variation of the index, statistically significant at one-per cent level.

15 Thomas Gunton & K. S. Calbick, 'The Maple Leaf in the OECD: Canada's Environmental Performance', a study prepared for the David Suzuki Foundation and the School of Resource and Environmental Management, Simon Fraser University (June 2010).

16 Top income data from The World Top Incomes Database. Highest top 1 per cent income data since 2005 are used, except late 1990s data for Germany, the Netherlands and Switzerland due to data availability. Average tax ratio of 1975-2008 based on OECD data.

17 Gini coefficients for people aged 18-65 based on OECD data from the late 2000s.

18 As an illustration of the importance of taxes and transfers in society, representative average tax ratios and changes in inequality are correlated. The average tax ratio of 1975-2008 explains about 69 percent of the variation of differences between

Gini before taxes and transfers and Gini after taxes and transfers calculated based on OECD data from the late 2000s. The relationship is statistically significant at one-per cent level.

19 Countries can then be compared by converting their GDP per capita into US dollars on the basis of the purchasing power of that country's currency (the purchasing power parity rate).

20 In part, the Nordic average is so high because of the high per capita income in Norway, but even without Norway the per capita income in the other three Nordic countries is higher than the Anglo-American average at $40,012.

21 Data from OECD. The dashed line shows the direction of the relationship between the GDP per capita (2011 data, US$, current prices, current PPPs) and average tax levels (1975-2008) among the OECD-20, but the relationship is not statistically significant.

22 See Anthony B. Atkinson, Thomas Piketty & Emmanuel Saez, 'Top Incomes in the Long Run of History', (2011) 49(1) *Journal of Economic Literature* 3–71, p. 9.

23 Facundo Alvaredo, Anthony B. Atkinson, Thomas Piketty & Emmanuel Saez, The World Top Incomes Database, http://g-mond.parisschoolofeconomics.eu/topincomes. The UK bottom 90 per cent average income series started in 1963. All three UK series ended at 2009. The US and Swedish series ended in 2010. The UK income series changed the unit of analysis from adults in 1989 to tax units in 1990. The pre-1990 UK average income series is based on married couples and single adults.

24 Calculations based on World Bank data used by Gapminder at http://www.gapminder.org/data/.

25 Data refer to the period 1975-2008.

26 The Innovation for Development Report 2010–2011: Innovation as a Driver of Productivity and Economic Growth (Palgrave Macmillan, 2010).

27 The Global Innovation Index 2012: Stronger Innovation Linkages for Global Growth (2012).

28 Global Innovation Index, 2012. Average tax ratio, 2005-9.

29 Global Competitiveness Index, 2012. Average tax ratio, 2005-9.

30 The argument and the idea for the following two graphs borrows from Thomas Piketty, Emmanuel Saez & Stefanie Stantcheva, 'Optimal Taxation of Top Labor

Incomes: A Tale of Three Elasticities', CEPR Discussion Paper 8675, December 2011.

31 Tax rates based on the Urban Institute-Brookings Institution Tax Policy Center dataset 'Historical Top Marginal Personal Income Tax Rate in OECD Countries'. The tax data refer to the period of 1975-2008 except Denmark, for which 1976 was used instead of 1975.

32 Top income data from The World Top Incomes Database; tax rate data calculated based on the Urban Institute-Brookings Institution Tax Policy Center dataset 'Historical Top Marginal Personal Income Tax Rate in OECD Countries'. Rate cuts explain about 43 per cent of variations of change in the top 1 per cent income share. The relationship is statistically significant at one-per cent level. The maximum top 1 per cent share in 1975-8 and the minimum top 1 per cent income share in 2006-8 are used for most countries. Data for other countries are used due to best data availability. The tax data refer to the period of 1975-2008 except Denmark, for which 1976 was used instead of 1975.

4 Plutocracy, Climate Change and the Fate of the World

1 United Nations Environment Programme, *HFCs: A Critical Link in Protecting Climate and the Ozone Layer* (UNEP, November 2011).

2 Author interview with Robert Watson, Washington, 25 March 2003, originally reported in Linda McQuaig, *It's the Crude, Dude: War, Big Oil and the Fight for the Planet* (Toronto: Random House, 2003). See pp. 147–54.

3 Nina Chestney, 'Effects of climate change to claim 5 million lives a year, report says', Reuters, 26 September 2012. Perhaps the lack of action on climate change by the industrialized world can be explained by the fact that 90 per cent of the deaths are expected to be in developing countries. But even if we assume that we in the 'advanced' world are so callous that we dismiss the importance of deaths in poor countries, this still leaves ten million deaths in our own countries, which we would presumably care about.

4 James E. Hansen, 'Climate change is here – and worse than we thought', *Washington Post*, 3 August 2012.

5 Richard Elliot Benedick, 'The Improbable Montreal Protocol: Since, Diplomacy and Defending the Ozone Layer', Case Study Prepared for the 2004 Policy

Colloquium of the American Meteorological Society, reproduced in Donald Kaniaru (ed.), *The Montreal Protocol* (London: Cameron May Ltd., 2007).

6 Bill McKibben, 'Global Warming's Terrifying New Math', *Rolling Stone*, 19 July 2012.

7 Sabrina Fernandes & Richard Girard, *Corporations, Climate and the United Nations* (Ottawa: Polaris Institute, November 2011), p. 3.

8 Quoted in Fernandes & Girard, *ibid.*, p. 14.

9 *Ibid.*, p. 12.

10 Mark Townsend & Paul Harris, 'Now the Pentagon tells Bush: climate change will destroy us', *The Observer*, 22 February 2004.

11 Frederick Solt, 'Economic Inequality and Democratic Political Engagement', *American Journal of Political Science*, vol. 52, no. 1, January 2008, pp. 48–60.

12 Martin Gilens, 'Inequality and Democratic Responsiveness', *Public Policy Quarterly* 69, no. 5 (2005), p. 794.

13 Richard Elliot Benedick, 'The Improbable Montreal Protocol: Since, Diplomacy and Defending the Ozone Layer', Case Study Prepared for the 2004 Policy Colloquium of the American Meteorological Society, reproduced in Kaniaru (ed.), *The Montreal Protocol*.

14 Ross Gelbspan, *The Heat is On: The Climate Crisis, the Cover-Up, the Prescription* (Reading, MA: Perseus Books, 1998), pp. 76–7.

5 Why Bill Gates Doesn't Deserve His Fortune

1 The story of IBM's early dealings with Gary Kildall and Bill Gates is recounted in Harold Evans, *They Made America* (New York: Little Brown, 2004), pp. 402–19. See also Steve Hamm & Jay Greene, 'The Man Who Could Have Been Bill Gates', *BusinessWeek*, 25 October 2004.

2 Evans, *They Made America*, pp. 402–19.

3 James Essinger, *Jacquard's Web* (Oxford: Oxford University Press, 2004), p. 37.

4 *Ibid.*, p. 249.

5 Thierry Bardini, *Bootstrapping: Douglas Engelbart, Coevolution, and the Origins of Personal Computing* (Stanford, CA: Stanford University Press, 2000), pp. 81–102.

6 Gar Alperovitz & Lew Daly, *Unjust Deserts* (New York: The New Press, 2008), p. 58.

7 *Ibid.*, pp. 59–61.

8   *Ibid.*, p. 60.

9   Cited in *ibid.*, p. 63.

10 Robert M. Solow, 'Growth Theory and After', Nobel lecture, 8 December 1987, http://www.nobelprize.org.

11 Herbert A. Simon, 'UBI and the Flat Tax', *Boston Review*, October/November 2000.

12 Cited in Alperovitz & Daly, *Unjust Deserts*, p. 36.

13 *Ibid.*, p. 96.

14 John Stuart Mill, 'Land Tenure Reform', *Collected Works*, vol. 5 (Toronto: University of Toronto Press, 1967), p. 691.

15 John Stuart Mill, *Principles of Political Economy*, vol. 2, book 2, chapter 1, section 3, p. 208.

16 L.T. Hobhouse, *Liberalism and Other Writings*, James Meadowcroft (ed.), (Cambridge: Cambridge University Press, 1994), pp. 91–2.

17 Frank E. Manuel & Fritzie P. Manuel, *Utopian Thought in the Western World* (Cambridge, MA: Belknap Press, 1979), p. 466.

18 Bardini, *Bootstrapping*, pp. 6–14.

19 Alperovitz & Daly, *Unjust Deserts*, p. 144.

6   Why Other Billionaires Are Even Less Deserving

1   Quoted in Gregory Zuckerman, *The Greatest Trade Ever* (New York: Random House, 2009), p. 192.

2   *Ibid.*, p. 95.

3   *Ibid.*, pp. 3, 8.

4   Martin Wolf and Simon Johnson, online interview, Yahoo Originals, 21 April 2010.

5   This analogy is an adaptation of one made by Phil Angelides, head of the federally appointed Financial Crisis Inquiry Commission, and cited in Dean Baker, 'Goldman's Scam #5476, Yes, It Can Get Even Worse', *The Guardian*, 19 April 2010.

6   Wolf and Johnson interview.

7   Henry Paulson is not related to John Paulson.

8   In fact, Goldman bought more of this insurance from AIG than any other bank.

See Richard Teitelbaum, 'Secret AIG Document Shows Goldman Sachs Minted Most Toxic CDOs', Bloomberg.com, 23 February 2010.

9   Les Leopold, 'The Preposterous Reality', Alternet.org, 10 April 2010.

10 Joseph Stiglitz, 'Skewed Rewards for Bankers, CEOs', *Korea Herald*, 30 March 2010.

11 Evans, *They Made America*, pp. 413–14.

12 *World Wealth Report 2007*, Merrill Lynch.

13 Cited in Anatole Anton, Milton Fisk & Nancy Holmstrom, (eds), *Not for Sale: In Defense of Public Goods* (Boulder, CO: Westview Press, 2000), p. 3.

14 *Ibid.*, p. 14.

15 Robert Nozick, *Anarchy, State, and Utopia* (New York: Basic Books, 1974), pp. 177–80.

7   Bobby Moore and the Myths about Motivation

1   Robert E. Lane, *The Market Experience* (Cambridge: Cambridge University Press, 1991).

2   Robert H. Frank, *Luxury Fever: Money and Happiness in an Era of Excess* (New York: The Free Press, 1999), p. 65.

3   *Ibid.*, p. 73.

4   Lane, *The Market Experience*, p. 345.

5   Hindery, Weill & Griffin quoted in Uchitelle & Cox, 'The Richest of the Rich, Proud of a New Gilded Age'.

6   Quoted in Frank, *Luxury Fever*, p. 122.

7   *Ibid.*, p. 120.

8   Richard A. Posner, 'Are American CEOs Overpaid, and If So, What If Anything Should Be Done about It?', *Duke Law Journal* 58, no. 1023 (2009).

9   *Ibid.*, p. 102. See also Sanjai Bhagat & Bernard Black, *The Non-Correlation Between Board Independence and Long-Term Firm Performance, Journal of Corporation Law* vols 27, 231, 263 (2002).

10 Interview with John C. Bogle, 21 September 2011.

11 Quoted in Daniel Knowles, 'Sorry, but tackling executive pay isn't equivalent to communism,' *The Telegraph*, 22 November 2011.

8 John Maynard Keynes and the Defeat of Austerity

1 Paul Krugman, 'The Big Fail', *The New York Times*, 7 January 2013.

2 The hearings of the US Senate Finance Committee in February 1933 are described in Sidney Hyman, *Marriner S. Eccles: Private Entrepreneur and Public Servant* (Stanford, CA.: Graduate School of Business, Stanford University, 1976) pp. 3–8.

3 Up until June 1933, the US was on the gold standard. But the gold standard didn't impose the same constraints on the US that it did on Britain, because the US was a creditor nation. This meant that it didn't need to deflate its prices in order to maintain the external value of its currency. However, despite its greater latitude, those running the US Federal Reserve had the same attitude as central bankers in England in the early years of the Depression, and kept US interest rates high.

4 Quoted in William Greider, *Secrets of the Temple: How the Federal Reserve Runs the Country* (New York: Touchstone, 1987), p. 300.

5 *Ibid.*, pp. 304–21.

6 The account of Keynes here is drawn largely from Skidelsky's comprehensive biography. See Robert Skidelsky, *John Maynard Keynes* (London: Macmillan, vol. 1, 1983; vol. 2, 1992). See also D. E. Moggridge, *Keynes* (Toronto: University of Toronto Press, 1976); Dudley Dillard, *The Economics of John Maynard Keynes* (Englewood Cliffs, NJ: Prentice-Hall, 1948); and Linda McQuaig, *The Cult of Impotence: Selling the Myth of Powerlessness in the Global Economy* (Toronto: Penguin Books Canada Ltd., 1998), pp. 172–213.

7 Quoted in Skidelsky, vol. 1, p. 38.

8 Quoted in Geoffrey Ingham, *Capitalism Divided? The City and Industry in British Social Development* (London: Macmillan, 1984), pp. 182–3.

9 Quoted in Skidelsky, vol. 2, p. 449.

10 *Ibid.*, p. 306.

11 See Walter S. Salant, 'The Spread of Keynesian Doctrines and Practices in the United States', in Peter A. Hall (ed.), *The Political Power of Economic Ideas: Keynesianism across Nations* (Princeton, NJ: Princeton University Press, 1989), p. 38.

12 Quoted in Skidelsky, vol. 2, p. 580.

13 *Ibid.*, p. xxiii.

9 Triumph of the Welfare State

1 Quoted in Paul Addison, *The Road to 1945* (London: Jonathan Cape, 1975), p. 130.

2 Nicholas Timmins, *The Five Giants: A Biography of the Welfare State* (London: HarperCollins, 1995), pp. 25, 44.

3 Quoted in *ibid.*, p. 25.

4 Richard Cockett, *Thinking the Unthinkable: Think-Tanks and the Economic Counter-Revolution 1931 to 1983* (London: HarperCollins, 1994), p. 62.

5 Quoted in Timmins, *The Five Giants*, p. 47.

6 Michael Sullivan, *The Development of the British Welfare State* (Hemel Hempstead: Prentice Hall, 1996), p. 29.

7 *Ibid.*, p. 31.

8 Timmins, *The Five Giants,* p. 62.

9 T. H. Marshall, *Citizenship and Social Class and Other Essays* (Cambridge: Cambridge University Press, 1950), pp. 10–18.

10 Timmins, *The Five Giants,* p. 247.

11 Colin Leys, *Politics in Britain: From Labourism to Thatcherism* (London: Verso, 1989), p. 68.

12 *Ibid.*, p. 179

13 Angus Calder, *The People's War* (London: Pimlico: 1992), p. 322.

14 Leys, *Politics in Britain*, p. 68.

15 John Kenneth Galbraith, *The Great Crash 1929* (Boston: Houghton Mifflin, 1961), p. 7.

16 David Madland, 'Growth and the Middle Class', *Democracy: A Journal of Ideas*, Issue 20, Spring 2011.

17 Frederick Solt, 'Economic Inequality and Democratic Political Engagement', *American Journal of Political Science*, vol. 52, issue 1, January 2008, pp. 48–60.

18 Alan S. Blinder, 'The Anatomy of Double-Digit Inflation in the 1970s', in Robert E. Hall (ed.), *Inflation and its Effects* (Chicago: University of Chicago Press, 1982), p. 261.

19 Cockett, *Thinking the Unthinkable*, pp. 25–34.

20 Timmins, *The Five Giants*, p. 167.

21 Cockett, *Thinking the Unthinkable*, pp. 102–3.

22 Hayek note, cited in *ibid.*, p. 104.

23 *Ibid.*, p. 122.

24 Fisher quoted in *ibid.*, pp. 123–4.

25 Quoted in *ibid.*, p. 176.

26 Quoted in *ibid.*, p. 174.

27 *Ibid.*, p. 307.

28 Quoted in Kim Phillips-Fein, *The Invisible Hand* (New York: W. W. Norton & Company, 2009), p. 119.

29 Dwight D. Eisenhower, in L. Galambos & D. van Ee, 'The Papers of Dwight David Eisenhower', doc. 1147.

30 Phillips-Fein, *The Invisible Hand*, p. 165.

31 Lee Edwards, *The Power of Ideas* (Ottawa, IL: Jameson, 1997), p. 9.

32 Phillips-Fein, *The Invisible Hand*, pp. 169–72.

33 Yasha Levine & Mark Ames, 'Charles Koch to Friedrich Hayek: Use Social Security!', *The Nation*, 27 September 2011.

34 Harry G. Frankfurt, 'Reflections on Bullshit', *Harper's*, February 1987. Frankfurt later developed his theory into a bestselling book, *On Bullshit*, published by Princeton University Press in 2005.

10 Revamping the Ovarian Lottery

1 Norbert Haring & Niall Douglas, *Economists and the Powerful* (London: Wimbledon Publishing Company, 2012), p. 1.

2 Adam Smith, *The Wealth of Nations* (London: Penguin Books, 1999), p. 857.

3 Hugh Stretton & Lionel Orchard, *Public Goods, Public Enterprise, Public Choice: Theoretical Foundations of the Contemporary Attack on Government* (New York: St. Martin's Press, 1994), p. 20.

4 Karl Polanyi, *The Great Transformation* (Boston: Beacon Press, 1957), p. 163.

5 R. H. Tawney, *Religion and the Rise of Capitalism* (Toronto: Penguin Books, 1990), p. 73.

6 Henry Simons, *Personal Income Taxation* (Chicago: University of Chicago Press, 1938), p. 29.

7 Henry Simons, *Economic Policy for a Free Society* (Chicago: University of Chicago Press, 1948), p. 6.

8 Smith, *The Wealth of Nations*, p. 725.

9   *Ibid.*, p. 842. Interestingly, while Adam Smith appears to support a progressive income tax, Karl Marx thought the idea was rather lame and that it fell considerably short of the kinds of changes needed. 'Tax reform is the hobby-horse of every radical bourgeois, the specific element in all bourgeois economic reforms,' Marx wrote, along with Friedrich Engels, 'From the earliest medieval Philistines to the modern English free-thinkers, the main struggle has revolved around taxation… The further it slips from his grasp in practice, the more keenly does the bourgeois pursue the chimerical ideal of equal distribution of taxation…The reduction of taxes, their more equitable distribution, etc., etc., is a banal bourgeois reform.' Karl Marx and Friedrich Engels (1850), 'Review: Le Socialisme et L'Impôt, par Emile de Girardin', in K. Marx and F. Engels, *Collected Works*, 1978 (ed.), vol. 10 (London: Lawrence & Wishart), p. 326, pp. 330–1.

10 Adam Smith, *The Theory of Moral Sentiments*, part 1, chapter 3.

11 Quoted in Chuck Collins, Mike Lapham & Scott Klinger, *I Didn't Do it Alone* (Boston: United for a Fair Economy, 2004), pp. 1–2.

12 J. K. Rowling, 'The Single Mother's Manifesto', *The Times*, 14 April 2010.

13 John C. Bogle, commencement address, Georgetown University, 18 May 2007.

14 Institute for Fiscal Studies, *The Structure and Reform of Direct Taxation* (London: Allen & Unwin, 1978), p. 316.

15 HM Revenue & Customs, 'The Exchequer effect of the 50 per cent additional rate of income tax', March 2012.

16 Robert Winnett, 'Two-thirds of millionaires left Britain to avoid 50p tax rate," *The Telegraph*, 27 November 2012.

17 Emmanuel Saez, Joel Slemrod & Seth Giertz, 'The Elasticity of Taxable Income with Respect to Marginal Tax Rates: A Critical Review', *Journal of Economic Literature* 50 (1), pp. 3–50.

18 Piketty, Saez & Stantcheva, 'Optimal Taxation of Top Labor Incomes: A Tale of Three Elasticities'.

19 Simons, *Personal Income Taxation*, pp. 18–19.

20 Patrick Wintour, 'Treasury reveals how little tax the super-rich pay', *The Guardian*, 15 April 2012.

21 Warren E. Buffett, 'Stop Coddling the Super-Rich', *The New York Times*, 14 August 2011.

NOTES

22 Alan S. Blinder, 'The Under-Taxed Kings of Private Equity', *The New York Times*, 29 July 2007.

23 Interview with John C. Bogle, 21 September 2011.

24 A good deal has been written on tax havens in recent years. Two of the best descriptions and analyses are Ronen Palan, Richard Murphy & Christian Chavagneux, *Tax Havens: How Globalization Really Works* (Ithaca: Cornell University Press, 2010), and Nicholas Shaxson, *Treasure Islands: Tax Havens and the Men Who Stole the World* (London: Vintage Books, 2012).

25 Tax Justice Network, 27 January 2011.

26 'Greece would have avoided a bailout if it were not for tax havens, says former PM', *The Telegraph*, 30 August 2012.

27 Ed Howker & Shiv Malik, 'Cameron family fortune made in tax havens', *The Guardian*, 20 April 2012.

28 'Revealed: Tax havens of the top 20 UK companies', *This Is Money*, 24 January 2011.

29 Fajeev Syal & Martin Williams, 'Tory treasurer wants UK to become more like a tax haven', *The Guardian*, 21 September 2012.

30 *Ibid.*

31 Tom Bergin, 'Special Report: How Starbucks avoids UK taxes', Reuters, 15 October 2012.

32 Nicholas Shaxson, *Treasure Islands: Tax Havens and the Men Who Stole the World* (London: Vintage Books, 2011).

33 Before the imposition of the fixed charges, Richard Murphy estimated the annual revenue loss to be in excess of £4.3 billion. Richard Murphy, 'The UK domicile rule costs £4.3 billion in lost tax a year', www.taxresearch.org.uk, September 2007.

34 'Cameron refuses to reveal when he found out Tory peer Lord Ashcroft was a non-dom', *MailOnline*, 2 March 2010.

35 John Maynard Keynes, *The General Theory of Employment, Interest and Money* (New York: Macmillan, 1936), p. 156.

36 Quoted in Charles Duhigg, 'Stock Traders Find Speed Pays, in Milliseconds', *The New York Times*, 23 July 2009.

37 For an excellent discussion of the FTT and its relevance to today's high frequency

trading markets see Ross P. Buckley, 'A Financial Transactions Tax: The One Essential Reform', *Intereconomics: Review of European Economic Policy*, vol. 47, no. 2, March/April 2012, pp. 99–103. See also an insightful piece by Lee A. Sheppard, 'Rationales for the Financial Transactions Tax', *Tax Notes*, 28 May 2012, pp. 1087–91.

38 Buckley, *ibid*.

39 John D. Brondolo, 'Taxing Financial Transactions: An Assessment of Administrative Feasibility', IMF Working Paper 11/185, August 2011, p. 5.

40 Stephen G. Cecchetti & Enisse Kharroubi, 'Reassessing the impact of finance on growth', conference draft of paper prepared for the Reserve Bank of India's Second International Research Conference, Mumbai, February 2012.

41 Dean Baker et al., 'The Potential Revenue from Financial Transaction Taxes', Working Paper no. 212, Center for Economic Policy Research, December 2009.

42 Ron Suskind, *Confidence Men: Wall Street, Washington and the Education of a President*, 2nd edition (New York: HarperCollins, 2011), p. 365.

43 Heather Stewart, 'Robin Hood tax: 1,000 economists urge G20 to accept Tobin tax', *The Guardian*, 13 April 2011.

44 Warren E. Buffett has described his concept of the Ovarian Lottery on a number of occasions, including a lecture at the University of Florida School of Business, 15 October 1998.

45 Lily L. Batchelder, 'Taxing Privilege More Effectively: Replacing the Estate Tax with an Inheritance Tax', Discussion Paper, Hamilton Project, Brookings Institution, June 2007.

46 *Ibid*.

47 Institute for Fiscal Studies, *The Structure and Reform of Direct Taxation* (London: Allen & Unwin, 1978).

48 The Commission on Taxation and Citizenship, *Paying for Progress: A New Politics of Tax for Public Spending* (London: Fabian Society, 2000).

49 *Ibid*., p. 286 ff.

50 Bruce Ackerman & Anne Alstott, 'Why Stakeholding?', *Politics & Society* 32, no. 1 (March 2004): pp. 41–60.

51 *Ibid*., pp. 55–6.

acknowledgements

We'd like to thank a number of people for their invaluable assistance. In particular, Thaddeus Hwong, professor of tax law and social policy at York University in Toronto, generously gave his time and expertise, and was particularly helpful in the research and preparation of graphs.

We also greatly appreciate the assistance and expertise of Michael Wolfson, as well as Daniel Wright, Barbara Nichol, Douglas Peters, David Peters, Nelson Oliveira and Miriam Spevack.

We're also grateful to the terrific crowd who worked on the book for Oneworld Publications, including Mike Harpley, Andrea D'Cruz, Ruth Deary and Tamsin Shelton. Their enthusiasm for the project and their excellent editing skills contributed enormously.

Our agent, Chris Bucci, was always helpful.

Linda also thanks Peter Langille, for his sharp intellect, great ideas, and for being supportive and wonderful.

index

Note: *t* following a page number denotes a table. This is only used where there is no textual discussion of the topic on the same page.

INDEX

INDEX

about the authors

Described as 'Canada's Michael Moore' by the country's *National Post*, Linda McQuaig is an award-winning investigative reporter and columnist for the *Toronto Star*. She is the author of seven Canadian bestsellers, which have earned her a reputation as a fierce critic of the establishment. Neil Brooks is director of the Graduate Program in Taxation at Osgoode Hall Law School, York University, Toronto. He has published extensively on income tax issues and has been a consultant on tax policy and reform issues to numerous governments around the world.